Hübner / Dunkel (Eds.)

Recent Essentials in Innovation Management and Re

I0004495

GABLER EDITION WISSENSCHAFT

Kasseler Wirtschafts- und
Verwaltungswissenschaften; Band 1

Herausgegeben von Dr. Heinz Hübner, Dr. Jürgen
Reese, Dr. Peter Weise und Dr. Udo Winand,
Univ.-Professoren des Fachbereiches
Wirtschaftswissenschaften, Universität-Gh Kassel

Die Schriftenreihe dient der gebündelten Darstellung der vielfältigen
wissenschaftlichen Aktivitäten des Fachbereichs Wirtschaftswissenschaften der Universität-Gh Kassel. Er umfaßt die Fachgebiete Be-
triebswirtschaftslehre, Volkswirtschaftslehre, Verwaltungswissen-
schaft und Wirtschaftsinformatik. Die Reihe ist jedoch auch offen für
die Veröffentlichung von Arbeiten aus „verwandten" Fachgebieten
und Ergebnissen aus interdisziplinären Projekten mit ausgeprägtem
Bezug zu ökonomischen Fragestellungen.

Heinz Hübner / Torsten Dunkel (Eds.)

Recent Essentials in Innovation Management and Research

Networking, Innovation Systems, Instruments, Ecology in International Perspective

Springer Fachmedien Wiesbaden GmbH

Gabler Verlag, Deutscher Universitäts-Verlag, Wiesbaden

© Springer Fachmedien Wiesbaden 1995
Ursprünglich erschienen bei Betriebswirtschaftlicher Verlag Dr. Th. Gabler GmbH 1995

Höchste inhaltliche und technische Qualität unserer Produkte ist unser Ziel. Bei der Pro-
duktion und Auslieferung unserer Bücher wollen wir die Umwelt schonen: Dieses Buch ist auf
säurefreiem und chlorfrei gebleichtem Papier gedruckt.

Die Wiedergabe von Gebrauchsnamen, Handelsnamen, Warenbezeichnungen usw. in
diesem Werk berechtigt auch ohne besondere Kennzeichnung nicht zu der Annahme, daß
solche Namen im Sinne der Warenzeichen- und Markenschutz-Gesetzgebung als frei zu
betrachten wären und daher von jedermann benutzt werden dürften.

ISBN 978-3-8244-6253-7   ISBN 978-3-663-08911-7 (eBook)
DOI 10.1007/978-3-663-08911-7

Dedication

It is a pleasure and honour for me to start the series of publications of the faculty of **Business Management and Economics** at the University of Kassel with a volume dealing with the "Management of Technology and Innovation" in practice as the object of innovation research requiring an interdisciplinary approach.

The disciplines represented by the authors and participants, the content of the articles and the documentation of the results of the Working Groups show clearly this interdisciplinarity.

By this book, the editors hope to be able to provide a stimulus for future-oriented topics and issues in the area of Innovation Research and transfer of results into reality.

When dealing with current and urgent political issues like, e.g., the tranformation of former communist economies and societies, as well as with societal and economic problems like damage and destruction of the ecosphere, solutions are **not** possible without application of findings of Innovation Research, coupled with experience from innovation practice. This elucidates the **high rank of an Innovation Research** which should **not be confined to technical product innovation**.

In this sense, this book shall be dedicated, in the first place, to all those who are dealing, as experts and managers in the economic system in the broadest sense, in politics and public administration, with the phenomenon of innovation. Moreover, the volume is dedicated to all those who are occupied with this phenomenon under a scientific point of view, including students.

In this context, it is appropriate always to keep in mind the Janus-headed character of innovation as "creative destruction" according to Schumpeter, the founder of Innovation Research: Referring to a sentence of the Austrian poet Anton Wildgans, it is a characteristic of culture **not** to "presume all at once a gospel behind everything new".

Heinz Hübner
Speaker of the Editors

VI

Dear Reader,

Instead of the "Preface" usually appearing in this place, we would like to address you more personally in this way:

This book is a **special kind of documentation** of results of a special kind of conference, namely as a **working** conference. Therefore you will find, in addition to the "papers" presented, a special kind of **information**, which **normally** is **not published** within any conference proceedings: The documentation of **discussions and results worked out by Working Groups** involved in four different Topics, namely

- Strategic Networking within (Inter-)National Innovation Systems
- The Innovation System of the Company as a Frame for the Management of Innovation Projects
- Instruments as Management Technology
- Ecological Problems as a Trigger for Innovation.

While reading this, you will almost feel like a member of the pertinent Working Group!

A "by-product" of the group work is the identification of unsolved current problems of innovation practice as **"Fields of Future Research"**.

Though discussions and common search for approaches, procedures, and models have been emphasized during this special kind of **Working** Conference, the book includes, like common proceedings, the papers which have been presented within the Working Groups initiating their discussion.

It is evident that the structure of the book follows the structure of the Conference: It consists of four parts corresponding to the Topics, each including all the papers covering the specific Topic, followed by the documentation of discussions and results worked out by the Working Group.

For a better understanding of what has been discussed and worked out within the Working Groups, further particulars on the Topics are given in advance.

Therefore, it is **strongly recommended** for a better understanding to read these explanations before reading the papers and group work documentations.

Finally, we hope that this book will meet your needs in a way that will induce you to participate in another ISPIM (Working) Conference.

Heinz Hübner   Torsten Dunkel

Contents

The Innovation System of the Company as a Frame for the Management of Innovation Projects

Instruments as Management Technology   141

Ecological Problems as a Trigger for Innovation

Scope, Structure and Organization of the Conference

Motivation

Attending conferences of "usual" structure, more and more uneasiness can be felt with respect to the following:
Lack of time for discussion (not scheduled or no time - discipline of speakers);
- Too many parallel sessions do not allow to get an overview on all Topics discussed;
- Lack of opportunities for Topic-focussed work;
- Lack of possibilities for better personal acquaintance.

Based on this, the Working Conference was designed as an opportunity for
- participation,
- presentation of a key note speech,
- taking the moderator's function,
- proposals for special subjects for, or fitting into, a Topic,
- other comments.

During its meeting on the occasion of the IXth International ISPIM (International Society for Professional Innovation Management) Conference at the Eindhoven University of Technology in September 1993, the Board of ISPIM decided that the Department of Management Science - Technology Impact & Innovation Research at the University of Kassel (**TWI**) should organize such a conference. Professor Hübner is engaged in Innovation and Impact Research and established an interdisciplinary course of supplmementary studies designated as "Innovation Management, considering Technology and Product Impact Assessment" at the University of Kassel some years ago.

Scope

Competition in innovation as a specific kind of competition has become the dominant one in most branches of economy. This is true not only for the company but also on the level of national economy and bigger economic regions.

Confronted with this fact, professional and efficient design and realization of innovation processes is of crucial importance for the company. With regard to the importance of innovation for the economy of a region, country, or nation, public administrations and the political systems are supporting activities of companies by a lot of measures including government-driven R&D activities.

Professional and efficient Management of Technology and Innovation has to be oriented or guided by applying results of Innovation Research in the way of approaches, models, instruments, etc.

Though Innovation Research as a discipline of its own has been growing up since about 25 years only, a lot of results have been worked out, mostly based on empirical research, well suited for application in practice[*]. To proceed in Innovation Research meeting the real main problems in practice related to the Management of Technology and Innovation, the Conference has been based on **some general assumptions**:

- As in other scientific disciplines, there is the danger that Innovation Research is focussing on some "fashion topics".
- Therefore, other unsolved problems in the field of Innovation Management in the real world are neglected ("Highway-Jungle Dilemma").
- Concentration on product innovation in theory and practice is blocking the view on other possible fields of innovation (production, organization, management technology, service, etc.).
- Pseudo-scientific approach by "combining naïve dogmas to a theory[**]".

Consequently, the **general goals of the Conference** are defined as follows:
- Broadening up the problem understanding by
- Identifying problems of innovation management in practice, which until now have been neglected by Innovation Research[***],
- Developing and defining procedures and methods suited to work out solutions by doing respective research after the conference.

---

[*] In this connection, the results of former ISPIM Conferences may be mentioned:
Hübner, H. (Ed.): The Art and Science of Innovation Management: An International Perspective, Amsterdam 1986 (ISPIM Conference 1985);
Rothwell, R./Bessant, J. (Ed.): Innovation: Adaptation and Growth, Amsterdam 1987 (ISPIM Conference 1987);
Allesch, J. (Ed.): Consulting in Innovation: Practice - Methods - Perspectives, Amsterdam 1990 (ISPIM Conference 1989);
Geschka, H./Hübner, H. (Ed.): Innovation Strategies; Theoretical Approaches - Experiences - Improvements, Amsterdam 1992 (ISPIM Conference 1991)
[**] Bierfelder, W.: Innovationsmanagement, München 1987, page 15
[***] These problems are fields of future research and, therefore, topics for further ISPIM Conferences

Conference Structure

To reach these goals, a special structure as **Working Conference** was used which is shown below:

<u>**Thursday, 25.8.94**</u>

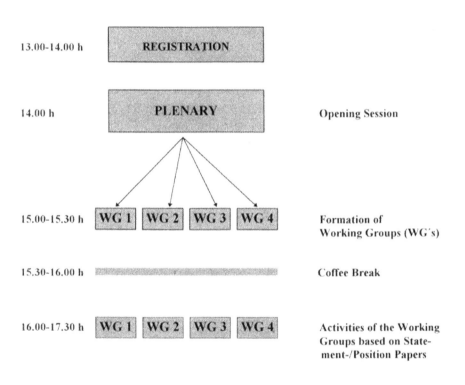

13.00-14.00 h	REGISTRATION	
14.00 h	PLENARY	Opening Session
15.00-15.30 h	WG 1 WG 2 WG 3 WG 4	Formation of Working Groups (WG's)
15.30-16.00 h		Coffee Break
16.00-17.30 h	WG 1 WG 2 WG 3 WG 4	Activities of the Working Groups based on Statement-/Position Papers

Friday, 26.8.94

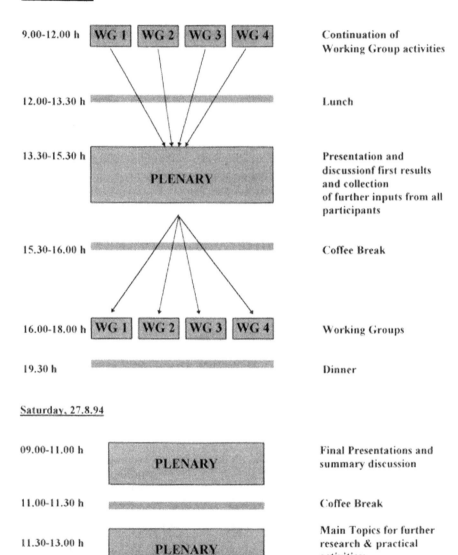

9.00-12.00 h	WG 1 WG 2 WG 3 WG 4	Continuation of Working Group activities
12.00-13.30 h		Lunch
13.30-15.30 h	PLENARY	Presentation and discussionf first results and collection of further inputs from all participants
15.30-16.00 h		Coffee Break
16.00-18.00 h	WG 1 WG 2 WG 3 WG 4	Working Groups
19.30 h		Dinner

Saturday, 27.8.94

09.00-11.00 h	PLENARY	Final Presentations and summary discussion
11.00-11.30 h		Coffee Break
11.30-13.00 h	PLENARY	Main Topics for further research & practical activities; Planning of the next Working Conference?

End of the Conference

International Advisory Board

Per Dannemand Andersen, Riso National Laboratory, Denmark
Jens H. Arleth, Innovation Management U3, Denmark
W. P. Brouwer, Philips Consumer Electronics B.V., The Netherlands
Michel Brylinski, Consultant, France
Ferdinando Chiaromonte, Studio Chiaromonte sas, Italy
Horst Geschka, Management Consulting & Seminars, Germany
Knut Holt, University of Trondheim, Norway
Heinz Hübner, University of Kassel, Germany
Manos Iatridis, Creativity and Innovation Center, Greece
Takaya Ichimura, Nihon University, Japan
Arshad M. Khan, Norwegian School of Management, Norway
Dale Littler, University of Manchester, England
Richard J. Marsh, SBD International, USA
Arie Pier Nagel, Eindhoven University of Technology, The Netherlands
Walter K. Schwarz, Kodak Office of Innovation, Austria
Markku Tuominen, Lappeenranta University of Technology, Finland
Vilkko Virkkala, R&D, Finland
W.J. Vrakking, Holland Consulting Group, The Netherlands

Conference Chairman

Univ.-Prof. Dipl.-Ing. Dr. Heinz Hübner
Head of Department
Management Science - Technology Impact & Innovation Research
(TechnikWirkungs- & Innovationsforschung, abbreviation **TWI**)
Faculty of Business Management & Economics
University of Kassel

Local Programme & Organizing Committee

Heinz Hübner
Torsten Dunkel
Stefan Jahnes   TWI
Ursula Harbusch   University of Kassel
Gertraut Berthold
Hans-Dieter Schwabe, Chamber of Industry & Commerce, Kassel

Acknowledgements

I want to express in this way my grateful thanks to all who helped in preparing, carrying through, and "after-treatment" of the Conference, whether by their active personal service or by financial support. In contrast to the usual type of conferences, the Conference structure chosen required the service of additional experts to act as Moderators for the individual Working Groups, and as "Reporters" for documentation of the results of such group work. These persons have been named, just like the Speakers, in the individual chapters, so I may confine myself to a general thanks in this place.

Special thanks are dedicated to my colleague and friend Prof. Takaya Ichimura of the Nihon University, Tokyo, who fortunately had been staying as a Visiting Professor at our Department in the spring of 1994; a lot of helpful recommendations and experience contributed by him could be adopted in the preparation, performance, as well as in the present Proceedings.

Thanks to all members of the Local Programme & Organizing Committee, as well as for the convenient cooperation with H.D. Schwabe of the Chamber of Industry & Commerce in Kassel, and to the ISPIM President.

Finally, my special thanks are dedicated, on the one hand, to Ursula Harbusch - in particular for her unselfish service prior to and during the Conference - and to Gertraut Berthold, who helped to transform the manuscripts of the texts originating from the TWI into the necessary shape and saw to it that - hopefully - not too many "Germanic" expressions remained in them.

Heinz Hübner

Opening Remarks by the President of ISPIM

Prof. Dr. Heinz Hübner and Dipl.-Oec. Torsten Dunkel organized, with the help of their associates of the University of Kassel and the Kassel Chamber of Industry & Commerce, the first International Working Conference on Innovation Management and Research.

This kind of conference, where the participants not only held presentations but had the opportunity to discuss in length one of the four topics, was an innovation in itself. And it worked out very well. "Normally I hate conferences", one of the delegates remarked, "but this one I loved. We had time to discuss my favourite subject this time. Normally you run from session to session and come home with a lot of business cards. In this conference the quality stood above the quantity."

The results of the working conference were also ideas and fields for future conferences as well as for future research. In this way, the next discussion will be able to benefit from Kassel.

Thank you very much, Heinz Hübner and Torsten Dunkel !

ISPIM - International Society for Professional Innovation Management

As the President of ISPIM, I would like to explain to the readers what ISPIM is like and what you get if you become a member.

ISPIM is an international network of leading academics, business leaders, management consultants, and other professionals of various responsibilities, dedicated to the creation, development, and implementation of effective innovation management skills for the benifit of those we serve. Our organizational vision is one of professional strength rather than a great many members. As innovation and bureaucracy do not mix well, we are avoiding complex administration of our efforts. We think you will enjoy the convivial atmosphere of our gatherings and the spirit of mutual support. Our most important activity consists in holding conferences and workshops, where ISPIM members and other experts and managers meet every year to share experience and maintain personal relations and also develop new contacts and opportunities. The other benefits of your memberships include:

- access to an international network of researchers, consultants and practitioners occupied with innovation on a professional, long-lasting and informal basis;
- subscription to ISPIM-NEWS;
- opportunity to participate in international and country-wise ISPIM conferences at reduced rate;

- reduced rate for subscription to PDMA (Product Development and Management Association, USA).

ISPIM's "quality of people" strategy

Our membership strategy emphasizes quality rather than quantity. This means:
- A membership limited to 200 persons to provide a high level of effective communication and a more personal supportive climate;
- Balanced international representation;
- A well-distributed mix of academics, business leaders, consultats and others to assure effective bridging between theory and practice;
- Members are among the leading individuals in their country in terms of their knowledge of the innovation process, experience or other qualifications contributing to, and gaining from, our network.

Our networking activities

The means for fulfilling our mission are international conferences, workshops and publications, leading to personal contacts and friendships, research projects and business activities across nations and cultures.

Some of the ISPIM history

ISPIM originated from an initiative taken by Prof. Knut Holt at the University of Trondheim in the 1970ies. He initiated and organized a programme of comparative cross-cultural studies on Needs Assessment and Information Behaviour: The NAIB Programme. The objective was to present an array of tools, as well as guidelines for their practical application, for the assessment of user needs in product innovation processes. During the NAIB Project, an international group formally founded ISPIM in Trondheim/Norway on 15th June 1983. Through our activities, ISPIM has succeeded in developing a strong international network.

ISPIM has up till now organized nine international conferences or workshops on innovation management. These conferences and the number of participating coutries are:

1974	Trondheim	Norway	5
1979	Frankfurt	Germany	5
1983	Trondheim	Norway	9
1985	Innsbruck	Austria	17
1987	Brighton	England	19
1989	Berlin	Germany	7
1991	Jerusalem	Israel	7
1993	Eindhoven	The Netherlands	13
1994	Kassel	Germany	11
1995	Rome	Italy	under preparation

ISPIM Members

ISPIM presently has around 100 personal and institutional members (June 1994). ISPIM members are from 19 countries: Australia, Austria, Barbados, Belgium, Czechoslovakia, Denmark, Finnland, France, Germany, Greece, Israel, Italy, Japan, Liechtenstein, Norway, Sweden, The Netherlands, UK, USA. The ISPIM membership list includes a number of people internationally recognized for their professional distinction, the majority being academics and with a relatively large number from the Scandinavian countries and The Netherlands.

We believe our "quality of people" strategy is creating recognition of the professional distinction of ISPIM members and thereby adding to the standing of innovation management as a whole.

Dr. A.P. Nagel
ISPIM President
Eindhoven University of Technology

Recent Essentials in Innovation Management and Research, edited by H. Hübner / T. Dunkel
Gabler, Wiesbaden/Germany, 1995

Explanation of the Topics

Heinz Hübner
Management Science - Technology Impact & Innovation Research
University of Kassel

For better understanding of what has been discussed and worked out within the Working Groups, further particulars on the Topics are described here. Generally, the definition of the four Topics, on the one hand, is based on proposals of participants according to the Invitation for Participation, mailed instead of the usual "Call for Papers"; on the other hand, the Topics are - at least partly - covered as fields of research within the Department of Management Science - Technology Impact & Innovation Research at the University of Kassel. It is obvious that the Topics **cannot** *cover all fields of Innovation Management and Research. As far as other fields were touched, they are described within the Group Work documentations.*

Strategic Networking within (Inter-)National Innovation Systems

With respect to the importance of innovation for the economic position of national economies, most governments have established a lot of **institutions** engaged in innovation; these - **together with companies** - may be understood as the **concrete part** of a national Innovation System.

Additionally, a lot of measures have been worked out to ensure, together, a **public climate for innovation** to stimulate and support the innovation behaviour of companies. The measures creating the public climate for innovation may be undestood as the **abstract part** of the **national Innovation System** (Hübner, H., 1993)

Altogether, the national Innovation System may be understood as consisting of the components shown in Figure 1.

According to Freeman (1987, p. 1),*"the network of institutions in the public and private sectors whose activities and interactions initiate, import, modify and diffuse new technologies may be described as the* **"national system of innovation."**

In this context, **Strategic Networking** is of high importance, as the degree of autonomy generally is decreasing in the field of innovation, especially considering all the functions necessary for technical innovation. This is true for companies as well as for a national economy. Therefore, Strategic Networking has to be understood as an important means for designing and optimizing the Innovation System on government as well as company level.

2

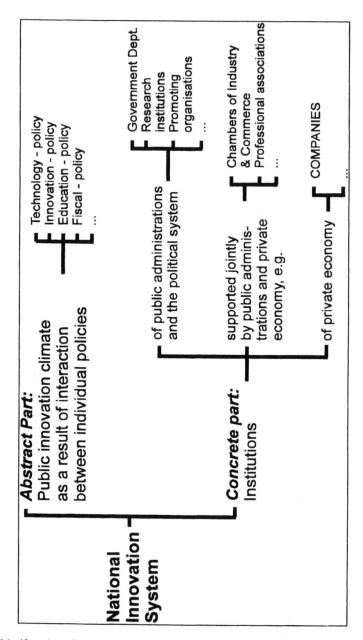

Fig. 1: Manifestation of the innovation System of a national economy

Main questions for group work could be

a) on company level: In which way potentials of the (inter-)national Innovation System can be used by Strategic Networking?

b) on government level: In which way can Strategic Networking with institutions of other countries/nations support political, economic, and social interests?

The Innovation System of the Company as a Frame for the Management of Innovation Projects

Explaining the first Topic, it was shown that the company may be understood as just one component of the (inter-)national Innovation System. But the company itself may be considered as a system, too: According to the system approach, the borders of a system may be defined on considerations of expediency.

Considering the dynamics of competition in innovation, companies' concentration on the specific innovation processes will not ensure to keep successful in future: Rather, the design of an Innovation System within the company seems to be necessary which - beyond other partial systems - will ensure successful overall innovation behaviour of the company. It appears helpful for the discussion, instead of a definition, to explain the Innovation System of the company in greater detail.

*The **Innovation System** is one of several partial systems of the company; as Innovation Management is an interdisciplinary task, which generally may require experience and know-how of all departments, the border of the Innovation System must not form a sub-system, but has to be identical with that of the company, forming a so-called Aspect System (Hübner, 1982). The components of this system are the different innovation potentials (men, technical equipment, information, know-how in technology, based on natural and engineering as well as other fields of science (including Management Technology etc.) which are interrelated.*

As the needs for designing such a system and main functions are described in more detail in the paper "How to Structure the Innovation System of the Company", there is no reason for giving further details here.

It is obvious that there are certain relationships between this Topic and Strategic Networking.

Instruments as Management Technology

As has been worked out by Booz-Allen & Hamilton (1982) in an empirical study[*] , a well-structured procedure within the processes of innovation is one main criterion of companies which are very successful in Innovation. In addition, the existence of an experience curve could be identified with cost reduction of 29% on each doubling of the number of innovation projects; this effect is mainly based on a methodological control of the process. Based on these more general results, Cooper/Kleinschmidt (1986) ascertained in greater detail, as a result of another empirical study, the deficits considering methodological certainty and professionality: On a scale ranging from 0 to 10, the average value was identified between 5 and 6, and the greatest deficits in respect of knowledge and application of methods were identified for the following phases:
- First idea selection,
- Rough market assessment,
- Detailed market analysis.

Another result seems of greatest importance for Innovation Managment and Research in general as well as for the Working Group discussions:

Incompleteness in the execution of the individual phases **of the innovation** process (against a well-structured procedure) **and poor methodological** professionality together are in strong correlation with **failures in product innovation.**

Considering these results, the importance of methods and instruments for being successful in innovation is evident.

With regard to this importance of competence in using instruments in a broader sense, these may be understood as an autonomous field of know-how of the company in the way of **"Management Technology"** (Hübner, 1992), including
- Approaches,
- Ways of thinking,
- Models,
- Methods and principles,
- Auxiliary equipment (computer support, check-lists, etc.).

---

[*] An overview on several empirical studies as well as a summarizing conclusion in German language is given by Geschka, 1989

In contrast to this importance and although a great number of different kinds of instruments are available, the diffusion and application in practice of corporate planning and Management of Technology & Innovation is unsatisfactory up to now. Therefore, **the diffusion of instruments appears to be of greater importance than the development of new ones**.

Main questions for the Working Group could be

-     how to diffuse Management Technology into practical use and
-     how to reduce barriers against applying instruments within a systematic procedure.

Ecological Problems as a Trigger for Innovation[*]

There is no doubt that ecological problems are mainly caused by industrial production and mass consumption in the industrialized countries (compare, among others: Worldwatch Institute, 1992; Bossel, 1990). Experts and decision-makers in governments or companies, and all of us in our consumption behaviour, are responsible for avoiding further destruction of the ecosphere; however, the dominant role of companies as a "pillar" of economy is evident.

While until now ecological problems mostly have been considered as a threat only, causing additional costs etc., some developments in theory and practice are showing that ecological problems may be understood as a chance for the company and as a trigger for innovation.

Although several approaches for handling ecological problems on companies' level have been developed, it seems appropriate to focus on the product, considering all stages from its origin, production, distribution, usage, and the stage after end of usage.

An increasing number of governments have established institutions for Technology Assessment - following in this respect the OTA (Office of Technology Assessment), Washington, D.C.; but there is a need for implementing these tasks in the way of Technology and Product Impact Analysis into the companies to advance from "after-caring" to preventive integrated environment protection. To be successful in this way, companies are again forced to apply efficient Management of Technology and Innovation, which is necessary to change the directions and goals of innovation towards the principle and vision of an overall **"sustainable development"**, defined as *"development that meets the needs of the present without compromising the ability of future generations to meet their own needs" (World Commission, p. 43)*. It contains within it two concepts:

---

[*]   The content of this Topic was first introduced into ISPIM activities at the Brighton Conference in 1987 (Hübner, H., 1987); it is my hope that this Topic will be growing up as an important field relating to Innovation Management and Research in general and within ISPIM.

6

- The concept of 'needs', in particular the essential needs of the world's poor, to which over-riding priority should be given; and
- The idea of limitation imposed by the state of technology and social organization on the environment's ability to meet present and future needs".

References

Booz-Allen & Hamilton (Ed.): New Products Management for the 1980's; Booz-Allen & Hamilton Inc., New York, 1982

Bossel, H.: Umweltwissen - Daten, Fakten, Zusammenhänge, Berlin etc. 1990

Cooper, R./Kleinschmidt, E.: An Investigation into the New Product Process: Steps, Deficiencies and Impact; The Journal of Product Innovation Management, Vol. 3 (1986), No. 2, p. 71-85

Freeman, C.: Technology Policy and Economic Performance: Lessons from Japan; London, 1987

Geschka, H.: Erkenntnisse der Innovationsforschung - Konsequenzen für die Praxis; in VDI (Hrsg.): Neue Produkte - Anstöße, Wege, Realisierungen, Strategien, VDI-Bericht Nr. 724, Düsseldorf 1989, p. 21-47

Hübner, H.: Das nationale Innovationssystem als Grundlage der Behauptung im Innovationswettbewerb; internal Working Paper, TWI, University of Kassel, 1994

Hübner, H.: "Innovations- und Technologiemanagement, ganzheitliches" and "Technologie", in: Gabler Wirtschaftslexikon, 13th, completely revised edition, Wiesbaden 1992, p. 1628 - 1637 and p. 3249

Hübner, H.: The Aspect-System-Approach - An instrument for reducing complexity in systems design and its application to Information-Systems planning, in Trappl, R./Hanika, P./Tomlinson, H. (Ed.): Progress in Cybernetics and Systems Research, Vol.X, Washington, D.C., USA, 1982, p. 263-268

Hübner, H.: Innovation - Quo vadis? 1987, available as Working Paper No. 5, TWI, University of Kassel, 1990

World Commission on Environment and Development (Ed.): Our Common Future, Oxford University Press, Oxford/New York 1987

Worldwatch Institute (Ed.): State of the World 1992, W.W. Norton & Company, New York

Strategic Networking

within (Inter-)National

Innovation Systems*[)]

For better understanding, it is recommended to read first the particulars on the Topic, given under Explanation of the Topics (pages 1-6)

·

Recent Essentials in Innovation Management and Research, edited by H. Hübner / T. Dunkel
Gabler, Wiesbaden/Germany, 1995

A Design Typology of Inter-Organisational Networks: A Tool for Network Development in Practice

Louweris Hop

Ger Post

Eindhoven University of Technology

Abstract:
In this paper we describe a typology of inter-organisational networks to facilitate the development of innovation networks in practice. This typology is based on literature research and empirical research on innovation networks in Dutch industry. This typology represents the main structural dimensions of inter-organisational networks and the main design options on these dimensions.

1. Introduction

The dominant perspective of academic attention on product innovation can be characterized as the "lonely innovator syndrome". Many studies in this field focus on the independent producer as the initiator and executer of the product development processes. The idea of the lonely innovator has also affected organisational practitioners. Many business owners or company managers see product innovation as an internal issue.

During the last years a growing attention for joint innovating between business partners can be observed (Von Hippel, 1976; Biemans, 1989; Håkansson, 1987; Teece, 1986; De Bresson and Amesse, 1991; Freeman, 1991; Shaw, 1993). In joint innovating an important part of the development process takes place in the form of relations and interaction between different actors. Consequently, innovation should not be seen as the product of one actor but as the result of an interplay between actors who are coupled together in a network form of organisation. According to De Bresson and Amesse this network form of organisation can be seen as a privileged way of innovating (De Bresson and Amesse, 1991).

Presently much attention is paid to this new theme in organisation theory. In scientific work as well as in management literature the network form of organisation is held for flexibility, innovation and organisational learning. Many business and service organisations - often due to economic developments - have adopted (or are doing so) these ideas about modern organisation and are facing (corporate) change programs to improve organisational effectiveness. The impact of this theme on management practice and academic research is large enough to claim the title of paradigm in organisation theory.

However, the accessibility of this new field of research (and practice) is not very great. Using a metaphor introduced by Koontz (Weihrich and Koontz, 1993) the management theory jungle has grown by the addition of a new jungle section: organisation and network.

In this paper we try to cultivate a (small) part of this network theory jungle. In this we take an action perspective. In addition to descriptive objectives resulting in a better understanding of organisational networks the paper primarily aims to contribute to design problems in practice.

First the network phenomenon is described and defined. Second, specific attention is paid to the topic of network organisation structure. The paper offers an overview of landmark contributions on this topic. Third, a typology of network organisations is developed and the practical value of this typology will be illustrated with an example of the development of an innovation network. The network typology represents the design options for inter-organisational networks and is developed to facilitate the creation process. The paper closes with some concluding remarks and implications for future research.

2. What are networks?

According to Webster's dictionary of the English language a network is an interconnected or interrelated chain, group or system. The connections or interrelations between these elements can be physical (as with computer networks or infrastructural networks) or social (as with personal networks).

The field of studies on organisation and network is somewhat broad. The contributions by scholars and management differ on many dimensions. Three mainstreams within network literature can be distinguished:

- social network theory (*personal networks*);
- information technology and the impact on management (*physical or infrastructural networks*);
- organisational network theory (*organisational networks*).

In this paper we concentrate on organisational networks. From the perspective of networks, organisations can be seen as:

- conglomerates or corporations build up by more or less autonomous units;
- autonomous organisational entities interacting (or cooperating) with other organisations.

In other words the network may be inside or outside the organisation. In the first case we speak of intra-organisational or internal networks. The second type is called inter-organisational or external networks. Today, *internal networks* generally originate from relative large, integrated organisations by a process of "disentanglement". The development of *external networks* usually originates from a process of "interweaving" and integration. Very often external networks are considered in small business management. The different background of internal networks on the one hand and external networks on the other results in similarities as well as in differences. Despite the existence of several similarities, the problems of internal networks differ to a certain level from the problems and attributes of external networks. Therefore the research questions and aims of both (academic) researchers and management consultants studying internal or external networks show some differences as well.

A frequently stated premise is that all organisations are networks - patterns of roles and relationships - whether or not they fit the network image (Baker, 1992; Nohria, 1992; Laumann et al, 1978). From the ontological point of view this statement is true but we refuse such a formal definition. Although every organisation can be seen as being composed of an internal network structure and participating in an external network or organisation set (Evan, 1966) the ideal type of network organisation differs strongly from the classical functional mechanistic type of organisation. In this paper network organisation is considered to be an empirical phenomenon with characteristics that are different from other types of organisation.

As well for internal as for external networks one of the basic characteristics is that the system as a whole can be described as "loosely coupled" (Weick, 1976). In terms of transaction theory the network form stands midway between market and hierarchy.

The literature on organisation and network offers a colourful range of definitions and characterizations. These definitions of the phenomenon organisational network differ according to the point of reference taken by the author.

In most definitions organisational autonomy and the absence of (dominant) hierarchical relations is chosen as a critical aspect of network organisations (Miles and Snow, 1992; Perrow,

12

1992). The participation of individual organisations or organisational parts is based on free choice and the belief (and trust) that participation will benefit. Except from internal networks this is true for all network organisations. Even for internal networks it may be true that the choice to participate in an internal network is an autonomous one. However, this choice may be influenced by hierarchical relations.

Some authors claim that an organisational network allows to gain and sustain competitive advantage or economies of scale. Usually the concept of (collective) goals and objectives is taken as a central part of some definitions (Jarillo, 1988). Table 1 offers a brief overview of definitions and characterizations quoted from management literature and organisation science.

Table 1: Some definitions and characterizations concerning organisational networks

- Long term purposeful arrangements among distinct but related organisations that allow those firms in them to gain or sustain competitive advantage vis-a-vis their competitors outside the network (Jarillo, 1988).
- Cluster of organisations that makes decisions jointly and integrates their efforts to produce a product or service (Alter and Hage, 1993).
- Cluster of firms or specialist units coordinated by market mechanism instead of chain of commands (Miles and Snow, 1992).
- Cluster of very small (10 employees) firms interacting as well as competing with one another surrounded by an infrastructure that is essential for their survival and for the economics of network scale. The architecture of the Small Firm Network (SFN) is characterized by multiple upstream and downstream relationships between participating organisations. (Perrow, 1992).
- "Self-designing organisation" (Eccles and Crane, 1987).
- A market mechanism that allocates people and resources to problems and projects in a decentralized manner (Baker, 1992).
- A network organisation is integrated across formal boundaries; interpersonal ties of all types are formed without respect to vertical, horizontal, or spatial differentiation (Baker, 1992).
- Distinction between "thick" networks (integration across boundaries of multiple types of socially important relations) and "thin" networks (firms with extensive electronic communication networks, (Nolan and Pollock, 1986; Baker, 1992)).

In this paper we are interested with inter-organisational networks. We define an inter-organisational network as a set of at least three autonomous organisations or parts of organisations bond by more or less stable and non-hierarchical relationships that facilitate transactions between participants in order to achieve a specific goal. For innovation net-works this goal is the development and commercialization of a new product or technology.

The most striking element of our definition is the focus on networks that consist of at least three participating organisations. The rationale for this is that there is a vast array of theoretical literature and practical experience on the development of bilateral relationships between two partners. Far less is known about cooperation between more than two organisations. It is likely to expect that the organisational and managerial problems that arise in (the creation) such multi-actor networks are more complex than in two-actor "networks".

We are primarily interested in the *structural characteristics* of inter-organisational network organisations with objectives directed towards product innovation. In scientific research as well as in management consulting, researchers often are confronted with managerial problems concerning structural characteristics of network organisations. From a scientific point of view many of these questions need to be investigated in future research. One of the tools needed in future network research is a typology of inter-organisational networks. In the next section an overview of typologies of network organisations is summarized and used to develop a preliminary typology of small business innovation networks.

3. Developing a network typology

Organisational networks can be encountered in various forms. In Europe and Japan often we are confronted with a form that can be described as Small Firm Networks (Perrow, 1992). The objectives and "raison d'aitre" of these networks can be either joint development, knowledge transfer, subcontracting or other.

Typical of the American situation a different form of network is strategic alliance of large (multidivisional) organisations. As for small firm networks the nature of the alliance can be various. Often these alliances are created to gain and sustain competitive advantages and to increase market share.

A third form of appearance can be encountered in subcontracting and joint ventures. This type of network is found in the building industry and the Japanese automobile industry. This type of network differs from Small Firm Networks concerning the durability, the stability and legal formalisation of the relationship between the business partners.

Other examples of network forms can be described. In fact the diversity is numerous. In the following we try to draw some lines and present a concise overview of network typologies. Table 2 offers a brief overview of landmark typologies.

14

Table 2: Overview of typologies concerning network organisations

Author	Dimension(s)	Types
Warren (1967)	uniformity of goals;	social choice context, coalitional context, autonomy federative context, unitary context
Godfroy (1993)	network function	exchange network, circuit, policy network, network of technical facilities
Teulings (1992)	morphology	organisation set, action set, grid, configuration
Haas en Drabeck (1973)	autonomy; control	simple exchange system, mediated system, delegated system, hierarchical system
Können (1984)	intensity of bond	transaction network, "control network", "personnel union", constellation of organisations
Lehman (1975)	distribution of power; influence	simple feodal field, intermediary field, organisational empire, corporate guided field
Wissema and Euser (1988)	basis for goal formulations	structure based network, application based network, technology based network
Miles and Snow (1992)	stability; internal context	internal network, stable network, dynamic network
Alter and Hage (1993)	resource dependency; degree of regulation (autonomy)	self sufficient network with autonomy, self sufficient network with constraint, dependent network with autonomy, dependent network with constraint
Alter and Hage (1993)	vertical dependency; task scope	(unnamed; only entitled by numbers 1 to 4)
Ibarra (1992)	degree of alignment	workflow network, influence network, expressive network

Reflecting on the large number of typologies five patterns can be distinguished.

First, networks can be classified as *internal or external* networks (e.g. Warren, 1967; Haas and Drabeck, 1973; Lehman, 1975; Miles and Snow, 1992). This distinction is already discussed in the preceding section. The basic dimension of this classification is the presence or absence of hierarchical relations within the network. In fact a dichotomized classification does violence to the real life situation where differences are gradual (networks are "more or less" dominated by hierarchical relationships).

Second, networks can be classified on the basis of the *goals and objectives* of the individual participants and of the network in full (e.g. Warren, 1967; Wissema and Euser, 1988; Huyzer, 1990). Objectives are: transfer of knowledge or skills, "trade agreements" and technological cooperation. Often the rationale for jointly undertaken activities is based on economies of scale, expertise supplementation, coalition building, flexibility and uncertainty reduction.

Third, networks can be classified on the basis of the *domain of the interaction* (e.g. Godfroy, 1993). Domains of interaction are: research and development, production, logistics, finance, purchase, marketing, recruitment, and so on.

Fourth, networks can be classified on the basis of the *legal form* of the relationships (e.g. Wissema and Euser, 1988). Different legal forms are: joint venture, franchise, license and "project contracts".

Fifth, networks can be classified on the basis of *structural dimensions* (e.g. Haas and Drabeck, 1973; Lehman, 1975; Können, 1984; Miles and Snow, 1992; Teulings, 1992; Alter and Hage, 1993). Dimensions of these typologies reflecting the structure of network organisations are similar to the dimensions used for other forms of organisation.

According to our research interests our typology of inter-organisational networks developed in this section is based on structural characteristics.

Our own research on network organisations in practice demonstrates that several types of network organisation can contribute to joint product innovation. In practice several design options occur for the design and realization of product innovation networks. In the following a shortlist of main design questions is worked out to develop a preliminary typology of inter-organisational networks.

1.   What will be the size of the network? Or: How many actors (organisations or parts of organisations) are necessary for the creation of the network?

2.   What types of services must be available in the network and what is the degree of differentiation among the organisations in the network? Or: What is the complexity of the network?

3. How are the actors related to each other in the network? Or: What is the morphology of the network?

4. What is the degree to which the network relies on rules and procedures to direct the behaviour of the organisations within the network? Or: What is the degree of formalization?

5. Is it necessary to create a central organisational entity which support and manage the network? Or: What is the management and resource centrality of the network?

These questions are taken as an input for the development of an inter-organisational network typology. The main discrepancies between the networks we have investigated were strongly related to two dimensions: (the degree of) *formalization* and the *management and resource centrality* of the network. Formalization relates to the extent to which a network actor's role is defined by formal documentation like rules, procedures and contracts. Management and resource centrality relates to the degree to which the network itself (apart from the participating organisations) has managerial, personnel, material or financial resources to bring into action.

Given these two dimensions four basic forms of inter-organisational networks emerge. This is depicted in figure 1. With respect to management and resource centrality we emphasize that not only decision making but also some staff functions can be concentrated within a "central" unit.

Before describing these basic forms we will emphasize that our typology is still in an early stage of development. More research in necessary to test and improve this typology.

Management and Ressource Centrality

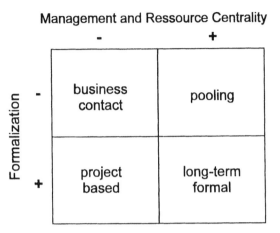

Figure 1: Inter-organizational networks

The first basic form is called *Business Contact*. A business contact network is a set of relationships between industrial organisations in order to realize interchange of business thoughts or ideas and coalition building. Often this network form is used as a starting point for closer cooperation. This is the most informal network form: decision making is based on consensus and the relationship between the member organisations is merely based on trust.

An example of the business contact network is the Japanese 'Igyoshu Koryo' in the interchange step in the development of these networks. In this stage the Igyoshu Koryo are loosely organized and aimed at the transfer of knowledge between participants. (Van Kooij, 1990). Quite similar the Eindhoven Innovation Center organizes business contact circles. The main objective of these circles is to facilitate the transfer of knowledge and practical experience concerning new technologies. Areas in witch these business contact circles operate are: R&D, CAD/CAM, robot welding, and others.

The second basic form is called *Pooling*. In order to solve collective problems the members work closely together. The member organisations establish a central organisational entity for the coordination and integration of the interdependent activities. Although there are no (formal) hierarchical relations within the network, decision making is dominated by the 'manager(s)' of the network.

An example of the pooling network form is the research-sponsor pool. In this form, industrial organisations pool their funds to sponsor research at universities or other institutions. Under the flag of the network the members work closely together with each other and with the research institute in order to develop a new technology that is of common interest to the member organisations. The members use the output of the network - the new technology - as input for the development of there own new products.

The third basic form is called *Project Based*. In this situation the member organisations only cooperate with regard to a specific project and retain their autonomy in all other areas. Project based networks tend to be somewhat temporary. When the project is completed the operational network activities are suspended until another project comes along that is of common interest to the member organisations. During this period acquisition activities and others will be continued.

The member organisations have specialized roles and tasks within a project. There are explicit task descriptions, organisational rules, and clearly defined procedures covering work processes. Because of the short-term orientation of the network there is no need for a central organisational entity.
Examples of project based networks can be found in the Dutch building and construction industry. Also in other industries many joint ventures are project based and similar to our project based network type.

The fourth basic form is called *Long-term Formal*. In this situation the member organisations cooperate with regard to a range of various projects and areas. The member organisations create a more or less free-standing organisational entity for the management and services to support the network. The formalization of this form is comparable with the project based network.

An example of the long-term formal type is a multi-technology network between SME's operating in the areas of metals, electronics and plastics. This network functions as a main supplier for the European automobile industry. The central office is responsible for the acquisition of new projects, the formation of project teams and the coordination of projects under execution. The authority of the central office management includes the expulsion of members who perform weakly or don't live up to contract agreements. In addition to this managerial activities the network uses formalisation techniques like procedures and contracts.

4. A practical example of a product innovation network

To illustrate the practical value of this typology we describe the rise and nearly fall of a product innovation network in Dutch industry. In a period of three years this inter-organisational network evaluates from a business contact network to a project based network.

The start of a business contact network.

In 1991 five executives of industrial organisations started to deliberate on the possibilities for cooperation. From these organisations two of them were involved into product development respectively specialized in mechanical engineering and electronics, the other three were medium sized suppliers for the metal industry. The first meeting was arranged by a local government agent who knew that these organisations endeavoured to cooperate with regard to production and product development. During and after this meeting the executives were enthusiastic about the potential cooperation opportunities and they decided to investigate the cooperation possibilities in depth.

From a business contact network to a project based network.

This investigation almost took one year and the main result was a commission for the development and production of a new product for a customer of one of the member organisations. Together with this customer they worked out a plan for the realization of this project. In this plan the project was worked out in detail: product specifications, task descriptions, responsibilities, planning of the project and the formulation of milestones and the distribution of cost and benefits. The customer was a trade organisation and had no development nor production facilities. He was the financier and the "owner" of the product. His main task was the commercialization of the product.

The two engineering organisations started with the development of the product. During this stage they needed detailed information about the production facilities (production technologies and production capacity) of the other member organisations. At that moment these members realized that this production knowledge was vital for their own competitive advantage in the metal industry. They didn't want to share this knowledge open minded with others which were potential competitors. As a result, the three suppliers left the network. The other two and the customer decided to go further with the network and to search for a substitution of production capacity. However they decided to relinquish from involvement of potential competitors into the network. Supported by a consultant organisation they succeeded to get in contact with three producers active in the different fields of plastics, metal and electronics. The project became a success and the customer was willing to continue the relations with this network. The different specialisms of the members of the network made obvious that complementarity gives more room for open minded communication and applications of different technologies.

At present the members of the network are working on a business plan for new activities. They intent to look for a central office manager charged with acquisition and coordination. It can be said that in the framework of our typology that this network organisation is moving from a project based network to a long-term formal network.

5. Conclusion and implications for future research

We have tried to develop a typology to characterize a network organisation on the basis of two organisational structure dimensions : Formalization and Management and Resource Centrality. We depicted only one case to make obvious that this typology was helpful to follow and to characterize a development process of a network.

In the future we intent to improve and test our typology. Networks are mostly dynamic and therefore longitudinal research schemes are of interest. For each of the distinguished network types indications and contra-indications need to be revealed in order to facilitate the structuring of inter-organisational networks in practice. Also attention will be given to the factors affecting the process of (innovation) network development.

In common with other experiences and research findings it seems that competition can be an important road block for the continuation of the relations especially for project based networks and that complementarity seems to be a success factor. In future research special attention will be given to this issue.

References

Alter, C. and J. Hage, 'Organisations Working Together', Sage, London 1993.

Baker, W.E., 'The Network Organisation in Theory and Practice', In: Nohria, N. and R.G. Eccles (ed.), 'Networks and Organisations: Structure, Form and Action', Harvard Business School Press, Boston, pp. 397-429, 1992.

Biemans, W.G.,'Developing innovations within networks-With an application to the Dutch medical equipment industry', dissertation E.U.T., Eindhoven, 1989.

DeBresson, C. and F. Amesse, 'Networks of innovators: A review and introduc-tion to the issue', Research Policy, Vol. 20, no. 5, pp. 363-379, 1991.

Eccles, R.G. and D.B. Crane, 'Managing Through Networks in Investment Banking', California Management Review, Vol. 30, pp. 176-195, 1987.

Evan, W.M., 'The Organisation-set: Toward a Theory of Interorganisational Relations', In: J.D. Thompson (ed.), 'Approaches to Organisational Design', University of Pittsburgh Press, Pittsburgh, pp. 175-191, 1966.

Freeman, C., 'Networks of innovators: A synthesis of research issues', Research Policy, Vol. 20, no. 5, pp. 499-514, 1991.

Godfroij, A.J.A., 'Interorganisational network analysis', In: Beije, P., J. Groenewegen, O. Nuys (eds.), 'Networking in Dutch Industries', Garant, Leuven, pp. 69-93, 1993.

Haas, J.E. and T.E. Drabeck, 'Complex Organisations: A Sociological Perspective', Macmillan Publishing Company, New York, 1973.

Håkansson, H. (ed.), 'Industrial Technological Development: A Network approach', Croom Helm, London, 1987.

Hippel, E. von, 'The Dominant Role of Users in the Scientific Instrument Innovation Process', Research Policy, Vol. 5, pp. 212-239, 1976.

Huyzer, S.E., Strategische Samenwerking, Samsom, Alphen a/d Rijn, 1990

Ibarra, H., 'Structural Alignment, Individual Strategies and Managerial Action: Elements Toward a Network Theory of Getting Things Done', In: Nohria, N. and R.G. Eccles (eds.), 'Networks and Organisations: Structure, Form and Action', Harvard Business School Press, Boston, pp. 143-164, 1992.

Jarillo, J.C., 'On Strategic Networks', Strategic Management Journal, Vol. 9, pp. 31-41, 1988.

Können, E.E., 'Ziekenhuissamenwerking, Fusie en Regionalisatie', Erasmus Universiteit Rotterdam, 1984 (dissertation in Dutch).

Kooij, E.H. van, Technology transfer in the Japanese electronics industry, Economic Research Institute for Small and Medium-sized Business, Zoetermeer, 1990.

Laumann, E., Galaskiewicz, J. and P. Marsden, 'Community structure as interorganisational linkages', Annual Review of Sociology, Vol. 4, pp. 455-484, 1978.

Lehman, E.W., 'Coordinating Health Care: Explorations in Interorganisational Relations', Sage Publications, London, 1975.

Miles, R.E. and C.C. Snow, 'Causes of Failure in Network Organisations', California Management Review, Vol. 34, pp. 53-72, Summer 1992.

Nohria, N. and R.G. Eccles (ed.), 'Networks and Organisations: Structure, Form and Action', Harvard Business School Press, Boston, 1992.

Nolan, R.L. and A.J. Pollock, 'Organisation and Architecture, or Architecture and Organisation', Stage by Stage, Vol. 6, pp. 1-10, 1986.

Perrow, C., 'Small-Firm Networks', In: Nohria, N. and R.G. Eccles (ed.), *Networks and Organisations: Structure, Form and Action*', Harvard Business School Press, Boston, pp. 445-470, 1992.

Shaw, B., 'Formal and informal networks in the UK medical equipment industry', *Technovation*, Vol. 13, No. 6, pp 349-365, 1993.

Teece, D.J., 'Profiting from technological innovation: implication for integration, collaboration, licensing and public policy', *Research Policy*, Vol. 15, pp. 285-305, 1986.

Teulings, A.W.M., 'Interorganisational Network Analysis and Network Theories', paper presented to a Stip workshop on September 15, 1992.

Warren, R.L., 'The interorganisational Field as a Focus for Investigation', *Administrative Science Quarterly*, Vol. 12, pp. 420-439, 1967.

Weick, K.E., 'Educational Organisation as Loosly Coupled Systems', *Administrative Science Quarterly*, Vol. 21, no. 1, pp. 1-19, 1976.

Weihrich, H. and H. Koontz, *'Management: A Global Perspective*', McGraw Hill, 1993.

Wissema, J.G. and L. Euser, 'Samenwerking bij technologische vernieuwing: De nieuwe dimensie van het management van innovatie', Kluwer Bedrijfswetenschappen/NEHEM, Deventer, 1988 (in Dutch).

Recent Essentials in Innovation Management and Research, edited by H. Hübner / T. Dunkel
Gabler, Wiesbaden/Germany, 1995

Experiences on implementing cross-border networking with the Technology-oriented Development Programme EUREGIO

Rick Garrelfs

Innovatie adviesbureau Van der Meer & van Tilburg

Enschede, The Netherlands

1. Introduction

Van der Meer & van Tilburg has conducted a project with the aim to establish cross border co-operation in technology projects in the EUREGIO, the Dutch-German border region between the Rhine, Ems and IJssel. We will first introduce the backgrounds for cross border co-operation (§2) and how network strategies can play a part in regional development (§3). In order for networks to grow without continuous effort from an independent bureau, we have defined within the current project some innovation mechanisms (§4). The central question is what other mechanisms might be used for initiating and continuing networks (§5).

2. The need for cross border co-operation

National borders have historically presented barriers for integration and cohesion of neighbouring regions. These barriers have had political, social and economic effects. Firms located in border regions were faced with half of their geographical span spread to the other side of the national border. The introduction of the European market will directly effect these firms as even regional functions will both be open for new competition and at the same time provide enlarged markets. In order to facilitate integration of border regions and the use of until now unrealized synergies, the European Union stimulates cross-border co-operation. Along the internal European borders, about forty Euregions -- organized regions that cover both sides of the border --, have been established. The EUREGIO is the Dutch-German European region that is located between the Rhine, Ems and IJssel.

One of the aims of the EUREGIO is to stimulate cross border co-operation in the field of innovation and technology transfer. Van der Meer & van Tilburg is commissioned to establish a

Technology oriented Development Programme [TDP] which must lead to a creative climate for innovation and technology transfer and result in a set of co-ordinated innovation and technology projects for the period 1994-1999.

3.   Networks and an innovative climate

Regional policies that are initiated by or targeted at the needs or problems of a specific region and that are extended to the building of an industrial region, are sometimes referred to as technopolis policies. In an interesting article, Charles points out that for these technopolis approaches there seem to be three main options:

1.   The **market-led approach**, where high growth regions develop based on concentrations of high technology industry and R&D without the presence of an overt regional technology strategy. These regions usually do not necessarily demonstrate a high degree of interaction within the region, but often have national and international relations.

2.   The **directed technopolis**, where strong emphasis is placed on installation of infrastructure and inward investment. The two major planning concepts that are associated with this approach are the new towns and the growth pole. With this strategy emphasis is placed on attracting outside investors and local integration does not necessarily occur.

3.   The **network strategy**, which is focused on the networking of a number of local initiatives and organizations to promote indigenous development and, secondary, to attract outside investment. The aim is to link together organizations and institutes to exchange information, develop joint projects, make use of complementary skills and market access etcetera. Emphasis is placed on innovation and technology transfer throughout the entire region. The aim to realize indigenous development potential seems to make networking a strategy of regeneration rather then of new development.

It is this focus on realization of indigenous development potential that makes networking the preferred strategy for development within the TDP. Indigenous development comes from the benefits firms and organizations realize by the establishment of these new contacts. Faced with ongoing globalization of markets, fast paced technological developments and high turbulence in markets that is associated with shortening of product/market/technology-lifecycles, firms put in continuous effort in rationalization of costs and increase in flexibility. Networking has shown to improve the ability for creative adjustment within firms and can be categorized as a flexibilization strategy.

What are the potential benefits a company can expect from a co-ordinated innovation effort? Hagedoorn has made an overview, based on literature research, of motives why companies would want to co-operate in their efforts to innovate. These motives can be related to R&D, the innovation process, and market access. Motives related to R&D include the increased complexity of new technologies, cross-fertilization of various disciplines and fields of technology, enlarged access to know-how and complementary technology, and reduction of uncertainty and costs in R&D. Motives related to the innovation processes include capturing of the partners' tacit knowledge of technology and speeding-up innovation. Motives related to market access include improved monitoring of changes and arising opportunities, enlarged (foreign) market entry, and expansion of the product range.

There are several forms in which this co-operation with respect to technology development can be established. Many of these forms are based on one-to-one relationships. In the TDP the aim is to co-ordinate efforts between a number of companies and institutions (public-private-partnerships) in a strategic network. In the definition of Sydow, a strategic network is a strategic organizational form, led by one or more firms, for co-operation in strategic economic activities aimed at the realization of competitive advantages. This organizational form holds the middle between hierarchy (like vertical integration) and market relationships. They are comparatively stable relationships between autonomous companies who usually have an interdependent relationship in the market.

When the number of contacts and the intensity with which the communications are taking place is high, clusters of entrepreneurial activities can come into existence. Often, clusters are referred to as a number of companies in a region with similar activities. However, here clusters are defined as a group of companies in a region between which intensive relationships exist and who together add value to their markets. The relationships can be horizontal (a group of companies with similar activities in similar markets; for instance: Philips and Siemens in the Megabit project), vertical (a group of companies from different levels of the same value chain; for instance: Toyota's keiretsu system) and even diagonal (a group of companies from different levels from various value chains; for instance: the recent clusters of computer manufacturers, cable networks and production companies and studios). Especially the diagonal clusters seem to be promising in a European setting and are already well researched. The importance of the existence of regional clusters as engines of regional economic growth seems to become ever more clear.

26

Scientific institutes (or similar public organizations) usually are the dominant organizations from which transfer of knowledge takes place. The relationship between companies and scientific institutes can often be described as 'fetching' knowledge. However, when the relationship can be seen as a form of co-makership between companies and scientific institutes, this relationship is called a Public-Private-Partnership (PPP).
An overview of the structure of networks is given in figure 1.

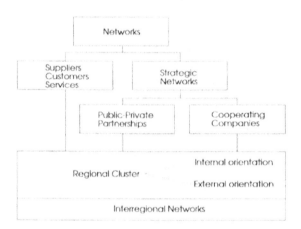

Fig. 1: The Network Structure

The preferred course of development for the regional clusters is dependent on the nature of the business activities. If the regional companies really have an external orientation only, potential synergies in the region will not be realized; there is a lack of regional coherence. On the other hand, if regional companies are primarily intraregionally oriented, it is expected that innovative ability within the region will diminish: the region will choke.

4. Networks as instruments for innovation

The objective of stimulating network organizations is to create entrepreneurial activity that is distinguished by its innovative ability, or, as it was put by an interviewee: 'the region should be oozing with applications [...of technology...]'.

An innovative climate will exist there, where public organizations (public offices, intermediairy organizations, scientific institutes, andsoforth) and private organizations are in a modus of intense interaction, founded on a coherent social base. The best chances for a creative climate to develop will be where the three main elements come together.

Fig. 2: Elements for an innovative climate

When the premise is that regional development should primarily stem from indigenous development potential, it is necessary to get a clear overview of the strong and weak points of the region relative to other reference regions and the spread of strong and weak points within the region itself. From this overview, areas can be defined where with a given effort and budget the best results can be expected. If these areas can be defined as particular technology themes, then these are the themes with which the region can establish a clearly discernible position relative to its environment. 'On some essential points a kind of Mecca should be created'.

It is a prerequisite that these essential points are carried by market demand. Clearly, the definitive success of a network will be defined by its superior performance of its members in the marketplace. Since initiatives originate not only from high technology companies but also from companies that have applied new technologies in only a few aspects of the product or production process, and since often these initiatives lead to incremental improvements in relatively large numbers of companies in the region, it is clear that less R&D intensive sectors should be included in realizing innovation processes. Networks should consist of high-, combi- and low-tech firms.

5. The Technology-oriented Development Programme EUREGIO [TDP]

The question now is: How can the relevant companies, organizations and informal networks be identified, the developments in the field of innovation and technology transfer in the EUREGIO be ascertained, and cross border technology projects be initiated?

Van der Meer & van Tilburg used a phased approach for the attainment of these goals:

1. **Face-to-face interviews** with a number of key figures in the EUREGIO. The key figures are mainly representatives of intermediary organizations. Goal was to identify which technology trends were considered to be important in the EUREGIO and which companies fulfilled a leading role in these developments.
2. **Telephone interviews** with a number of companies mentioned in the face-to-face interviews. Goal was to ascertain the current technological development efforts and the interest in cross border co-operation in these companies.
3. **Workshops** with rerpesentatives from intermediary organizations with the goal to make a listing of current technological themes in the EUREGIO.
4. **Workshops** around specific technological themes with representatives from companies, public organizations and knowledge institutes.
5. **Project groups** where project ideas were worked out into project plans.

In addition to gathering regio-specific information it was the objective to define five cross-border project initiatives that would build up sufficient momentum to continue themselves and initiate new projects. It is known from innovation projects in companies that the enhancement of an innovative climate by the use of enabling mechanisms (innovation mechanisms) improves the innovative capability of most of the organizations; for each individual company there seems to be an 'ideal mix'. Therefore, special focus was placed in the TDE on the definition of innovation mechanisms.

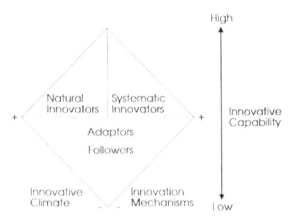

Fig. 3: Types of innovators

In the workshops the most likely hindrances for a successful start of cross-border technology projects were identified. These hindrances essentially cover two points: unfamiliarity with the 'other side' and fear for competition. Therefore, mechanisms were identified that focus on informing on and introducing entrepreneurs to the activities at the other side of the border. A bouquet of mechanisms, varying in degree to how well established contacts between participants were, was identified. An example of the mechanisms used in different phases is given in FIGURE 4.

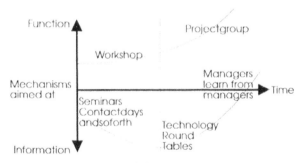

Fig. 4: Various mechanisms for network building

Technology Round Tables are sessions that are organized by the Dutch Innovation Centres where two experts and about twelve entrepreneurs present and discuss current technology trends. Interested entrepreneurs can subsequently obtain consultancy services from the Innovation Centres in Holland.

Managers Learn From Managers is a coherent long term group of entrepreneurs from different industries, who regularly discuss their innovation problems amongst each other, assisted by an innovation consultant. Van der Meer & van Tilburg has good experiences with this mechanism.

Workshops are organized on a specific technology theme. After inventarization of the interests of the participants, follow-up is organized in project groups.

Project groups are used for preparation of cross-border technology projects. Usually, the partners have complementary knowledge, skills or resources, either within a specific technological themes or between specific technological themes. Examples of complementarity are:

- companies with similar technology needs (R&D, transfer, consultancy);
- companies with mutually reinforcing product components;
- co-ordinated product development or market entry;
- new supplier or user webs;
- new webs within the subcontractor network ;
- similar needs for external services;
- andsoforth.

With the abovementioned objectives and mechanistics in mind, the EUREGIO was analysed. First, the different technology policies were described and analysed. For the Netherlands the policies were worked out on national and provincial level, for Germany on Bundes, Länder and Kreis level. Secondly, all relevant scientific institutes were listed with their respective technology focus. Thirdly, the key figures were interviewed in order to get an overview of technology themes that provided the best opportunities for further development in cross-border technology projects. On this basis, various project ideas were identified and five projects were initiated within the programme. A list of promising technology themes in the EUREGIO and project ideas in the TDE is given in table 1.

6. Conclusion

In the Technology-oriented Development Programme EUREGIO, interweaving of existing national networks as a means to define cross-border technology projects and thus to stimulate cross-border contacts between intermediary organizations and companies has proven to be a viable strategy. However, experience shows that much energy and effort is needed for the establishment

Technology theme	Project idea in TDE
- Information technology	xxx
- Telematics	x
- Fuzzy Logic	
- Micro-electronics	
- Sensors & Actuators	x
- Signalprocessing	
- Production control & -automation	xxxx
- Mechatronics	
- Machinebuilding	
- Materials technology	
- Surface technology	x
- Laser technology	x
- Plastics	
- Membranetechnology	
Technology-application themes	
- Environmental technology	xx
- Recycling	xxx
- Alternative energy sources	x
- Medical technology	xx
- Rehabilitation technology	
- Biomedical Sciences	
- Food industry	
- Textiles	
- Transport & distribution	xx
- Logistics	
- Agrification	
Various	xxxx

Table 1 : Promising technology themes and project ideas in the EUREGIO

32

of the first contacts and control of the process to come to concrete results. It is therefore suggested that a central initiating function is a necessary condition in the first stages of establishing networks in the region. The TDE so far seems not sufficient to start a networking activity that has adequate momentum to prolong itself. A proactive attitude towards cross-border initiatives is therefore suggested for the coming years.

Literature

1. Adviesraad voor het Wetenschaps- en Technologiebeleid, *16 Technologiebeleid en Economische Structuur*, 1994.
2. Berkowitz, S.D., *An introduction to Structural Analysis*, The Network Approach to Social Research, Butterworth, Toronto, 1982.
3. *Beter samen*, rapport van de adviescommissie Enschede/Hengelo, september 1989.
4. Brouwer, N.M., A.H. Kleinknecht, *Technologie, werkgelegenheid, winsten en lonen in Nederlandse bedrijven*, SEO, OSA-werkdocument w114, februari 1994.
5. *Bundesbericht Forschung 1993*, Bundesministerium für Forschung und Technologie, Bonn, Juli 1993.
6. Charles, D, 'The design and evaluation of regional technology policies', *in: Technology Transfer Practice in Europe*, Conference Papers, TII and SPRINT, Hannover, April 28-29, 1994, pp.251-260.
7. COB/SER, *Nieuwe kansen voor bedrijven in grensregio's*, eindrapport, samengesteld door MERIT, 1994.
8. *Concept Werkplan technologie-beleid*, afdeling economische zaken Enschede, 1993.
9. *Concurreren met kennis, Beleidsvisie Technologie*, Ministerie van Economische Zaken, 's-Gravenhage, 1993.
10. Corvers, F. B. Dankbaar, R. Hassink, *Euregio's in Nederland, een inventarisatie van ontwikkelingen en beleid*, samengesteld door MERIT, COB/SER, 1994.
11. *Das neue Entwicklungsprogramm für den Kreis Borken*, Kreis Borken der Oberkreisdirektor, Dezember 1993.
12. *De economische produktiestructuur versterkt, plan voor acquisitie en behoud van bedrijvigheid*, afdeling economische zaken Enschede, augustus 1993.
13. *De ontwikkeling van arbeid, kennis en kapitaal in de regio Twente, een analyse van het economische draagvlak*, Stichting Maatschappij en Onderneming, 1994.
14. *Deutscher Delphi-Bericht zur Entwicklung von Wissenschaft und Technik*, Bundesministerium für Forschung und Technologie, Bonn, August 1993.
15. *Economische ontwikkelingsvisie van de Achterhoek*, Concept-rapport, Sociaal-Economisch Overleg voor de Achterhoek, Doetinchem, december 1993.
16. *Europees industriebeleid voor de jaren negentig*, Bulletin van de Europese Gemeenschappen, Supplement 3/91.

33

17. *Forschung in Europa, Aufgaben und Schwerpunkte der europäischen Forschungs- und Technologiepolitik während der deutschen EU-Präsidentschaft 2. Halbjahr 1994*, Bundesministerium für Forschung und Technologie, Bonn, Juli 1994.
18. *Forschungsplan 1992-1997*, Rheinisch-Westfälisches Institut für Wirtschaftsforschung, Essen, Januar 1993.
19. Garrelfs, R., J.J. van Tilburg, *Technologie in de EUREGIO, Technologie-georiënteerd Ontwikkelingsprogramma EUREGIO*, EUREGIO, opgesteld door Van der Meer & van Tilburg, December 1994.
20. *Grensoverschrijdend regionaal beleid*, CNV-visie op europees regionaal beleid, Utrecht, 1993.
21. *Groei, concurrentievermogen, werkgelegenheid, naar de 21e eeuw: wegen en uitdagingen*, Witboek, Europese Commissie, Luxemburg, 1994.
22. Haakansson, H., *Industrial Technological Development, a network approach*, Croom Helm, New Hampshire, 1987.
23. *Handlungsprogramm Wirtschafts- und Arbeitsmarktförderung* - Entwurf -, Kreis Borken, Januar 1994.
24. *Het bedrijfsleven in Nederland 1993*, Vereniging van de Kamers van Koophandel en Fabrieken in Nederland, Woerden, 1993.
25. Hinterhuber, H.H., B.M. Levin, 'Strategische netwerken: organisatievormen van de toekomst', *PEMselect, uit: Long Range Planning, jaargang 10, nummer 4*, juni 1994, pp. 53-66.
26. IHK Stärken- / Schwächenanalyse, *in: Wirtschaft*, IHK Osnabrück-Emsland, NR. 12, Dezember 1992.
27. *Jahresbericht 1993*, IHK Osnabrück-Emsland, 1994.
28. Jeu, M. de, Tj.N.M. Föllings, *Werkdocument operationeel programma Twente 1994-1998*, OOM advies.
29. Kreis Borken, *Das neue Entwicklungsprogramm für den Kreis Borken*, Dezember 1993.
30. Krijger, L., M. Peek, *Technologiebeleid en regio's, verslag van de workshop*, het Provinciehuis te Arnhem, economische zaken Provincie Gelderland, 8 december 1993.
31. Krolis, H.P., C. Machielse e.a., *Kiemen van vernieuwing, economisch-technologische ontwikkeling en ruimtelijke gevolgen voor Twente*, INRO/TNO, Delft, mei 1989.
32. Meffert, H., *Regionenmarketing, Münsterland, Ansatzpunkte auf der Grund-lage einer empirischen Untersuchung*, Westfälische Wilhelms-Universität Münster, Münster 1991.
33. *Mit Forschung die Zukunft gestalten, Das Ministerium stellt sich vor*, Bundesministerium für Forschung und Technologie, Bonn, März 1994.
34. Müller, M., Strategieansätze für Zulieferer, *in: Die Unternehmung*, vol. 3, 1993.
35. *Nationaal Platform Globalisering 24 maart 1994*, uitgave Min. van Economische Zaken, april 1994.
36. *Nationaal Platform Globalisering*, Verslag van de slotmanifestatie 1994, uitgave Min. van Economische Zaken, april 1994.
37. *Nederland in drievoud, een scenariostudie van de Nederlandse economie 1990-2015*, Centraal Planbureau, SDU uitgeverij, Den Haag, 1992.
38. *NRW, Bilanz der Zusammenarbeit des Landes NRW mit der EG, Belgien und den Niederlanden im Rahmen des INTERREG-Programms*, Dezember 1993.
39. *Provinciaal Economisch Beleidsplan '91-'94*, Provincie Drenthe.
40. *Ratgeber Forschung und Technologie 1993/1994, Fördermöglichkeiten und Beratungshilfen*, Deutscher Wirtschaftsdienst, Köln, 1993.

34

41. *Regionales Entwicklungsprogramm Münsterland*, September 1991.

42. *Scanning the future, a long-term scenario study of the world economy 1990-2015*, Central Planning Bureau, SDU publishers, The Hague, 1992.

43. *Sociaal-Economisch actieprogramma 1993-1994*, Provincie Overijssel, oktober 1993.

44. *Sociaal-economische projecten 1994*, Provincie Overijssel, juli 1994.

45. *Städtedreieck Enschede/Hengelo-Münster-Osnabrück, Rahmenbedingungen, Entwicklungschancen und Gestaltungsmöglichkeiten I*, Forschergruppe Städtedreick, Juni 1993.

46. *Städtedreieck Enschede/Hengelo-Münster-Osnabrück, Rahmenbedingungen, Entwicklungschancen und Gestaltungsmöglichkeiten II*, Forschergruppe Städtedreieck, Juni 1993.

47. *Stärken-/Schwächenanalyse des IHK-Bezirks Osnabrück-Emsland*, Zusammenfassung der wichtigsten die Grafschaft Bentheim betreffenden Aussagen aus der o.g. Untersuchung der IHK Osnabrück-Emsland vom November 1992.

48. *Strategische visie op de economische ontwikkeling van Twente*, Provincie Overijssel en RBA in Twente, oktober 1993.

49. Sydow, J., *Strategische Netzwerke, Evolution und Organisation*, Gabler, Wiesbaden, 1992.

50. *Technologie-Handbuch Nordrhein-Westfalen, 2., überarbeitete und erweiterte Auflage*, Ministerium für Wirtschaft, Mittelstand und Technologie des Landes Nordrhein-Westfalen, Köln, März 1993.

51. *Technologiebeleid in Gelderland '91-'95*, notitie technologiebeleid, Economische Zaken Provincie Gelderland, december 1992.

52. *Wirtschaftszahlen '93*, IHK Osnabrück-Emsland, 1994.

53. *Zukunftssicherung des Standortes Deutschland*, Bundesministerium für Wirtschaft, Bonn.

54. *Zukunftssicherung des Standortes Deutschland, Forum 8./9. Februar 1994*, Bundesministerium für Wirtschaft, Bonn, März 1994.

Recent Essentials in Innovation Management and Research, edited by H. Hübner / T. Dunkel
Gabler, Wiesbaden/Germany, 1995

The Importance of European Technology Policy for the German Research Landscape and its Influence on Cooperation

Guido Reger

Fraunhofer-Institute for Systems and Innovation Research (ISI)

Karlsruhe, Germany

Abstract:

The importance of the Commission of the European Communities as a policy agent in the German research landscape has increased over the last 10 years. German participants in the Second Framework Programme form a relatively small community; however, there is a large potential in Germany for future participation in EC programmes. One important impact of EC projects for participating enterprises, higher education institutes and non-university R&D institutes is the improvement of the knowledge base and scientific skills. Another crucial impact is the bringing together European R&D actors and supporting the creation of a "European technology community".

1.   Introduction: European Research and Technological Development Policy

When the Agreement for the Foundation of the European Economic Community (EC Treaty) was extended and changed by the Single European Act (SEA), ratified by all the Member States of the European Community (EC) in July 1987, research and technological development were placed for the first time on an equal footing with other political competences of the EC. In the newly added Articles 130 f - q of the EC Treaty the aims and policy measures are clearly formulated, thus giving the EC a real competence to act. The **main aim of European research and technological development policy** (RTD policy) is according to Article 130f of the SEA

- to strengthen the scientific and technical basis of European industry and the development of its international competitiveness,

- to support transnational cooperation between industry and science, and

- to integrate the area of research and technological development into the general concept for the realisation of the internal market of the European Community.

The main instruments of European RTD policy are the **"Community Framework Programmes"**, running for several years, in which the aims, priorities and financial dimensions are defined for a period of four to five years (cf. Kommission der EG 1990b). Up to now there have been three Framework Programmes, with a growing number of sub-programmes: the First Framework Programme (1984-1987) was followed in September 1987 by the Second Framework Programme (1987-1991) and in August 1990 by the Third Framework Programme (1990-1994) (cf. Kommission der EG 1987 and 1990a). The overlapping of the programmes in time is deliberate, and is intended to ensure the continuity of the RTD activities of the Commission of the European Community (CEC). The Fourth Framework Programme (1994-1998) is just discussed and will presumably start - with one year delay - in the end of 1994.

The growing political and economic integration of western Europe, and the conferring of the competence to act in the area of RTD policy, have led to **increasing importance of the EC as a policy agent in the German research landscape** over the last 10 years. In the Federal Republic of Germany the federal government is the main actor in RTD policy. However, in the course of the historical development of German RTD policy regional and supranational policy agents have also come to play an important role (cf.Meyer-Krahmer/Kuntze 1992, pp.92). Today, as well as the federal government, the "Länder", local authorities, semi-public and private institutions (such as chambers of industry and commerce, transfer institutions, Confederation of Industrial Research Associations (AiF)) at a national or regional level, and the EC at a supranational level, play an active role in the field of RTD policy in Germany.

A systematic attempt at a horizontal, cross-programme empirical examination of the impacts of EC RTD support in the Federal Republic of Germany (and in the other Member States) has not previously been undertaken. Therefore, and in consideration of the preparations for the Fourth Framework Programme, the **"IMPACT studies"** have been carried out at the request of the Directorate General XII (DG XII) of the Commission of the European Communities (CEC) in order to assess the relative importance and possible effects of European RTD policy for national policy in the Member States. The studies concentrated mainly on the Second Framework Programme (1987-91), because a lot of the supported projects have either reached their final stage or have been completed and it is therefore possible for statements to be made on the project results.

ISI was commissioned by DG XII to carry out the **German IMPACT study**. The methodological instruments applied were analysis of existing studies on the subject, data bank analysis of German participants in the Second Framework Programme, written questionnaires to participants (586 usable replies) and non-participants (560 usable replies), more than 60 interviews with different experts, and the discusssion of results in a Steering Committee. This contribution is based upon the German IMPACT study (cf. Reger/Kuhlmann et al. 1994).

2. Significance of the EC Technology Policy

2.1 Importance of the EC Technology Policy for the German Research Landscape

The **financial share of EC RTD support** in total expenditure on R&D in Germany is small. In the period from 1987 to 1991, a total of 1,308 thousand million DM was received by German actors from DG XII and DG XIII. Compared with the total German domestic expenditure on R&D in the same period (327.5 thousand million DM; cf. BMFT 1993), EC funding represented 0.4% of the financing of the R&D budget in Germany. Relative to expenditure by the Federal Government (1987-91: 72.4 thousand million DM), EC funding received by Germany represented an approximate 1.8% share, and relative to civil, direct project support by the Federal Government (21.9 thousand million DM, not including expenditure by the Federal Ministry of Defence (BMVg)) it represented ca. 5.9%. Figure 1 shows - in a simplified form and sometimes as estimates - the share of EC financing in the RTD expenditure of the most important actors in the German research and innovation system. In assessing the significance and impact of EC support, this limited financial proportion should always be borne in mind, in order not to overestimate the possibilities of Community funds.

Viewing the German research landscape as a whole, German participants in EC programmes form a relatively **small "community"**. There were 2,108 German participations in EC projects under the Second Framework Programme. However this number is substantially reduced if the frequency of participation is taken into account: the "top ten" large enterprises (most frequent participants) accounted for more than half of all participations in the group of large corporations, and the "top ten" higher education institutes for somewhat less than half of all participations in the higher education sector. German participants in the Second Framework Programme obviously form a stable clientele who - once they have entered the circle of EC consortia - cooperate several times on different projects. To newcomers (especially SMEs and higher education institutes), access to EC projects appears very difficult.

There is still **a large German potential for future participation** in EC programmes. This applies particularly to small and medium-sized firms, research groups at higher education insti-

38

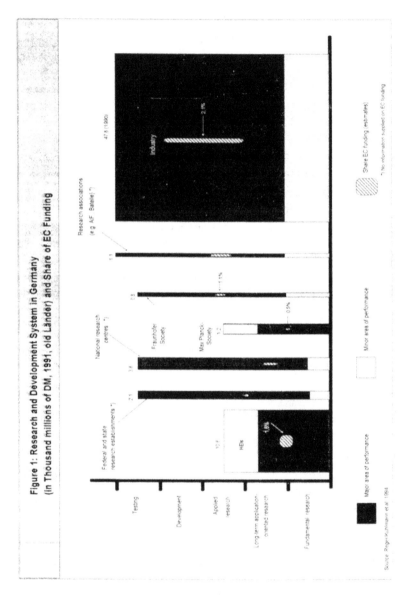

Fig. 1: Research and Development in Germany and Share of EC-Funding

tutes, private R&D institutes, and to some extent to large corporations in industrial sectors which have not been directly addressed by EC programmes so far. Reasons for non-participation are to be found primarily in information deficits about the possibilities of EC support, in an insufficiently European orientation, but also evidently in satisfaction with German RTD support up till now.

2.2 Strategic Importance of Participation in EC Programmes

The EC projects are an **integral part of the R&D portfolios** of the German participants. With the exception of some of the large corporations, projects belong primarily to the **strategic core area of technological competence** (see Figure 2). It is mainly the large corporations and non-university R&D institutes that are aiming to open up a potential new area. For all participants, the EC projects serve to **extend existing business or research fields**, and not so much to establish new ones. Higher education institutes and R&D institutes oriented towards basic research mainly apply to participate in EC projects when the topics fit into their given research context. Large enterprises, and to some extent SMEs, would in some cases have carried out their R&D project without EC support, but in a much less extended form and over a longer time period. The incorporation of the EC project into the strategy and thematic fields of R&D institutions certainly means that the project is useful for them, but reduces the **"value added"**. An absolute "value added" is not attainable in practice; the EC projects arise from existing R&D projects and deal with related problems.

The financial significance of EC support is described by large enterprises as small; it is - as one R&D head put it - "a drop in the ocean" (see Figure 2). For higher education institutes, R&D institutes and SMEs, however, EC funding may amount to between 10 and 20% of the R&D budget. For the SMEs, the average share of EC funding is actually higher than the share of federal funding. Generally speaking, Community support mainly enables R&D projects to be carried out **in an extended form** and **within a shorter time**.

With the exception of SMEs, all other groups in German research expect the **financial importance of EC support to increase**, and Federal and Länder support to decrease; thus great expectations are being placed in the European Commission.

Figure 2: Strategic Significance of EC Projects

	SMEs	BIGs	HEIs	RDIs
R&D Project Portfolio				
Integrated part	●	●	●	●
Few connections	◎	◎	⊖	◎
No connections	○	○	○	○
Role of Technology Competence				
Strategic technological area	●	◎	●	●
Potential new area	⊖	◎	⊖	◎
Just one technology among others	◎	●	◎	◎
Rather peripheral area	○	○	○	○
Role for Business Strategy				
Establish new research areas	◎	◎	◎	◎
Extension of a research area	●	●	●	●
No significance	○	○	○	⊖
Diversification	⊖	⊖	○	⊖
Cost reduction	○	◎	○	○
Role of EC Funding				
Independent of EC funding	⊖	⊖	○	○
Only with EC funding	●	◎	●	●
Larger scale possible through funding	◎	●	◎	◎
Faster through funding	◎	◎	⊖	⊖
Other goals without funding	⊖	⊖	○	⊖
R&D Budget				
Share of EC funding	⊖	○	⊖	⊖
Share of Federal Republic funding	○	⊖	◎	◎
Future Financial Significance of ...				
EC R&D funding	→	↗	↗↗	↗↗
Contracts from enterprises	↗	↗	↗	↗
R&D funding of Federal Republic/Länder	→	↙→	↙→	↙→

●	very important	→	constant significance	
◎	important	↙→	constant, rather decreasing	
⊖	less important	↗	increasing significance	
○	not important	↗↗	strongly increasing significance	

Source: Reger/Kuhlmann et al. 1994

3. Impacts of EC Projects on Innovation and Cooperation of Participants

3.1 Improvement of the Scientific and Technical Basis

The most important results and impacts of EC projects are **improved knowledge and scientific skills** (see Figure 3); this is equally true for all German participants. The higher education institutes also make use of EC projects to increase their R&D personnel, to enhance their scientific reputation and for PhD research. Viewed as a whole, the success of the Second Framework Programme lies in having promoted the exchange of ideas, technology and knowledge within the European Community and in having improved the scientific and technical basis.

In the course of the Second Framework Programme the **scientific and technical quality of the results**, sometimes considered unsatisfactory in the 80s, has been acknowledged by all groups of actors in German R&D. In some areas of technology, according to experts, leading positions have been achieved; however, these successes are limited and cannot be interpreted as signs of a broader breakthrough in the improvement of international competitiveness in the field of information and communication technologies.

EC projects provide opportunities for higher education institutes and non-university R&D institutes to extend their research activities in fields where they are already active. The relatively low participation of higher education institutes can be attributed, among other causes, to the good quality, the relatively good financial equipping and the functional autonomy of the German support system (through the German Research Society, DFG). Institutional funding, and the distribution of support funding via largely autonomous science organisations, provide a guarantee for science and research quality in Germany.

3.2 Impacts on Transnational Cooperations

One important aim of the Second Framework Programme was the support of transnational cooperation between industry and science. In this chapter, the cooperation behaviour and the achievement of a growing cooperation within the EC is described in detail for enterprises,higher education institutes and non-university R&D institutes.

Enterprises

For German firms, the idea of cooperating with one another as partners in Europe has definitely become more attractive: working together in EC projects has increased the general **willingness to cooperate** of large and small and medium-sized enterprises (SMEs). Because of their positive experiences in EC projects, more than half of the investigated enterprises have expanded their cooperation in the area of R&D, extending it especially to include cooperation in further EC projects. For four large companies, positive long term experiences have led to the setting-up of joint R&D establishments. One fifth of the firms have expanded **cooperation into other business areas**, particularly product development (see Figure 3). However, a favourable impact on cooperation in the areas of production, marketing and sales could not be established.

Since many firms have already engaged previously in cooperations, EC RTD programmes do not so much initiate totally new cooperative relations as support the **stabilising and reinforcement of cooperative relationships** at the level of the Community. Personal interviews with representatives of firms confirmed this favourable, stabilising element of European cooperation: many of the partners are known to one another from previous contacts, and apply to the EC's call for proposals as a ready-formed consortium or as the "core" of a consortium in which only a few of the partners are "new". In the opinion of interviewees, Community RTD support gives **SMEs** an especial opportunity to expand existing cooperations into areas other than R&D (e.g. joint sales or service), or to extend business relationships between suppliers and customers into the area of applied research and development.

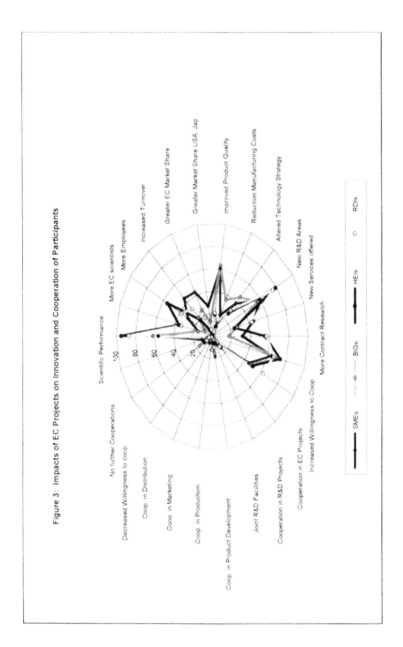

Figure 3: Impacts of EC Projects on Innovation and Cooperation of Participants

Source: Reger/Kuhlmann et al. 1994

Existing contacts and **cooperation in other EC projects** are important for firms when **selecting partners**. Conferences and publications by partners have a limited importance. The EC information data banks and the German federal and Länder public liaison offices play only a marginal role in the search for partners. According to statements in interviews with experts, one main reason for this is that although data banks and liaison offices can provide sufficient data quantitatively speaking, this does not suffice for a qualitative assessment of potential partners, nor for the "forging of networks". Personal contacts and cooperation experiences cannot be measured in terms of quantities of data; they still remain the best way of finding partners. The statement apply generally to large enterprises and to SMEs. However, if results are analysed more intensively and in more detail, it can be ascertained that personal contacts or personal mediation by other partners is even more important for SMEs. Large companies, on the other hand, make better use of publicly available sources of information and public liaison offices.

Higher Education Institutes (HEIs)

A large proportion of the higher education institutes (HEIs) analysed have already cooperated with external partners before participating in EC projects. It is clearly apparent that the great majority (95%) of HEIs work with other HEIs, both in and outside EC projects. Apart from these, the preferred partners are non-university R&D institutes. There are relatively few contacts with enterprises. By contrast, HEIs are most frequently named as cooperation partners by enterprises and by RDIs. Interview results reinforce the impression that the academic research groups and institutes that participate in EC projects are distinguished by an **above-average international orientation**.

In the search for partners for EC cooperations, **existing contacts** are the decisive **starting-point**. Previous cooperations in other EC projects (a factor which will continue to gain importance as the numbers of participants increase), and the typical academic communication channels of conferences and publications, also play a significant part in the search for partners. External assistance from the EC and Federal/Länder sources, such as the EC information data Bank, the EC offices of scientific organisations or public contact agencies of the federal government and the Länder, were evaluated as having little importance in the search for partners; however, it should be borne in mind that at the time when cooperations were being formed for the Second Framework Programme, these public contact agencies had either not yet been opened, or were still being built up. In the meantime, more and more higher education institutes are tending to install EC information offices or name officials in charge of European affairs; this emerges in the interviews. The external task of these offices or officials in charge is to make contact with the EC; their internal purpose is the diffusion of information and coordination of European activities within the university or technical college.

As a result of working together with European partners in projects supported by the EC, the **willingness of HEIs to cooperate has increased markedly** (see Figure 3). Experiencing the possibilities of European research cooperation is "irreversible", in the sense that cooperation horizons have been permanently broadened. Other studies also confirm this conclusion (cf. Tsipouri et.al. 1992).

Non-university R&D Institutes (RDIs)

Most non-university R&D institutes (RDIs) analysed have already cooperated with external partners before participating in EC projects. Cooperation is **primarily with HEIs** and other RDIs, **enterprises** as clients occupy a **secondary** place. Cooperation with competitors and consultants is mentioned least often.

Partnerships in EC projects usually originate from already **existing contacts**. Conferences and publications, and cooperation in other EC projects, are important sources in the search for partners. Mediation by other partners is slightly less important. By contrast EC mediation, EC data banks, public liaison offices and EC offices of scientific organisations appear to play a relatively minor role in the search for partners. Again, direct personal contact is usually the decisive factor in the search for partners. However, these services provided by the EC and German federal advisory offices are used more by first-time applicants to the EC than by applicants with previous EC experience.

For the great majority of institutes, previous cooperation in EC projects has led to a **general increase in willingness to cooperate and/or to extend R&D cooperation** (see Figure 3). No willingness or less willingness to cooperate following participation in an EC project was mentioned only in exceptional cases.

Summary: Growing Willingness for European Cooperation

Summing it up, one important effect of EC support in the sense of politically promoted "value added" is the increased willingness of all participants to cooperate with other institutions throughout Europe. The **important aim of bringing European actors together** and creating awareness of a **"European technology community"** has been attained by the Second Framework Programme, if one considers the statements of German participants. The EC programmes have succeeded in dismantling a preliminary reluctance on the part of industry to work with partners from other countries in strategic core technologies.

However, **two points relating to cooperation appear to be problematic**: firstly, the desired cooperation between industry and science takes place only to a limited extent. Secondly, it is noticeable that the wish to engage in further cooperations definitely focuses on cooperation within other EC projects; the intention to cooperate in transnational R&D projects that are not supported by the EC is expressed by only 10% of German participants. One fifth of SMEs, and one sixth of large enterprises, have engaged in cooperation on the development of joint products; in a few isolated cases up till now have EC partners cooperated in production, marketing or sales. Obviously - and this also emerged from interviews with enterprises - R&D goals are pursued jointly, but the results of EC projects are used and exploited separately.

4. Impacts on German Policy

One of the most important ways in which the European Community influences German RTD policy lies outside the EC Framework Programme: the **"Community Framework for State Aids for Research and Development"** (cf. Commission of the European Communities 1986) stipulates from a competition policy perspective a notification of all R&D promotion measures of Member Countries according to common criteria: science-oriented basic research may be financed 100% from public sources, industrial basic research up to 50%, and applied research from 25% up to a maximum of 50%. This has already **noticeably reduced the freedom of action of the German actors** in the field of industrially-oriented RTD policy, namely the BMFT, the BMWi and the "Länder" governments.

EC RTD policy in the narrower sense, as expressed in the Framework Programmes, gained influence in Germany slowly at first, then with increasing momentum: up to the mid 80s, it was regarded as a marginal factor; with the Second and particularly the Third Framework Programme it has become a recognised actor in the German research landscape, although **not yet** of **central** importance. The impacts of EC RTD promotion have mainly been in the stimulation of original, **additional research and development efforts** in industry and in the industrially-oriented research system. From a national RTD policy point of view the Community support was considered as an additional effort which is welcome but not vital. Only in the (important) area of information technology was this different to some extent: here the significance of the EC efforts is above average.

Over the previous decades, a tentative **distribution of tasks** has arisen in the RTD policy efforts between the Federal Government, increasingly strong in research policy, and the "Länder", whose resources since the 1970s have been taxed to the full by the rapid expansion of the higher education sector. This working arrangement now appears to be endangered by the coordination requirements of EC RTD policy: the Länder see themselves being permanently affected by decisions in Brussels, but do not feel that they are adequately represented there.

Many policy actors in Germany fear that as EC RTD promotion gains importance, there will be **too high a concentration** of related tasks and competences within the **policy administration system of the Community**. They are afraid that the planning, decision-making and control processes of EC research administration, although acceptable in themselves, may become untransparent and eventually ineffective. Against this background there are calls for decentralisation of the institutions and processes of European research and technological development policy. However, it is still an open question whether this decentralisation regards only the administration of (sub-)programmes, or whether it also includes the processes of developing an informed opinion prior to policy decisions.

5. Outlook: Requirements to European Technology Policy

Important reasons for the present high degree of acceptance of Community support in Germany are the **transnational cooperation** towards which the EC programmes are directed and the orientation towards **medium-term or applied research.** Provided the participating enterprises do not have to worry about distortions of their competitive situation or know-how "leaks" to competitors they will participate in a joint R&D project. Thus, from the viewpoint of many German actors, **the orientation towards applied research** is a "conditio sine qua non" for the shaping of future EC programmes.

In the future, the EC policy guideline of "strengthening the international competitiveness of European industry" will have to be understood in a broad and problem-oriented sense: technology as the basis for industrial innovation and competitive production at the beginning of the 21st century cannot be understood or dealt with from a conventional standpoint. **Various fields of technology are progressively fusing and overlapping**. The science-based technology of tomorrow requires the sustained support of appropriate fundamental research. Not only does this increase the importance of the classic transfer from basic research to industrial

48

research; the feedback **transfer from industrial problems into basic research** also acquires new significance.

Furthermore, the **global nature of ecological and social challenges** will mean that the CEC, as a transnational authority, will be pressed by a growing number of urgent problems that can no longer be dealt with at the level of small and medium-sized countries as in Europe. This implies the necessity to link visionary applications of new technologies with new research tasks, without eroding the present responsibilities of the actors.

EC RTD policy in future will have to promote not only R&D cooperations within Europe, as it has done until now, but will have to specifically envisage the support of **cooperation with partners in the "triad"** (USA, Japan) and with **developing regions**.

References

BMFT (Bundesministerium für Forschung und Technologie) (1993):
Bundesbericht Forschung 1993, Bonn
Commission of the European Communities (1986):
Official Journal of the European Communities, 86/C 83/02 of 11.4.1986, Brussels/Luxembourg
Kommission der EG (1987):
Amtsblatt der Europäischen Gemeinschaften L302 vom 24.10.1987, 30. Jahrgang, Brüssel/Luxemburg
Kommission der EG (1990a):
Amtsblatt der Europäischen Gemeinschaften L117 vom 08.05.1990, 33. Jahrgang, Brüssel/Luxemburg
Kommission der EG (1990b):
Forschungs- und Technologieförderung der EG, 2. Auflage, Brüssel
Meyer-Krahmer, F./ Kuntze, U. (1992):
Bestandsaufnahme der Forschungs- und Technologiepolitik. In: Grimmer/ Häusler/ Kuhlmann/ Simonis (Hg.): Politische Techniksteuerung, Opladen
Reger, G./ Kuhlmann, S./ Bierhals, R./ Pilorget, L. (1994):
European Technology Policy in Germany. The Impact of European Community Policies upon Science and Technology in Germany, Heidelberg
Tsipouri, L./Gonard, Th./Kuhlmann, S./Morandini, C. (1992):
Analysis of the Value Added due to Multinational University-industry Partnerships in EC Research Projects, Athens et al. (MONITOR-SPEAR study no. 5.7)

Recent Essentials in Innovation Management and Research, edited by H. Hübner / T. Dunkel
Gabler, Wiesbaden/Germany, 1995

The National Innovation System in the Russian Aerospace Industry

Brian Shaw

Oxford Brookes University
Oxford, England

1. Introduction

The objectives of this research were first to identify the nature of the innovation system in this industry. Having identified the process, it was then necessary to attempt to understand how this system came into being, what is happening presently and where the present major players and academics see it developing.

The (former) Soviet Union's research, development and innovation (RDI) system has the longest history of any centrally administered national innovation system (Hanson and Pavitt (1987).

The need for new customers, collaboration with Western aircraft and component manufacturers coupled with the funding crisis in Russia are resulting in significant changes in the actors and the relationship between them in the sophisticated network which determines the innovation system in this industry.

2. Research Methodology

The methodology was in-depth interviewing, normally lasting some two hours, with senior politicians, academics, directors and managers. The sample included such interviewees as the Chairman of the Committee on Education and Science, Supreme Soviet of the Russian Federation, Chief Designers of Design Bureaux, General Directors of Aircraft, Engine and Rocket Plants, Vice-Rectors and Chairs of Departments of Universities. In total 30 people were interviewed, of whom 2 were Government Ministers, 11 were Senior Academics, 7 Design Bureaux Heads/Chief Designers and 10 Plant Directors/Senior Managers, with 5 being interviewed twice, once in April/July 1993 and again in April 1994. These interviews were carried out with personnel in the White House in

Moscow, in ex KGB buildings and in plants and design bureaux which previous to August 1991 were impenetrable. In fact, the majority of the interviews were carried out in Samara (the previously forbidden city of Kuilbyshev), the centre of aircraft manufacture. The interesting mix of the key actors in and the authorities on the system enabled a balanced view of the way that the system worked to be gained.

3. The Innovation Network

The present innovation network is illustrated in figure 1. Before August 1991 the following actors were not in this network: Department of Aviation Industry, Furthest Abroad Subcontractors, Federal/Joint Aviation Authorities, and the only customers were the Department of the Military Industry of the Central Committee of the Communist Party and the governments of CMEA countries.

The Design Bureaux

These bureaux and their manufacturing plants were guaranteed monopoly sales and payments for the aircraft that they designed and manufactured. The Chief Designer had his lobby in the Ministry-Industrial Commission, which existed within the Council of Ministers of the Soviet Union. More important was the Department of Military Industry of the Central Committee of the Communist Party, as they managed the annual budget for the bureaux. The regional communist committees were also powerful and, in particular, the Samara region due to its concentration of aircraft manufacture. However, the Central Committee sought advice from the Politburo where guidelines were developed. It was, therefore, necessary also to lobby the Politburo, especially as it recruited personnel from the other regions and different branches of industry whose support was needed. This previous lobby system was reasonably stable and once the decision to support a particular aircraft design was made, state funding was decreed and material supplies assured. As a result of the stability of this system the Design Bureaux have long histories with for instance Tupolev celebrating its 71st birthday. Ilyushin its 61st and Beriev its 60th in 1994. They also became the focal actors in this network being responsible for all the stages in the innovation process illustrated in Figure 2 ie the design, testing, certification, launch, marketing and continuous development of all aspects of the aircraft over its lifecycle, coupled with oversight of the production so as to ensure that the safety criteria demanded in the certification are met.

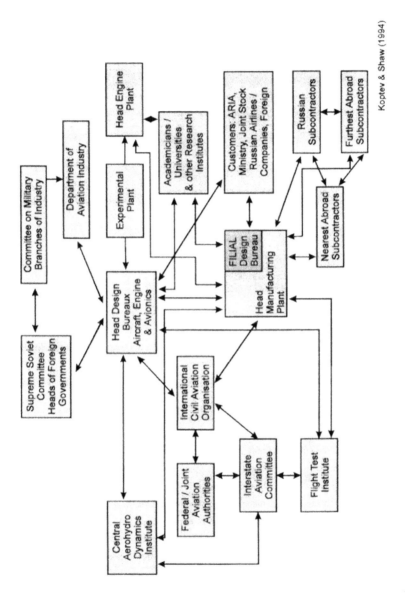

Koptev & Shaw (1994)

Fig. 1: Network in the Design, Development & Manufacture of Aircraft in the Russian Aerospace Industry

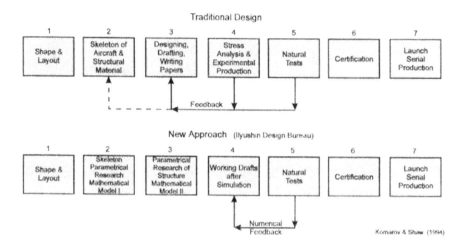

Fig. 2: The Innovation Process in the Russian Aerospace Industry

The dramatic change of and relationships with the customer in 1994 was made very clear by Gorlov (1993) when he stated, the Committee on Military Branches of Industry has not given a new order for military aircraft for three years and the Design Bureaux and manufacturing plants are now ultimately responsible for finding their own customers.

The second major change, as stated by Shorin (1993) to impact on this stage was "Before August 1991, 60 per cent of the science and research budget came from the State and 40 per cent from industry. By the middle of 1992, the Research Institutes had stopped receiving funds from industry and the share from the state had decreased threefold. Added to this, the most advanced scientists were concentrated in the military context and the military complex is now in the disastrous process of conversion. There is also a critical lack of State investment in industry and with the State restriction, industry has a long and painful process of recovery, but meanwhile is plunging deeper into the situation of being the 'raw material appendage to the West'".

As a result of this the Ministry orders for civilian aircraft given before the formation of Aeroflot Russian International Airlines (ARIA) as a joint stock company, have been delivered, but only minimal payment has been forthcoming with, for instance, the powerful Ilyushin Design Bureau (Katyrev (1994)) and the Frunze Motor-Building Production Association (Shitarev (1994)) being the most successful in receiving one third of the payments due to them. However, the Samara AVI.S aircraft building plant is owed billions of roubles with the result that they are working only a three day week, with a high proportion of that time being spent producing civilian goods. A possible lifeline, short term, is the new contract as sub-contractor for wing manufacture, for the US aircraft manufacturer, McDonnell-Douglas (Koptev (1994)).

Western Collaboration

The entrepreneurial Ilyushin bureau forecast some of the potential chaos, with the break up of the USSR, and at the end of 1990 started negotiations which resulted in the incorporation of Pratt and Whitney engines into the Ilyushin aircraft IL96M and IL96T in 1993. Eighteen US components manufacturers subcontract to Pratt and Whitney as main contractor and each of the actors taking part in the aircraft development are sharing the risk and funding their part of the project (Katyrev 1993). Rockwell Collins supply the traffic alert and collision avoidance systems (TCAS) for these aircraft and also to the TU204 designed by the Tupolev Design Bureau. The TU204 also has Rolls Royce engines, Hunting Aircraft seats, Smiths Industries avionics and Litton's inertial reference system. All of these Western parts impact on the design of the aircraft and must be accommodated in the mathematical models now developed to create the IL96.

The Experimental Plant

This carries out the prototype tests. To assist the experimental plant the first prototype is sent to the *Flight Test Institute*, which tests all Russian aircraft and, therefore, has `priceless experience'. (Koptev (1994)) The test aircraft are flown by the Bureaux test pilots, who carry out the test plan that has been devised by the Head Designer in collaboration with the Head of the Test Institute. The aircraft are also sent to Russia's *Central Aero Hydrodynamic Institute* (TsAGI) for instance, the Tupolev TU334 has sent one airframe to TsAGI for static structural test. Five prototypes will be produced. The fourth will be used for ground lifetime cyclic structural tests and the fifth (actually the third flight test model) will become the pattern for future production.

Certification

The key issue now being faced by the civil aviation industry in Russia is certification to US Federal Association Rules (FAR), ie FAR 25 and 23, and the Joint Aviation Rules (JAR) of Europe, JAR 25 and 23, which, if received, will enable them to market their aircraft worldwide. The Russian Interstate Aviation Committee (IAC) is responsible for Russian certification. It is the responsibility of the Aircraft Design Bureaux to gain certification for their aircraft. The Flight Test Institute and the Research Institutes such as: Ts AGI, Institute of Research into Aircraft Engine Building, Research Institute of Engine Technology and Production, Research Institute of Raw Materials Used in Aviation, Research Institute of Aviation Technology and Go NIIAs, the Research Institute for Avionics, for instance, who all have continuous linkages with the industry are also asked for their expert advice by the Russian Interstate Aviation Committee and FAA when verifying the certification claims of the manufacturers.

One of the major reasons for collaboration with the Western partners is to gain certification faster so that they can enter the world market, but also to lock into the worldwide maintenance and service systems of these partners. Katyrev (1994) is convinced that a bilateral agreement will forthcoming in early 1996 between Russia and the USA on certification, when Russian certification will be acceptable to the Federal Aviation Authority (FAA).

The final stage is serial or mass production, which, if the Head Designer has not designed correctly for "makeability" will create the need for new drawings or remodelling. These major modifications go back to the Main Design Bureau in Moscow with the Filial Design Bureau seeing itself as trying to solve the manufacturing/design conflict problems on site.

The Filial Design Bureaux

These Bureaux have been set up at most aircraft manufacturing plants. They advise the main Bureau on faults in the aircraft design when moving into serial production and also act on behalf of the main Bureau as the supervisor of mass production as it refers to design. In 1994, these Filial Bureau were instructed by the Minister to become independent joint stock companies and they have now become part of the new complexes being set up. (Grischenko (1994))

The Manufacturing Plant

One great problem that the manufacturing plants have is that they were designed to produce everything for the aircraft, because of the supply constraints during World War II, with the need to be a complete stand-alone manufacturing unit. This tradition still applies to some extent with 240,000 parts for AN124 and a similar number for TU204 being manufactured and stored in the Ulyanovsk plant. This increases significantly the cost of manufacture in comparison to the Western system where the just in time supplies are delivered to an assembly plant, such as those of Boeing and Airbus (Gulyaev (1994)).

The Head Aircraft Manufacturing Plants also used to ensure full capacity through manufacturing aircraft for two or three bureaux (Gulyaev (1994)) and by ministerial directives, sometimes resulting in an inability to manufacture the newer aircraft, eg the AVI.S plant were not able to take on the TU204 in replacement for the TU154 and lost the contract to the newest plant built from 1985 onwards at Ulyanovsk. (Tyuchtin (1993)) Now with the most plants underemployed, competition is fierce to gain new work.

This competitiveness now also applies to the Engine Plants, who normally employed 20-25,000 people in a 'feudal village'. The Ministry used to direct, to some extent, which plant produced the engines, but now it depends on the availability of capacity and potential financial support by the engine plant for final development work and sales. In this they are supported by the two major Bureaux, the Kuibyshev Scientific and Production Association (TRUD), designing Kuznetsov engines and Soloyov with its PERM engines. The engine contract for the Beriev BE103 was bid for by three plants because they could see that it could be made quickly and be sold to the third world countries. The contract went to a military plant which could fund the development and had experience of selling military aircraft to the third world. (Konoplev (1994))

Subcontractors

For all the design bureaux, the plants, the research institutes etc another great problem is the secession of the Republics from the USSR creating the "nearest abroad" mentality in negotiating for supplies which were previously obtained from the USSR monopolist supplier. The Ilyushin Bureau had 500 different suppliers. This problem is further aggravated by the nearest abroad suppliers, eg the Ukraine, trading their copper pipes, for instance, with the "furthest abroad", eg Western countries, for hard currency and then buying in roubles from Russian suppliers, but demanding dollars for their goods. (Koptev (1994) With the rouble becoming a harder currency, the imposition of import duties and the problems of shipping through the Ukraine and Belarussia, the search for Russian suppliers is becoming urgent. (Ermolov (1994))

Universities

Supplying all of these organisations with trained staff are the universities, such as Moscow State University, Moscow State Technology University, Moscow Aviation Technology University, Moscow Energy Institute, Moscow Institute of Physics and Engineering and Samara State Aerospace University. Graduates were guaranteed employment with the network, the best going to the bureaux. Now there are problems with the bureaux reduced level of activity and the loss of funding of the research institutes, the graduates are going into computing and banking, etc, where work is available. (Balakin (1994)) The professors in the specialist aviation universities have all worked in the bureaux or plants before entering the university and have continuous research links with them. Their doctoral research is normally carried out in collaboration with the bureaux/plants and is funded by them. The present crisis is potentially even more damaging in that the peak staff intake into the bureaux was in the mid-fifties and they are now of retiring age. The tragedy would be the loss of transfer of their knowledge and experience to the new generation of scientists and engineers and, therefore, the loss to Russian science for ever. (Komarov (1994)) The Academies, such as the Russian Academy of Science, the International Engineering Academy and Natural Science Academy also do basic and applied research of benefit to the industry.

Complexes

To attempt to overcome the problems of limited government funds and a backlog of payments on aircraft already bought by the government, the Bureaux are creating complexes of the Design Bureau, aircraft manufacturing plants, engine and avionic plants in order to sell the aircraft to fund the next one and, therefore, have no need 'to beg for money'. (Konoplev (1994) For instance, the Ilyushin Design Bureau, with Chernomyrdin's approval in April 1994, joined the Voronezh Aircraft Plant, the experimental plant Avia Exports, previously the State Export Agency and some banks to form the Ilyushin Corporation, where the new board will make the decisions. The major decisions will include Western collaboration, the fixing of the price for the aircraft, when to deliver, certification, maintenance and service and delivery of spares. (Katyrev (1994)) Beriev have also set up BETA Air, made up of Geneva ILTA Trade Finance SA of Switzerland, the GM Beriev Taganrog Aviation Scientific Technical Complex (TASTC), the Taganrog Aviation Production Plant (TAPO) and Irkutsk Aviation Production Plant (IAPO). (Konoplev (1994)) TRUD has joined with the Kazan Design Manufacturing Association, the Design Bureau for Engines, the Engine Plant in Samara, Kazan Engine Plant and JS Company "Metallist" Samara to form the TRUD complex, again run by its board of directors. (Grischenko 1994))

There we see that the sophisticated network of actors linking the government, universities, research institutes, bureaux, plants, sub-contractors, certifying agents and customers is adjusting to the post Perestroika world relatively quickly. However, at the same time, it is trying to ensure that the key elements of the networks stay in place to ensure continuity and protection of the invaluable stock of knowledge and experience built up over the 50 years of development.

Bibliography

Hanson P and K Pavitt (1987), The Comparative Economics of Research, Development and Innovation in East and West: A Survey, Harewood Academic Publishers GmBH, Chur.

Koptev A N and B Shaw (1994) (Figure 1), "Network in the Design, Development and Manufacture of Aircraft in the Russian Aerospace Industry."

Komarov V A and B Shaw (1993), (Figure 2), "The Innovation Process in the Russian Aerospace Industry".

References

Balakin Victor L (1993), Vice-Rector Samara State Aerospace University, Samara, Russia.

Ermolov Oleg (1994), General Director Samara State Enterprise AviaaGregat, Samara, Russia.

Gorlov Victor V (1993), Deputy Department Director, Ministry of Transport of Russia, Department of Air Transport, Moscow, Russia.

Grischenko Eugeny A (1994), President Kuibyshev Scientific Production Association (TRUD) Samara, Russia.

Gulyaev Anatole A (1994), Deputy Director General Aviastar Joint Stock Company, Ulyanovsk, Russia.

Katyrev Igor Y (1993 & 1994), Chief Designer, Ilyushin Aviation Complex, Moscow, Russia.

Komarov Valery A (1994), Professor, Head of Chair Aircraft Structure Design, Samara State Aerospace University.

Konoplev Vladimir N (1994), Assistant President G M Beriev Taganrog Aviation Scientific Engineering Complex, Taganrog, Russia.

Koptev Anatolii N (1993 and 1994), Professor, Aircraft Design, Samara State Aerospace University.

Shitarev Igor L (1994), General Director Motor-Building Production Association after M V Frunze, Samara, Russia.

Shorin Vladimir P (1993), Chairman of the Committee on Education and Science, Supreme Soviet of the Russian Federation.

Tyuchtin Pavel S (1993), General Director, AVI.S Aircraft Manufacturers, Samara, Russia.

Recent Essentials in Innovation Management and Research, edited by H. Hübner / T. Dunkel
Gabler, Wiesbaden/Germany, 1995

Results of Discussion and Fields of Future Research

Strategic Networking within (Inter-) National Innovation Systems

Torsten Dunkel, University of Kassel
Isabelle Le Mouillour, University of Kassel

Participants:

Moderator: Arie Nagel, Eindhoven University of Technology (NL)
Torsten Dunkel, University of Kassel (D)
Rick Garrelfs, Van der Meer & van Tilburg, Innovatie Adviesbureau (NL)
Louweris Hop, Eindhoven University of Technology (NL)
Richard Hübner, University of Innsbruck (A)
Isabelle Le Mouillour, University of Kassel (D)
Jean-Pierre Médevielle, INRETS, Lyon (F)
Ger Post, Eindhoven University of Technology (NL)
Guido Reger, Fraunhofer Institute for Systems and Innovation Research (D)
Brian Shaw, Oxford Brookes University (GB)

The Working Group agreed on the following procedure: After each key note speech there will be a discussion and inputs for future research will be collected, which will be reviewed at the end of the session.

Discussion after the key note speech of Hop/Post "A Design Typology of Inter-Organisational Networks: A Tool for Network Development in Practice"

1) What is the difference between co-operation and networks?

Speaker (S.): A network is a system that facillitates a co-operation. The difference is not so obvious. You could find some criteria to differentiate co-operations from networks such as the organization model. Co-operations are organised hierarchically; networks horizontally.

2) What was the need for developing another typology?

S.: You need a typology to allow the dialogue. The existing typologies in the literature are following these patterns: internal versus external networks, listing according to the goals of the networks, to their domains of interaction, their legal construction or their structural dimensions in terms of human resources or capital, etc.

In practice we were faced with many questions of structure morphology, but these did not go beyond the capacity of networks itself with co-operating organisations. This morphology includes, for instance sleeping and active networks, formal and informal networks, short or long term networks, e.g. a project-based network composed of two actors, who could not do it by themselves, ends after having reached its aim.

A network struggles between co-operation and competition and, thus, is not stable. According to our typology, it would go through various forms and degree of formalization and centralisation from a mere business contact to a real pooling of resources.

Besides, there may be competing and co-operating actors in a network at different stages as well as formal and informal ones.

Disussion after the key note speech of Garrelfs "Experiences on implementing cross-border networking with the Technology-oriented Development Programme EUREGIO"

1) How can one improve a region's competitiveness?

S.: We try to set up a balance of competing companies according to their external and internal orientation. We make an inventarisation of companies, i.e. who is the technological leader?

2) How do you to find out the companies' orientation efficiently and effectively?

S.: We try to get managers to meet one another in workshops formed as a technology round table, brainstorming sessions, or in „managers learn from managers" sessions. Our way of doing could be symbolised in the following figure:

3) How do you measure the innovative climate?

S.: You have to distinguish between indigenous and exogenous actors. You set up dimensions such as: credit allowance, similarity in the structure of the regions, their economic structures. We noticed, for instance, an asymmetry between the Dutch and the German part of the region in terms of population, different industrial policies, etc. For instance, North-Rhine Westphalia is more open to the projects than the Belgian region, the policy effects on industrial development in the regions, etc.

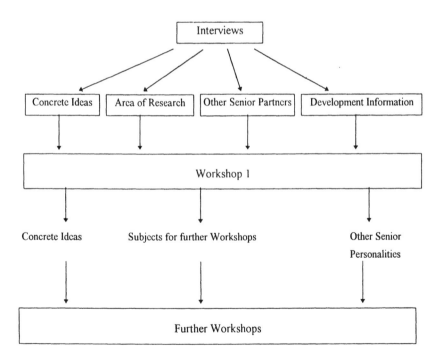

4) You mentioned the setting up of a service centre. Who funds it?
S.: It is like in the UK's R&D Clubs. Members pay a fee.

Conclusion of Speaker:
After all you want to know what is behind the border!?

Discussion after the key note speech of Reger "The Importance of European Technology Policy for the German Research Landscape and its Influence on Cooperation"

1) In which context was the study carried out? What is the basis of European technology policy?
S.: The study was carried out on the second framework programme 1988-1992 to study the impacts of that programme, among others the impact of the EC policy on the national level.
You have to apply in a network and you need four more partners from different member states, that is to say a German network cannot apply for a European R&D project.
We sent a questionnaire to German firms, universities, etc. asking about the impact of EC on their organization, on innovation and co-operation. Most impact of the EC project is on scientific performance, and in scientific and technological knowledge exchange (cf. Figure 1 in my paper).

2) When you talk about co-operation between European R&D institutions, are you using that term in the sense of all players of the R&D institutions? And for all kinds of companies?
S.: This is for all R&D players: SMEs, large companies, university and non-university R&D institutions.
The German research landscape consists of industry, higher education institutions, non-universitarian R&D institutes, policy actors (Federal Ministry, Länder Ministry, etc.), transfer institutions, contact and liaison actors.

3) Is it easier for the bigger firms or are they trying harder? Do the "bigger" firms get more funds?

S.: This is a reflection of the division of labour in a national R&D system, the SMEs carry out development, they do not help carry out research in any form, they are very strongly market-oriented: they have to develop a product now, and it has to be on the market one week later, they do not have the funds to finance a period of 1,2,3,4 or 5 years. Only large firms can afford this.

The second framework programme of the EC was strongly oriented to basic and applied research. Clearly, only the large enterprises, which carry out that type of research, apply for this programme.

It depends on their activity. Only the big firms carry out basic research and, therefore, they will apply for EC funds. SMEs are very important for the diffusion of technology but they carry out research on a short-term perspective, oriented towards the market (which does not fit in the framework). There used to be another programme within „BRITE/EURAM" named "CRAFT", which was more oriented towards those firms.

As a conclusion, I would say it reflects the division of labour in a national R&D system. If you want SMEs to participate in European technology policy, you have to change the framework programme to provide an opportunity of application.

It is important for the European R&D system and technology policy that they should apply because often, as far as we know in our innovation research, these SMEs are very important for the diffusion of technology.

4) Is it possible for a SME to enter a network? Is there a possibility for small firms to unite and to enter a network and then embark on a European programme research? Does it happen?

S.: Yes, we have to differentiate between the SMEs participating:

On the one hand, we have the spin-offs, very small high-tech firms like in Aachen, capable to perform applied research through contacts to universities, etc., but these are no typical SMEs in the innovation system.

On the other hand, there is a second type of SME doing some things like engineering bureaux, which are still in a network with other SMEs, for example with a developer of software. They apply for EC funds in a network with their customer, and this is also a possibility to support the access of such SMEs to EC technology policy.

5) A question about your methodology: One of the basic problems in all our presentations until now has been how to measure the impact of improvement programmes at any level: international, national, industrial, corporate, etc. Did you use questionnaires? One of the dimensions you measured was the willingness to co-operate; How did you deal with the fact of social desirability to co-operate?

S.: We analysed the pertinent literature, and we used data bases to get the structure of the participants. We sent a questionnaire to most of participants of the project and to non-participants. We conducted interviews with experts, and if you combine these three things you get a very good impression of what happenes in reality. All questionnaires are limited, and our own methodology was not to trust a questionnaire, but if we did, we made some interviews to get the feeling of what had happened. Then we checked the questions and the results of questionnaires with the different experts of the different R&D actors.

6) What is the significance of the European framework programme?
From the European programme, the whole financial support is used to start the project, but maybe only 1 % is initiating really new projects? You cannot base your analysis just on the percentage. How did you appreciate the nature of the projects?

S.: We asked not only for the financial significance but also for the strategic significance of each EC project. We had several indicators to measure this, for example we asked:

What is the ranking of EC projects in your whole R&D projects portfolio?

What role does this EC project play for your technological competence?

What role does it play for your business strategy?

What is the role of EC funding on the base of the institution? R&D budget?

Which role does EC funding play in applying for funds for national-based firms and institutions?

What will be the future financial significance of EC funding?

We asked for figures but a major question is also: Would you have done that research without EC funds?

All that information gave the indication to evaluate the strategic significance of EC projects for all participants. We differentiate them as SMEs, large firms, universities and non-universities.

7) What was the main result of the questions?
S.: Most of the EC projects have a strategic position in the R&D strategy of the participants. They do not participate in an EC project, if they are not sure to use the results for themselves,

and they do not apply just for funds. There is a clear impact and this means there is a value added because of the European technological policy, but it will be difficult to measure how large it is.

8) As for the long-term effect: Is there a direct relation between input and result?
S.: This is difficult to conclude. It is a general problem of how to measure the results of R&D.

9) Were the firms taking part in this programme already co-operating or are they looking for a new company?
S.: Most of the firms had already co-operated before. They apply for the EC project as a network. This network often gives access to new partners with whom they are entering into new co-operation within EC projects.

10) How long do these co-operations last after the end of the EC project and its funds?
S.: They try to apply for a new EC project.

11) As for the EC funds, do they play a role as a motivator? How important are the funds?
S.: They are important, but they are not the only reason to apply. Prospective participants want to get contacts in the European context. They apply to perform their own research and to increase their knowledge.
The share of the EC in their own R&D budget may be 10% to 15 %, which is a lot for an SME. The projects are too large, and sometimes the EC contribution amounts to 20 - 30 % of their budget. This means, if eight persons are working in the R&D group, four of them are financed for two or three years by the EC.
Inside the EC project, the EC funding is most important followed by funding from national, private and public institutions on the scientific level. The problem of the community is well known to the European Commission but it is not from the national federal state level. Within the enterprises, the top management does not have the same power in allocation of resources inside the institutions, and this is another problem besides the problem of subsidiarity (cf. paper).The EC is very important for those who participate! They have taken the chance to use this opportunity.

Besides, there is the political discussion: One problem is that the European parliament and commission are playing an increasing role in the national technology policy. A lot of German actors are afraid of a centralisation of the European technological policy in Brussels. There will be no influence from the national level, and it is not clear how programmes are generated, where the money is distributed, which fields of technology are put in the programme and so forth. This political discussion could not be measured in our questionnaire.

I have the feeling the European technology policy will play an increasing role in future, and I am not sure if this role will be good.

A topic for a future discussion could be the inter-relationships of different R&D systems or innovation systems.

Final comment from the group:

At a national level all people do not share the same goal. The jobcutters can cut R&D budget for other purposes but they do not realise that they do not direct anything and this is very important. In your paper you describe the big countries and the small countries. There will be a split-off among the three major countries and the others inside the EC about the European R&D policy, if the Parliament and the Commission are not aware of these aspects.

Discussion after the key note speech of Shaw "The National Innovation System in the Russian Aerospace Industry"

1) Could you give a definition of "complexes"?

S.: If you look at the figure on page 51, you will see what is happening: You have the design bureau, the aircraft manufacturing plants, the engine and avionics plants all joining together. For instance, the Beriev complex in Southern Russia „BETA Air" is made up with a finance company in Switzerland. The actual Beriev aviation scientific technical complex is the design part of the system, the actual production plants are located in Taganrog, and also the production plant is in Irkutz and the design bureaux for engineers. All those complexes are very, very new: BETA was set up in March 1994, the TRUD complex had also just been agreed.

Now, nobody knows how it is going to work. What they are doing is just aping the American system, I do not think it is the right way to do. It would be interesting to observe. All of them have been to America looking at what is happening there, all have been to Europe. Those people are powerful people in Russia, they all have their own private aircraft.

2) There will be a hidden problem concerning the informatics system being very specific. Is the use of American computers more appropriate in this context?
S.: They are using their own computer. Komarov as head of design department of some aerospace investors has created mathematical models for the Ilyushin Design Bureau. The Ilyushin 1996, which is the passenger aircraft coming off now was a complete computer-aided mathematical model; obviously, it had to be modified to incorporate the American parts. The software is supposed to be as good as the American one, if not better.

3) How is the chance of survival of this industry?
S.: You get a sequence like, "You are exactly in the situation we were in after World War II, when we had 25 million people killed by the Germans; Most of those were top best young men, and we are now 30 years later in power." They have the same mentality presently, saying "we are in an absolute crisis", as Churchill stated, "but we will do it!" and you can see them making it work. This complete collapse or supposed collapse of this network is not actually worse. What they are concerned with is conserving what they have: a high level of technology competence because they are trained. What they are also worried about is that the most of design bureaux's influence and power was at ist best in the 50s, most of these were set up and developed in the fifties. As Professor Komarov related, they are worried about the fact that there are no jobs for all the young men now in aerospace. They are going into computing or banking. Thus, there might be no transfer of this knowledge bank from the old to the young persons.

4) That is good for innovation!?
S.: Yes, but you need a good mix, what worries is that you still need someone to take this immense bank of knowledge out. What they are concerned with is to conserve their knowledge, most of it being tacit knowledge and if you do not transfer it, it will be lost for ever.

5) This has been used by Dassault in their design system for 15 years: An exchange team of young and old persons together to manage innovation. I have no doubt that the Rus-

sian aerospace industry makes good products but compared to the Western situation: Do they have the capacity to beat or to be comparable to the Western industry, when it comes to being first to market?

S.: The manufacturing plants were built to be self-sustained, they have got, for instance in one of their plants, two aircraft sitting there as inventory, both with 240.000 pounds each, and the costs are enormous, especially compared to Boeing.

They are aware all of these problems, you still have this mentality "I have 25.000 people to employ, what can I do?". In the old system, all of these aircraft plants had to produce civilian consumer products, "a kopeck to a rouble", that is to say, a 10% of their production had to be for civilian goods. That particular plant produced more refrigerator than the whole refrigerator industry.

6) Does it mean that they will have less problems with conversion?

S.: It is probably true. In one aircraft factory, they are already producing 5 billion syringes a year. They are desperately trying to transfer their expertise but it is a very specific expertise and very specific machines. That is their problem, they are saying: "It is cheaper for us to get rid off them a lot than trying to use these very sophisticated specialised machinery for those purposes, the cost is not worth".

A future field of research would be the dynamics and change of what is going to happen.

Fields of future research

- Place of networks and other mechanisms in the dynamics of innovation systems; (rules, forms, etc.);

- Life cycles of networks; Role and impact of moderators;Objectives of networks;

- European Union's dimension will be more relevant hence international networks;

- Structural change in industry/society and impact on innovation systems;

- Innovation Network Systems;

- Existence and Comparison of National Innovation Systems;

- Reasons for joining or not joining a Network; How to set up Networks;

- Indicators for Failure/Success of Innovation Networks;

- Faster Learning within Networks;

- Can Innovation Networks help Technology Management.

Further issues to be discussed

- As a result of the group process the following questions were raised

- How to create a network at a corporate level - structural dimensions?

- How to create network rules?

- How to build up the knowledge within the network? The region effect is based on pre-competitive R&D and the results have been used and it led to competition.

- Interaction of the participants:

- Role of central agent?

- Complementarity / Competition between participants?

- Can you have a network made up of only stakes in the network or do you need a moderator to have the network start, function and maybe disappear. The moderator could intervene through finance, his purpose should be defined by the participants. As for Garrelfs, the monitor's role is a passive one. The actors determine the nature, functions, structure, members, objectives and expected benefits of the network.

- In the pre-competition stage of a network actors have to perform pre-competitive R&D and make internal use of knowledge. The sources of competition that could endanger the network occur in the innovation process and in the access to the market.

- Are networks creating new patterns?

- What is the role of strategic networking at the corporate level?

- Change in the national innovation system: rules, competition (forms and areas of competition), climate, effectivity.

- What is the nature of a national innovation system? What are the characteristics?

- What causes differences in the system (EU finance)?

- Distinguish between EC-level, national level, regional level, industry level, firm level and network conversion of industry are taking place on an international or national level, whereas the SMEs are present on a regional level.

- International innovation system, national innovation system, regional innovation system, industry innovation system.

- Where is the border of a national system considered as a regional innovation system?

- Are the networks parts of the system?

- Innovation as an evolving complex system? Innovation is not a linear process.

- Networks and systems as paradigm for research?

- Is there a concept of networking and a concept of system?

- Have a look at specific cases to determine the accuracy of the new paradigm.

- Difference between innovation system and a network: a network as mechanism and an innovation system as an area?

- Where is the place of a network in an innovation system?

- Systemize other mechanisms that exist within the network.

- What is the nature of the dynamics of an innovation system?

- Role of networking in the value (added) chain;

- How does networking add value to the chain (medical industry)?

- How does innovation impact on the value chain?

- Are all cooperations hierarchically organised?

The Innovation System of the Company

as a Frame for the

Management of Innovation Projects^{*)}

---

*) For better understanding, it is recommended to read first the particulars on the Topic, given under Explanation of the Topics (pages 1-6)

Recent Essentials in Innovation Management and Research, edited by H. Hübner / T. Dunkel
Gabler, Wiesbaden/Germany, 1995

How to Structure the
Innovation System of the Company

Heinz Hübner

Management Science - Technology Impact & Innovation Research
University of Kassel

Abstract:
Engaged with the management of Technology and Innovation, up to now most companies are putting the emphasis on organizing single innovation processes. Meeting the competition in innovation in future will require a systematic use of external resources, taking into account measures of governments which create the public climate for innovation. Consequently, an Innovation System has to be established in the company, which itself may be understood as a component of an overall (inter-)national Innovation System. The paper deals with this need and with the question of how to design the company's Innovation System. The contribution includes some results of discussion within the corresponding Working Group, which altogether are documented hereunder.

1. Present Situation

Back in 1911, the Austrian Josef Schumpeter, the founder of Innovation Research, defined the creation of "new combinations" (Schumpeter, 1987, p. 100 & seq.) as a possibility "to evade competition". Meanwhile competition in innovation has become the dominant kind of competition in nearly all branches of economy; therefore, in present times innovation[*] is of **existential** importance for the company as well as for the economic welfare of a country.

However, the way of dealing with the question of innovation in literature and most areas of business practice meets this existential importance only to a low degree.

---

[*] The concept "Innovation" is explained/defined in the appendix of the paper together with other concepts used further on

If one concludes from the great number of publications on the activities of companies related to innovation, the emphasis is only on organization and management of single innovation projects and the design of the required innovative processes.

This concentration on the single process and the confinement to the resources presently available within the company is not sufficient to face the competition in innovation in the future. Own experiences resulting from discussions and projects with companys show that

- the establishing of innovation projects often depends on chance or power structures;
- innovation projects are often delayed;
- projects do not succeed because of lacking systematics and application of instruments as Management Technology[*];
- ideas remain hidden due to inadequate organization and innovative climate ("inner emigration" of employees);
- single-sided concentration on technical innovation blocks the possibilities for innovation in other fields;
- ...

In addition, the companys have to face a new situation, which is caused by the so-called Second Industrial Revolution: Besides the dynamic developments in economy and society, this "Second Industrial Revolution is science-based: The great inventions, such as penicillin or the transistor, are still products of individual genius. But ... today, science guides the invention process, provides explanations of why the inventions work, and shows the way to further inventions. As a result, every major technological breakthrough triggers of a competitive race in which technology is continuously improved and applied to uses other than those for which it was intended" (Ansoff, 1987, p. 29).

A decisive characteristic is:

- Partly simultaneous development;
- Cross-fertilization of research fields;
- Combination of knowledge from different research fields.

Considering the technological forecasts executed for the German governmental department of Research and Technology (Grupp/Ed., 1993; BMFT/Ed., 1993), a strengthening of these tendencies has to be expected:

---

[*]   comp. the Topic "Instruments as Management Technology"

"At the beginning of the 21st century, technology can no longer be split up according to traditional aspects. Even though the single lines of development may be quite different, they all interact in the end. It is arbitrary which general terms are formulated because individual topic areas in any case would have to be assigned to several of these general terms" (Grupp, 1993, p. 4).

2. The Need for and Main Functions of an Innovation System in the Company

The present situation, together with the tendencies mentioned, necessitates a drastical change of understanding in the company: Without misunderstanding the important role of the company, in order to be successful in the competition in innovation, a systematic search for external resources which are suitable for being used in the company's own innovation activities will be more and more required.

These external resources include all kinds of (research) institutions financed or supported by public administrations, accompanied by all measures of (semi-)public administrations and the political system which, together, create the public climate for innovation. Together with **all** institutions relevant for innovation - therefore, of course, **including the companies**, these measures may be considered as components of a(n) (inter-)national Innovation System.

To benefit from this "infrastructure" as far as possible, the company is challenged to establish a specific structure, as a layer of the company's overall structure, which can be considered as its Innovation System.[*]

Summing up, the following axioms and theses can be formulated:

Axioms[**]   (1)   Innovation, especially technical innovation, has an instrumental character to reach economic goals; this is true for the company as well as on the level of national economy;

              (2)   Thus, basic and applied R&D is based almost exclusively on economic interests;

              (3)   Results of R&D and innovation can be planned to a great extent.

---

[*]   comp. "Explanation of the Topics", page 2, Fig. 1.
[**]   Axioms and theses were presented in the Working Group and confirmed as a whole to be a suitable basis for further work within the Working Group.

Theses   (1)   To promote innovation activities of the companies, governments are establishing and supporting institutions and introducing measures to achieve a reasonable public climate for innovation which, together, create a national Innovation System;

           (2)   The company itself may also be understood as a component of the national Innovation System;

           (3)   The concentration on single innovation projects will not be sufficient in future;

           (4)   Due to the above-mentioned characteristics of the Second Industrial Revolution, the single company increasingly has to rely on cooperation with other institutions;

           (5)   To maintain its position in the competition in innovation, the company needs an Innovation System;

           (6)   Designing the Innovation System, the role of the company as a component of the national Innovation System has to be considered.

This understanding of the company as a component of a comprehensive national Innovation System, combined with the necessity of designing a specific Innovation System for the company, is essentially different from the way in which the professional literature as well as economic practice is predominantly dealing with the design of innovation processes and their concentration on specific partial fields of Innovation Management, such as the methods for idea generation.

Although the VDI Guidelines 2220, published in 1980, but still valid, are using the concept of a "product planning system" (p. 16), they do not describe the structure of such a system. Only Uhlmann (1978) is taking the system approach as a basis for structuring innovation activities.

It may be presumed that the greatly increased dynamics and complexity of innovation activities, which can be observed since Uhlmann's study was published, has acted strongly in favour of acceptance of a systematic approach in science and practice.

If the need for an Innovation System is accepted, the issue of the functions of such a system becomes crucial; some **main functions** of the Innovation System of the company can be identified:

- Frame for specific innovation processes;
- Absorption of ideas;
- Collecting and documentation of ideas for possible use in future;

- Ensuring integration, based on the common need for innovation;
- Solving of conflicts on goals of innovation (VDI 2220, p. 13), defining priorities, oriented on goals;
- Coordination of projects;
- Coordination and systematization of all activities for innovation within the company (VDI 2220, p. 13);
- Current search for possibilities
    - to benefit from measures creating the public climate for innovation (in Europe, actually, EC programmes)
    - for cooperation with other institutions within the regional/national/international Innovation System ("Strategic Networking");
- Formulation of contractual terms;
- (Supporting) Information Management (comp. Hübner, 1995);
- Building up a stock of knowledge on "Management Technology", making it available for the several projects and supporting its application;
- Identifying potentials, necessary to be successful in the competition on innovation in future, ensuring the further development of the Innovation System;
- Supporting further development of experts and managers in the field of innovation;
- ...

For better understanding, the difference between integration and coordination is worked out here briefly:

Integration is one criterion, constitutional for establishing an artificial system like a company; integration is reached by arranging integrative relationships as an ex-ante organizational design process to be performed once.

As against this, **coordination** includes all the tasks to be performed repeatedly to harmonize and synchronize several projects and processes respectively.

In this way, integration forms a structure which is used for coordination; therefore, integration is a prerequisite for coordination (Hübner, 1979, p. 30 & seq.).

Related to innovation, integrative relationships have to be established

- within the company,
- with other institutions,
    to be used for **coordination, necessary** to
- increase efficiency of companies' activities in innovation,

- prevent delays of projects,
- avoid double work,
- identify and use effects of synergy.

3. General Procedure for Designing the Innovation System Using the Aspect System Approach

It is hardly necessary to stress that the design of such an Innovation System will be far more complex for the company than the performance of specific innovation processes. However, the design of an explicit system will provide a better guarantee for

- better and goal-oriented utilization of innovation potentials outside and inside of the company;
- avoiding any "petering-out" of innovation impulses and projects within the company;
- ensuring (organizational) flexibility in accordance with environmental dynamics.

Aspect System Approach

According to the system approach, each institution, such as public administrations or companies, may be understood as an open, dynamic and goal-oriented sociotechnical system (Ulrich, 1972). The complexity of system design requires establishing of partial systems which are to be designed step by step; such partial systems normally are defined as subsystems, like the individual departments of the company. This "subsystem approach" cannot be used for the design of the Innovation System: Successful Innovation Management requires, as an interdisciplinary and multidisciplinary task, the engagement of all important departments. Therefore, the Innovation System has to be understood as one partial system of the company, the border of which is - like in a layer - identical with that of the company. This kind of partial system forms a so-called **Aspect System**: The reduction of complexity is not done - in contrast to the subsystem approach - by reducing the border of the partial system but by reducing the kind (and amount) of elements and relationships to be considered:

"An Aspect System includes only those elements of the entire system that are relevant to a specific aspect considered, and also determines the relations between such elements. Thus, an aspect system includes only a **certain part of all the relations** between the **relevant elements within the entire system**." (Hübner, 1982, p. 263)

Experience in applying this approach (Augustin/Hübner, 1984, p. 53) has shown that the design of such an Aspect System may be structured by developing, step by step, the following partial systems:

- System of Goals,
- System of Functions/Instruments,
- System of Responsibilities,
- System of Technical Equipment.

Applying this approach to the design of the Innovation System, innovation will, of course, be the **"relevant" aspect**.

The design of the partial systems mentioned is based on the analysis of the intensity of competition in innovation and technology competition in the respective economic branch, confronting the company with the following questions:

- What is the importance of the branch within the national economy?
- Which are the main forces of competition in innovation?
- Which strategic position can be reached by the company?
- What qualified potentials are existing within the regional/national/international Innovation System?
- In how far and in what form can these potentials be used for the company's own innovation activities?
- How can the interfaces towards Innovation Systems of other institutions be designed organizationally to ensure efficient communication?
- What additional qualifications (technical, managerial) are required for the own company?
- In how far can the company make use of measures of public innovative climate?
- In what way can the internal innovation climate be supported?
- ...

3.1 System of Goals

With respect to the character of innovation as a means for reaching the economic goals of the company, division, strategic business unit, etc., the goals to be fulfilled by the Innovation System have to be derived from these overall goals.

Generally, the goal of the Innovation System is to ensure reaching the position within the competition in innovation as defined by (corporate) strategy. To reach this general goal, several kinds of functions have to be executed by means of specific instruments forming together the System of Functions/Instruments.

82

3.2 System of Functions/Instruments

The Innovation System is, to a great extent, defined by the (partial) System of Functions/Instruments, as the requirements for personal and technical equipment are derived therefrom.

Decisions on **functions** to be performed within the Innovation System may be based on a general model of technological ontogenesis shown in Figure 1, which may be used for understanding the development of innovation outside of the field of natural and engineering sciences, too.

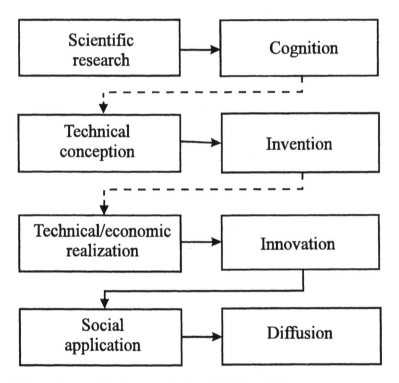

Fig. 1: Model of technological ontogenesis (Ropohl, 1979, p. 273)

Discussing this model, the Working Group accepted the general applicability of the model, as the same phases may be required for the development of non-technical innovations, too: As examples, the discovery of users' needs or the invention of new kinds of marketing were men-

tioned. Proposals for extending the model are described in the documentation of the results of discussions.

Based on this model, Figure 2 shows possible task areas of Innovation Management and supporting functions; this survey may help to define the functions of the Innovation System of the individual company.

As the execution of functions requires application of **instruments** in a broader sense, these are also **part of the System of Functions**.

The commonly used concept of "instruments" includes, in reality, a lot of "abstract" elements, namely

- approaches,
- ways of thinking,
- models,
- methods and principles,
- auxiliary equipment (computer support etc.),

forming together a specific area of know-how as Management Technology (Hübner, 1992, p. 3249).

The development of this area of know-how is one of the main functions within the Innovation System.

As in other fields of technology, it is impossible to be experienced in all the "instruments" available. The decision on instruments to be used requires knowledge on what (kind of) instruments are available; surveys and brief descriptions can be found in Haberfellner et al. (1993); a description based on application-oriented criteria is given by Hübner/Jahnes (1992) for about 30 "instruments" [*]. Depending on the frequency of application and complexity of the instrument, several **kinds of availability** may be distinguished:

- Permanently available,
- Available as required,
- Applied by external experts,
- Need-oriented (further) development of instruments.

---

[*] Based on this, a "Handbook of Management Technology" will be published in 1996 (Gabler, Wiesbaden)

84

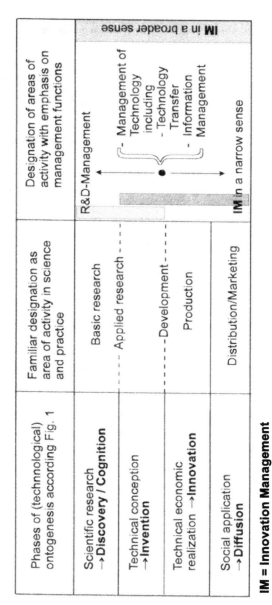

Fig. 2: Possible areas of achivity of an innovation system and assignment to phases of technical ontogenesis

3.3 System of Responsibilities

Establishing responsibilities within the Innovation System is as important as it is difficult:

(1)   As against the departments (Production, Purchasing, etc.) as subsystems, the Innovation System as an Aspect System is only one layer, but surrounding the border of the company or the planning unit respectively as a whole.

(2)   Though it is easy to define responsibilities for main functions of Innovation Management in a broader sense (as for the R&D department), the overall responsibility necessarily has to be spread upon several persons.

(3)   As most of these persons are involved in, and responsible for, functions in specific departments, the responsibility for innovation often is shared amongst these.

(4)   With respect to the main functions mentioned above (Fig. 2), responsibilities within the Innovaton System are quite different from those for one specific project.

Considering these difficulties together with the fact that, until now, the efforts to establish an Innovation System are rather negligible, it may be helpful to present the recommendations given in Guideline VDI 2220 (p. 13 & seq.) but concentrating only on product planning: The following possible kinds of institutionalization are recommended:

- Own position (several persons with different qualification);
- Team (consisting of experts/managers from different departments) established for long-time cooperation;
- Commission (like team, but established only for a short time for special tasks).
    ⇒   In any case, cooperation with experts and managers of the several departments is necessary, therefore competence and responsibilities will have to be defined.

With respect to the bigness of companies, it is recommended that responsibility should be given, in

- small companies (less than 200 employees), to Corporate Management, possibly supported by a team;
- medium companies (about 200 up to 1000 employees), to an individual post with 1 to 3 employees;
- bigger companies/units (more than 1000 employees), to an individual post with 2 to 5 employees, but not more.

For better understanding, here are some examples, based on project work and discussions with participants of a seminar on Management of Technology & Innovation:

Example 1, corresponding to the concept of an Innovation System:

> A company with about 450 employees, second place in the respective world market; innovation is considered as a strategic factor of success. Responsibility for overall innovation activities: **Own position**, according to VDI 2220, working out proposals for goals of innovation for Corporate Management; some other functions are:
> - Contact for in-house improvement proposals,
> - Contact for proposals from R&D department,
> - Information management,
> - Organization of specific innovation projects/processes.

Example 2, not corresponding to the concept of an Innovation System:

> A big company (more than 10,000 employees).
>
> Responsibility for overall innovation activities: Commission on Executive Board level, only considering product innovation. Proposals possible only via managers in high hierarchical position.

Example 3, not corresponding to the concept of an Innovation System:

> A big concern with central R&D laboratories intends to establish "Centres for Innovation" as a "specialized panel" within these laboratories.

3.4 System of (Technical) Equipment

The design of this system depends, to a great extent, on the technologies (product, production, research technology) typical of the specific branch of economy, as well as on the design of the system of functions as part of the Innovation System. Therefore, a general discussion does not appear to be helpful.

References

Ansoff, H.I.: Strategic Management of Technology; The Journal of Business Strategy, Vol. 7/No. 3, 1987

Augustin, S./Hübner, H.: Designing Computer-Supported Production Management Systems using the Aspect System Approach, in: Hübner, H. (Ed.): Production Management Systems - Strategies and Tools for Design, North Holland, Amsterdam 1984, p. 51-66;

BMFT (Ed.): Deutscher Delphi-Bericht zur Entwicklung von Wissenschaft und Technik, Bonn, 1993, ISBN 3-88135-267-8

Grupp, H. (Ed.): Technologie am Beginn des 21. Jahrhunderts, Physica Verlag, Berlin, 1993 (citation according to the brief version, FhG-ISI, Karlsruhe, 1993)

Haberfellner/Nagel/Becker/Büchel/von Massow: Systems Engineering: Methodik und Praxis, 7th ed., revised & enlarged, Ed.: Daenzer, W./Huber, F., Zürich, 1992

Hübner, H.: "Innovations- und Technologiemanagement", p. 1628 - 1637: "Technologie", p. 3249, in: Gabler Wirtschaftslexikon, 13th, completely revised edition, Wiesbaden, 1992

Hübner, H./Jahnes, St.: Instrumente als "Management-Technologie" für die Technikwirkungs-analyse - Technik- und Produktfolgenabschätzung im Unternehmen als Kern eines vorsorgenden Umweltmanagements; Kassel, September 1992

Hübner, H.: Informationsmanagement und strategische Unternehmensführung - Vom Informationsmarkt zur Innovation und Wettbewerbsfähigkeit, München/Wien, 1995

Hübner, H.: Integration und Informationstechnologie im Unternehmen; München, 1979

Hübner, H.: Management Technology, explication of term in Gabler Wirtschaftslexikon, Wiesbaden, 1992, p. 3249

Hübner, H.: The Aspect-System-Approach - an instrument for reducing complexity in systems design and ist application to Information-Systems planning, in Trappl, R./Hanika, P./Tomlinson, H. (Ed.): Progress in Cybernetics and Systems Research, Vol.X, Washington, D.C., USA, 1982, p. 263-268

Ropohl, G.: Eine Systemtheorie der Technik - Zur Grundlegung der Allgemeinen Technologie; München/Wien, 1979

Schumpeter, J.: Theorie der wirtschaftlichen Entwicklung, 7th edition, unchanged reprint of the 4th edition of 1934; Berlin, 1987

Uhlmann, L.: Der Innovationsprozeß in westeuropäischen Industrieländern; Band 2: Der Ablauf industrieller Innovationsprozesse; Berlin/München, 1978

Ulrich, H.: Die Unternehmung als produktives soziales System, Bern, 1972

VDI 2220: Produktplanung - Ablauf, Begriffe, Organisation; Düsseldorf, Mai 1980

Appendix: Explication of some terms

Innovation

The concept of innovation is based on a broad understanding of innovation dating back to Josef Schumpeter who is reputed as the founder of Innovation Research. Without explicitly mentioning the term, he introduced it into the economic discussion already in 1911, understanding thereby *"new combinations" related to the following cases:*

1. *"Manufacturing of a new... product or a new quality of a product;*
2. *Introduction of a new ... production procedure ...;*
3. *Entry into a new distribution market ...;*
4. *Opening up a new source of raw materials or semi-finished products ...;*
5. *Effecting a re-organization ... ".* (Schumpeter, J.: Theorie der wirtschaftlichen Entwicklung, 7th ed., unaltered reprint of the 4th ed. published in 1934, Berlin, 1987, p. 100 & seq)

Two pragmatic definitions may be added for better understanding:

Innovation *"means improved or new problem solutions related to*
- *products,*
- *services,*
- *procedures/processes and*
- *social systems*
using existing or new (technical) findings". (Working definitions of TWI, University of Kassel)

In the innovation concept of the Austriam Chamber of Economy (comp. Hübner, H. /Kaniowsky, H./Kutscherer, A./Mayer, F.J.: Unternehmen und Innovation, Ed.: Wirtschafts-förderungsinstitut der Bundeskammer der gewerblichen Wirtschaft, Wien, 1980), innovation is defined as follows:

Innovations are "operational novelties and changes which secure the existence and/or earning power of an enterprise by making a more efficient use of technologies and materials, harmonizing the products or services offered with changing market requirements, by making known products or services by means of technologies or materials which hitherto had not been used therefor, above all by offering new products or services".

A **system** consists of components which have specific characteristics and which are connected by relationships (common concept).

National Innovation System

(1)   *"A bundle of measures as well as the special environment of frame conditions, combinations, and amplifying factors."* (Wirtschaftskammer Österreich/Editor: Technologien für die Zukunft, Wien 1983, p. 20)

(2)   *"The network of institutions in the public and private sectors whose activities and interactions initiate, import, modify and diffuse new technologies, may be described as the 'national system of innovation'."* (Freeman, C.: Technology Policy and Economic Performance: Lessons from Japan; London, 1987, p. 1)

Innovation System of the company

The Innovation System is one of several partial systems of the company; as Innovation Management is an interdisciplinary task, which generally may require experience and know-how of all departments, the border of the Innovation System has to be identical with that of the company (Aspect System). The components of this system are the different innovation potentials (men, technical equipment, information, know-how in technology, based on natural and engineering as well as other fields of science (including Management Technology etc.) which are interrelated.

Management Technology

(1)   *"An autonomous field of know-how, including approaches, ways of thinking, models, methods & principles and auxiliary equipment".* (comp. Gabler Wirtschaftslexikon, Wiesbaden, 1992, p. 3249)

(2)   *"Production & Management Technology, not to be understood as a sub-section of business administration/management science, but handling questions of acceptance, organizational innovations, integration and coordination of departments of research, development or production which had been separated until now, new or re-definition of the importance of software & simulation for laboratory and production and a lot of others."* (comp. Grupp, H., 1993, brief version, p. 12)

Recent Essentials in Innovation Management and Research, edited by H. Hübner / T. Dunkel
Gabler, Wiesbaden/Germany, 1995

Economic Crisis - Innovation Crisis - Management Crisis?

Dietrich Legat
HEWLETT PACKARD
Geneva, Switzerland

1. Introduction

It is a great honor and pleasure to have been invited to this working conference. Heinz Hübner has given me the assignment to offer "food for thought and work" for the consecutive workshops, and I will try to fulfill this request by offering my view on some trends and problems which have become visible over the last few years in our economy.

I must apologize for the limitations within which my thoughts were developed:

- my observations are made in and from the point of view of business companies, therefore my considerations come mainly from the limited view of such an economical micro-cosmos,
- the company I work for is active in the field of electronics - computers, test and measurement - and thus my observations and thoughts may not be representative, as in such companies there are very high pressures from speed of change in both market and technology,
- it may be that the short term pressures which are experienced today in business are nothing than a momentary bottleneck, which will be overcome in the next few months - in which case I will have been proven to have a too pessimistic view of economy.

Personally however I work from the following assumptions:

- The observations from which I draw the conclusions presented are sufficiently representative to allow their generalization, - I found them confirmed with many European, US and Asian businesses with whom I work in my profession,
- the industry in which I work is a "pathfinder" industry - therefore, what is practice for us today will be practice for all businesses tomorrow.

2. Summary of Observations and Problems

I think we will all agree that something is basically "out of order" in our economical system. As always in such situations some people hope that the old state will return soon or a little later (some people look, full of trust, into the past). I do not have data that support this hope. Instead, my observations lead me to the conclusion that today's state of our economical and political system is defined by a paradigm shift of major historical dimensions[1]. I will attempt to illustrate this view by five observations which give rise to five problems:

Summary of Observations

I believe to have sufficient evidence to conlcude that our present economical problem is caused by an irreversible paradigm shift: the cycle times of most economic processes have been significantly and irreversibly reduced. Processes have become "superfast".

As a consequence the management process gets "out of synch" and has major difficulties to cope with the problems imposed by the externalities of the organization (market, technology).

It is correct that, at constant speed of process transactions, weaknesses of economies can be expected to be overcome be re-alignment of businesses to more attractive areas, thus creating somewhere else in the economy the jobs which are eliminated by outdated businesses elsewhere. If, however - as is the case today - process cycle times are reduced - then the posiive effect of adressing new business opportunities is over-compensated by reduction of process implicit work.

Problem Summary

Innovation so far has been mainly applied to the "value added" process. Now we need innovation of the management process: How do we apply innovation to the management process?

I will now attempt to grasp this situation in four specific problem statements - with the objective to give food for thought, analysis and further work for research in innovation:

3. Detail Observations and Problems

Observation Nr.1

One single new and irreversible paradigm change causes the economic difficulties of today: we have reduced the cycle times in all economic processes significantly:

---

[1] I believe that all major historical turning points have been created by paradigm breaks in key proccesses.

```
┌─────────────────────────────────────────────────┐
│                                                   │
│        Reduction of Process Cycle Times           │
│                                                   │
│                      1860          1992           │
│     Trip Paris to New York  11 Days   3 Hrs       │
│     Wash Laundry             8 Hrs    30 Min      │
│     Letter Paris-New York   14 Days   2 Days      │
│     Cook Chicken            1.75 Hrs  15 Min      │
│     Knit Pullover           1 Month   20 Min      │
│                                                   │
│                     16th Ctry    20th Ctry (*)    │
│     Build St.Peter's                              │
│     Cathedral               120 Years   3 Years   │
│                                                   │
│     (*) Cathedral in Yamoussoukro                 │
│                                                   │
└─────────────────────────────────────────────────┘
```

- We are not in a recession out of which "the next cycle will pull us".
- Instead, the rapid spread of IT networks have changed the rules for process cycles permanently.

This is not a phenomenon which our business processes are submitted to passively: it is planned in a systematic way into the process of change of our processes:

This observation leads me to stating

Problem Nr.1:

What are the full consequences of the arrival of "superfast processes" for our businesses and our economy?

Not only are products developed towards an increased reduction of cycle times, processes are submitted - in all businesses and countries - to radical reduction of cycle times by process re-engeneering

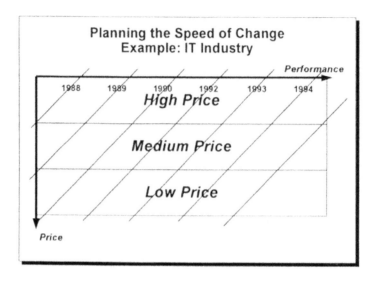

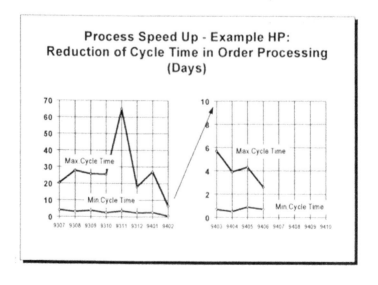

Observation Nr. 2:

This change has raised an issue which never before has been posed to man in physical reality as a survival question (although philosophers have been pointing the issue out theoretically before (1))

- The capability of processes to conform to all consecutive process customer requirements ("total consecutive conformance") decides, if a process will survive or be extinguished. Previously, conformance was nice to have to beat the competition, but not vital.
- "Useful" work is such that it provides consecutive conformance (utility) somewhere later in the process chain.
- If "total consecutive non-conformance" in a process is not reduced, then reduction of cycle times drives a process out of existence.
- However: if total consecutive non-conformance is reduced then unemployment grows: reduction on non-conformance means irreversible elimination of "useless" work. This explains why today jobs disappear in spite of the trend to higher output, productivity and profits. It is not automation which causes this trend, but management of non-conformance.

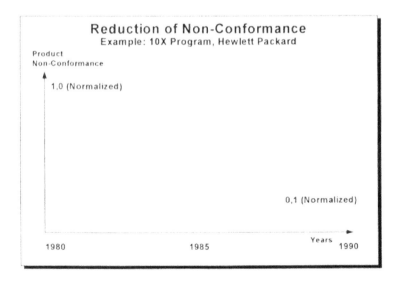

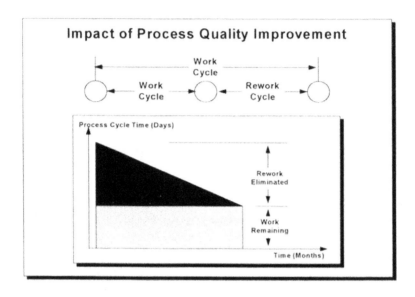

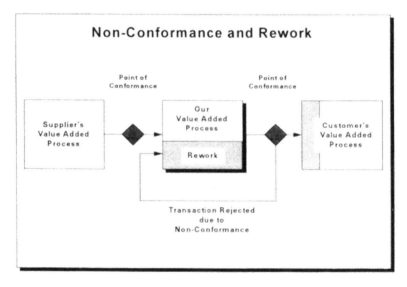

Problem Nr.2:

How would a society look like where all "useless" work has been eliminated?

Observation Nr.3:

Management is the design process for an organization:

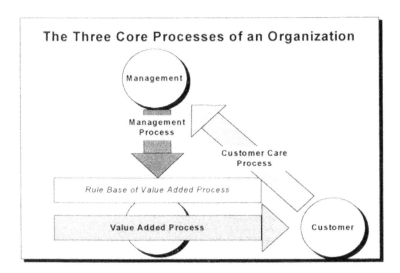

- Its output is the rule base (plans, policies, budgets) of the organization managed (3)
- The quality of this process can be measured. Data of companies in trouble shows that the quality of the management process is poor.
- Shortened cycle times in the value-adding process drives the management process "out of synch": the rule base of the organization gets out of synch with reality, thus drives the organization into "blindness". The shorter the cycle times the shorter it takes an organization to become blind.
- Thus, the management process becomes the prime cause of the non-conformance of the value- added process: it is the process with the highest need for process innovation. (2,3)

Problem Nr.3:

What are the principles of management of "superfast processes" ?

Observation Nr.4:

Innovation in the value added processes cannot sufficiently counteract this phenomenon. We need innovation in the management process: The issue cannot be resolved by the arrival of a new class of products or services:

- computer assisted reverse engineering and CAD have reduced the cycle time of the product and service adaptation process. So, there is less time left to exploit an innovative paradigm shift in the market.
- the innovation process in itself suffers from problems of non-conformance, due to the reduced cycle times.

Problem Nr.4:
How do we innovate the management process to the now required state?

Conclusion

Assuming my observations are both correct and representative we need answers to the four problems stated:

1) What are the consequences of the arrival of "superfast processes" for business and economy?
2) How would a society look like where all "useless" work has been eliminated?
3) What does management of "superfast processes" look like?
4) How do we innovate the management process to the now required state?

Workshop Additions

In the workshop and plenum discussion several comments and additions to these thoughts were developed:

1) Speed up of processes was confirmed, but at the same time speed of advance in technology has become very slow. Compare the two periods:
   1870-1910: telegraph, telephone, electric light, radio, radioactivity, roentgen, automobile, airplane
   1945-1994: computer, nuclear power plant, biotechnology.
   (Otala)

2) Technology and intellectual property are becoming strategic resources (Otala)

3) The definition of "not useful" work should include all three components of waste as defined in Kaizen: waste of work, waste of wait, waste of thinking.

4) The definition of conformance should include the conformance to the environmental requirements.

5) The assumption that process improvement reduces the amount of work in an economy is incorrect and is not substantiated by data. Instead this is a "one company" or "one industry" issue. Other companies or industries will compensate by creating work that is eliminated in others. Example given: software work will replace the work eliminated as describe above. (Plenum)

References

(1) Buber, Martin,"Ich und Du", Lambert Schneider, Heidelberg, 1974
(2) Deming, W.E., "Out of The Crisis", ISBN 0-911379-01-0
(3) Singh, Sarv Soin, "Total Quality Essentials", ISBN 0-07-059548-8

Recent Essentials in Innovation Management and Research, edited by H. Hübner / T. Dunkel
Gabler, Wiesbaden/Germany, 1995

Trends in cooperation between industry, R&D centres, and universities

Matti Otala

Robert Bosch GmbH, Stuttgart, Germany

Abstract:
Industry is presently experiencing rather fundamental changes in its operations, structure, mores and economies. These changes are caused by intensification of the international competition, restructuring of several large economic blocks, changing societal values and new organisational and competitive paradigms. The following is a terse, condensed summary of what the author sees as twelve major changes affecting the European research establishment in the ten forthcoming years. This is a strictly private view, based on personal experience gained in working in and managing of several European, American and Japanese large industries, and in working in and with several European universities and research centres.

Introduction

Something fundamental has happened to our business environment. Some of the basic business and political paradigms seem to have changed irreversibly. It may be that this is characteristic of all historical turning points, when new fundamental mores are replacing the old ones. In the present case, the main impetus comes from:

- simultaneous speeding up of economic, industrial and political processes; and
- their becoming strongly internationalised, interconnected and paralleled.

The corresponding business requirement is to identify and adapt to the new rules of the game rapidly, and to learn how to play the new game in an orchestrated manner. This has resulted in competitive advantage for organisations which have been able to adapt faster and to react more aggressively to the challenges of the competition than their competitors. Organisations of this kind are called *learning organisations*. They observe their environment keenly, and show an inherent interest in identifying, analysing and learning from all abnormalities in the marketplace.

A learning organisation has a corporate culture that encourages continuous learning and development of individual competencies, and favours flexible adaptation and smooth agility in individual and company reactions to external stimuli. Certain corporate cultures and organisational principles are in tune with the new competitive paradigms of *competition*, *focus* and *skill*, thereby explaining many of the success factors of these companies[1].

Trend 1	The overall need for technical research is increasing both in the industry and in the society. Advanced companies consider technology and intellectual property as a primary strategic resource to be created, acquired, shared, and traded. Coupling this resource with the company's operative business will be one of the principal issues in formulating the business strategy and the R&D targets of the company.

Trend 2	Technology development has grown swiftly in the newly industrialised countries, especially in the Far East. This trend is driven by significant system's and infrastructure differences; especially by less regulated business climate, different types of invisible government support, less costly or missing environmental regulation, easy availability of capital at low interest, high personnel productivity and individual motivation. For Europe, it will be of paramount importance to balance out these differences with better R&D focus, higher intellectual productivity, better cooperation and networking schemes, and new sources of employee motivation.

Trend 3	R&D units, both in the companies and in research organisations, are being required to manage their activities according to quantifiable business objectives. Research will be judged by productivity and quality measures identical to those used for measuring the performance of the operating functions of the company. This means a fundamental but positive change in the work environment of the R&D personnel.

Trend 4

In the wake of the general trend of internationalisation, corporations are developing towards the modern GLOCAL (*GLObally loCAL*) structures[2] and *Keiretsu*-type supplier chains[3]. This has increased the significance of regional research institutes (*i.e.*, those serving a culturally consistent geographic region, normally a group of nations) at the expense of international or global research providers. The regional research institutes are expected to be able to network closely with each other.

Trend 5

The trend in large industries is towards divisionalisation and decentralisation, thus breaking larger conglomerates into more manageable entrepreneurial business units. This has lowered the hierarchical level and increased the factual competence of the decision-makers. The old high-level or political contacts between the research institute and the top corporate management have lost much of their significance, and have been replaced by "*strictly business*" research deals. This trend has also resulted in dismantling many centralised functions, such as corporate research departments. Research centres are finding numerous new clients in the newly founded divisional R&D units, which have much more precise needs but considerably less tradition and international experience in research than the previous centralised units.

Trend 6

The trend in the industry is to focus on "**core**" matters, *i.e.*, **core business, core customers, core technologies** and **core competence**[4]. This means increasing selectivity on the industry's side when matching new technical inputs with the corporate strategy. The research organisations are finding it increasingly difficult to sell their own product ideas or technologies to the industry, unless the ideas are exactly focused on the company's needs. Similarly, selling of "*long-term scenarios for the future*" is becoming difficult because the industry feels this as their own core expertise, which they understand much better than any research establishment. The time of "*Think Tanks*" and the desire to diversify the company business portfolio is irrevocably past.

Trend 7	The shortening product life-cycles and the simultaneous need to secure new products faster to the market has led companies to short-term strategies and expectations of immediate return on investment. In the age of just-in-time product development, the research institutes are expected to provide "*quick fixes*" to precisely focused acute R&D problems. At the same time, advanced development of core product families is increasingly being done in industry's own laboratories. This will lead to increased use of research centres as a reservoir of knowledge rather than as a creator of it.

Trend 8	TQM *(Total Quality Management)*[5] is being increasingly used to overcome the severe problems of the Taylorian functional organisation[6], characterised by inefficiency, unproductivity, delays, and loss of employee motivation. The new organisational paradigm uses cross-functional teams, skunkworking[7], and the concepts of *kaizen, muda* and *gemba*[8]. It is based on a flat communicative team-working structure, reversing many of the previous western organisational dogmas. The result is that a contract research project carried out by a research organisation, including the personnel involved, is being tightly integrated into the operating structures of the contracting company.

Trend 9	Growing public budget deficits and normative supra-national legislation, *e.g.*, the "*1992*" directives of the EC, will limit the growth of public R&D spending and force the research establishment to seek more funding from the industry. This, together with the industry's sharpening "core" focus, may mean that the pure curiosity-oriented academic research may suffer.

Trend 10	The questionable performance of large national and international research projects is prompting the governments to look towards the industry for stronger leadership in the development of new technology. In spite of all its ambitions, the research community may not alone be successful in this task because of missing intimate contact with the reality of the markets and lack of proximity to the true end-user.

Trend 11	The rate of expansion of knowledge will continue to be high and the knowledge life-cycles will shorten further. This puts severe requirements on the broad adaptability and up-to-date competence of the research centre personnel. Extensive retraining (human recycling) of experienced scientists will be inevitable, and the requirement of managerial skills at the top of the research management will increase drastically. It may even be necessary to modify the traditional view of the "*scientific method*" and to concentrate on improving and updating the management processes of research organisations.

Trend 12	To meet the competitive pressures from other suppliers of research work, strategic alliances will grow between university research groups, research institutes, governmental organisations and industrial research laboratories. Networking between and within university research groups and research institutes will increase.

Explanations and references:

1. See, for instance, *Otala, M.,* **Paradigmawechsel in der Organisation: Organisatorische und technische Aspekte von Re-Engineering**. Invited Keynote Address in *IDG Kongress "Re-Engineering",* Oct. 1994, Frankfurt, Germany. *Proceedings, Part I*, pp. 270-286. (In German)

2. A **Glocal** (**GLO**bally lo**CAL**) structure is the emerging definition of an industry trend to rely on self-sufficient semi-autonomous operations, consisting of a full local Keiretsu and located in an area consisting of a reasonably homogenous customer group. A glocal is normally identified by the more or less homogenic culture to be served, for instance the Romanic, Germanic, Anglo-Saxon, Nordic and Slavic glocals in Europe. For further information, see for instance **Ruigrok, W., The Global Firm,** Proceedings of the Europrospective II Conference, Namur 1991.

3. **Keiretsu** describes the Japanese industrial structure, where a "mother" company works closely together with a host of exclusive subcontractors. As seen from outside, a Keiretsu operates like a single company, the mother usually taking care of the technological muscle and marketing power, at the same time providing the subcontractors with product designs and all the necessary training of the workforce.

4. **Core** denotes the trend in the industry to concentrate onto those things the company knows best. The focus can be defined as core customers, core markets, core competencies, core technology or core products of a company. For further information, see for instance **Prahalad, C.K. and Hamel, G., The core competence of the corporation.** Harvard Business Review, May-June 1990, pp. 79-91.

5. **Total Quality Management** is a principle stressing cross-functional co-operation, flat hierarchies and process-oriented thinking. Partial synonyms: Flat organisation, lean management, team-work.

6. **Taylorian** organisation is one that is based on extreme work division, atomising every task to elementary moves, which can be performed by people lacking intelligence or competence.

7. **Skunkworking** is a colloquial American term describing a business unit operating outside the official hierarchy but in competition with it. Partial synonym: Garage operation.

8. **Kaizen** (Kai = continuous Zen = good or God) describes the Japanese way of management, advocating the principle of continuous improvement. Kaizen concentrates, among other things, to the minimisation of **muda** (waste: either physical, material or mental) in processes, activities and thought. **Gemba** denotes the place where something happens. To solve a problem, "one must be in the gemba" (synonymous to "management by walking around"), also meaning that a manager must be "visible" to the employees. For further information, see for instance **Imai, M., Kaizen, the Key to Japan's Competitive Success.** McGraw-Hill, New York 1986, 254 p. ISBN 0-07-554332-X

Recent Essentials in Innovation Management and Research, edited by H. Hübner / T. Dunkel
Gabler, Wiesbaden/Germany, 1995

Innovation Mangagement System on Company Level

Takaya Ichimura (Nihon University, Tokyo, Japan)

Markku Tuominen (Lappeenranta University of Technology, Finland)

Petteri Piippo (Lappeenranta University of Technology, Finland)

Abstract:
The purpose of this research is to discuss the functions and elements of innovation management systems at the company level. We aim to clarify basic factors and problems to be solved in corporate innovation management. As the key points of discussion, we propose the elemental characteristics of the innovation management system. This system consists of three management levels: corporate level, business level, and activity level. Each level consists of several sub-levels created in order to accomplish each subgoal of management. The proposed concept and elements of an innovation system were verified by the discussion at the ISPIM Working Conference and by many comments from the participants. As a result of this process, we clarified the elemental activities of innovation management and the factors to be included in individual innovation management levels.

1. Introduction

Modern manufacturing companies face difficult conditions, such as decrease of demand caused by economic recession, severe competition in domestic and international markets, daily- progressing technological innovation, social needs in terms of ecological problems. In order to survive under these severe conditions, every company must find countermeasures against such difficulties by restructuring the conventional system or by adopting innovative management.

Promotion of innovation management is the focal point of management of the modern company to overcome such severe conditions, but the concept and subject of innovation management are widely recognized on the individual view point.

We have investigated the processes of product development and have clarified the basic model by analysing innovative activities and their decision-making process. In order to clarify the process, we analyzed the relationship between innovative product development and the managerial strategy. In order to establish a basic model for product innovation, the system must be structured as a sub-system of "innovation management system at company level".

The purpose of our presentation is to propose a seed of discussion on fundamental elements and functions of innovation management at company level.

2. Previous studies

"Innovation management system" is recognized very widely and defined variously by researchers and businessmen according to their perspectives and points of view.

F. Drucker[1] stated that "innovation" is a general and inevitable factor of all activities and innovation is a specific function of entrepreneurship, whether in an existing business, public service institution, or elsewhere.

On the structure and function of "management", many opinions have been disclosed. B.D. Henderson[2] insisted that strategy is necessary and is the most essential function enabling companies to obtain an unique advantage in order to survive in the competitive situation. N. Danila[3] classified the hierarchical structure of management as institutional strategy, corporate strategy, business strategy and technological strategy (engineering, R&D, manufacturing and marketing strategy). On the other hand, Sumii[4] noted that innovation is the most basic effort of management for the purpose of taking competitive advantage; he stated that innovation management is the most effective managerial method for surviving intense competition. He classified the subject of innovation management into process innovation, financial innovation, management innovation, and structural innovation. Thus innovation management consisted of a process of idea generation, promote idea and implementation. Kondo[5] clarified the steps of management to introduce new business and development of new technology, and he proposed substantial items to be examined and methods to be applied in each procedure of management. He concluded that such activities of themselves should be recognized as "innovation management".

Many researchers noted that the activities of technology development, R&D, project management, and new product development were innovation management. Some of them focused on product innovation activity as a subject of innovation management. Holt[6] focused his study on product innovation, and he investigated the process and method of new product development

[1] Peter F. Drucker, „The discipline of Innovation"
[2] Bruce D. Henderson, „The origin of strategy", Harvard Business Review, November-December 1989
[3] Nicolas Danila, „Strategic evaluation and selection of R&D projects", R&D Management, Vol. 19, 1989
[4] Kazuo Sumii, „Innovation management" (in Japanese), Japan Economic Newspaper Press, 1986
[5] Shuji Kondo, „Approach to new product and new business", Japan Management Association, 1989
[6] Knut Holt, „Product innovation management", Butterworths Pub., 1988

based on the fusion concept and proposed information behavior of innovation management. On the other hand, many studies on the process of product development and items to be examined have been investigated under the condition that the product group has been specified. Koppelmann[7] proposed a systematic analysis of product development steps, items to be examined and methods to be applied. He also developed a substantial method of analysis of market and product.

Concentrating on the fifth level of product development by Koppelmann, Kohno[8] attached weight to the process of generating commercial goods and described the procedures of new product development more precisely.

On the concept of "systems", Hübner[9] classified the innovation management systems into the international level, national level and company level, and he insisted that the interrelationship among levels should be clarified. Also he defined innovation management as a process of innovative problem solving and technological innovation by clarifying the function, information to be taken into consideration, and the rules to be adopted among company, governmental organization, university and institute to solve problems such as environmental and ecological problems. His main pint is the very good suggestion to clarify the interrelationship among system levels and elements of the system.

We proposed an idea for an innovation management system, with elements and functions to be considered by referring to previous researches.

3. An approach to the innovation management system

In order to clarify the innovation management system at the company level, we must take up the basic elements of the system, limited conditions, relationship among the elements, and the process of innovation management. As an approach to clarify the above items, our discussion on innovation management stands on the concept that innovation management is a continuous process of idea generation which creates an innovative new idea to solve confronted managerial problems. In general, management depends on the purpose of the company, and every managerial activity follows in order to achieve the stated purpose, which consists of several hierarchical levels.

As the first step of our approach to clarify the structure and function of the innovation management system, we have tried to elucidate individual innovative activities for the purpose of

---

[7] U. Koppelmann, „Grundlagen des Produktmarketing zum qualitativen Informationsbedarf von Produktmanagern", Verlag W. Kohlhammer GmbH, 1987 (translated into Japanese in 1984)

[8] Toyohiro Kohno, „Strategy for new product development", Diamond inc., 1987

[9] Heinz Hübner, „How to structure the innovation system", Preprint

achieving the specified goal at each hierarchical level of management. This means that each hierarchical level of management starts from recognized managerial goals; thus information, process and idea generation are necessary in order to attain the goal. If we can elucidate these goals and following processes, part of the innovation of activities, factors and functions of management at each level will be clarified.

We proposed a tentative idea for an innovation management system as a result of reference to previous studies and investigations; then we verified our proposed model by investigation and discussion at the Working Conference of ISPIM.

4.   Outline of the proposed innovation management system

4.1   Hierarchy of management and system element

We categorize innovation mangement at the company level into three hierarchical levels, corporate level, business level and activity level, according to the purpose of management, organization and object of activity.

The function of the **corporate level** is to establish basic corporate philosophy and policy, and to decide upon fundamental business and basic technologies and then to establish a long-range plan of management.

The function of the **business level** is to decide upon market and product strategy and a more exact business plan in order to achieve basic policy, and to strive to expand markets and increase profits in order to maintain a competitive advance position.

The function of the **activity level** is to manage actual and daily activities such as sales promotion, market expansion and extension of product life cycle.

The innovation management system can be described more exactly by clarifying the goals and activities included at each hierarchical level of management.

4.2   The function of innovation management at each hierarchical level

(1)   Corporate level

The purpose of management at the corporate level is categorized into three goals of individual levels; these are the establishment of an innovative management vision *(sub-level 1)*, introduction of innovative new technology and structuring of basic technology *(sub-level 2)*, and research for new business opportunities *(sub-level 3)*.

At *sub-level 1*, policy determination is dependent on the philosophy of the founder and fundamental policy of the company; then the basic concepts for management should be elucidated and long-range managerial strategy should be decided.

At *sub-level 2*, innovative and advanced technology should be selected after searching for and creating new technological capabilities.

At *sub-level 3*, plans and opportunities for new businesses, new product development and new markets should be issued according to the basic policy at the upper levels, and potential new technologies to be applied.

(2) Business level

The purpose of management at the business level is categorized into two goals of individual sub-levels; these are gain of competitive advantage position *(sub-level 1)* and increase of market share and profits *(sub-level 2)*.

In order to achieve a goal of *sub-level 1*, strategy for new markets and new product development should be planned. Thus more exact activity for new product development follows in order to attain a goal of *sub-level 2*.

(3) Activity level

The main functions of the above two levels, the corporate and business levels, are policy determination and strategic planning units. The activity level is a step to realize such policy and basic strategy as actual activities of daily management, which is categorized into three goals of individual sub-levels; which are increase of sales amount *(sub-level 1)*, market share increase and sales promotion *(sub-level 2)* and quality improvement to obtain long life cycle time of product and cost reduction *(sub-level 3)*.

In order to attain the goal of *sub-level 1*, product quality is improved, for *sub-level 2*, a service system which mainly includes sales channels is established, and then for *sub-level 3*, the manufacturing process is improved.

4.3 Relationship between management level and main activity of innovation management in company

Common activities of innovation management are listed in Table 1 by individual management level.

Management Level	Main Activity
Corporate Level	- Basic R&D
	- Organizational innovation
	- Introduction or development of new Technology (technological innovation)
Business Level	- Project management
	- Product innovation
	- Market creation
Activity Level	- Process innovation

Table 1: Main Activities of Innovation Management in Company

5. Verification of the proposed issue

5.1 Examination by questionnaire at the Working Conference

The main comments obtained by questionnaire and discussion are summarized as follows:

(1) On the meaning of „innovation management", there are two opinions:"all of the managerial activity performed innovatively in the company" and "management of activities such as technological innovation, process innovation and product innovation".

(2) Some recommend use of a more than three-dimensional chart which includes dimensions of R&D, marketing, distrubutor, manufacturing and so on. It is useful to discuss the activities of innovation management more precisely, but we concluded that a two-dimensional chart is sufficient for the purpose of our goal, which aims study to clarify the functions of innovation management by examining the purposes of management and extracting functions from them.

(3) On the problem of what measures of performance to adopt to classify the management level, there are different ways of thinking.

(4) The majority of respondents agree with our proposal to classify the management level into three levels.

Some of them who belong to companies where the founder exercises strong leadership or where there is a conceptual historical background put weight on determination of policy, and they insist that strategy at the *business level*, because the outline at the *corporate level* is directed by the founder or leader of the company.

At large-sized companies, the main function at the *corporate level* is to settle a platform rule and policy determination at the *business level*, from which all of the activities of the company follow.

(5)   On the activity of each level, several respondents answered that each management level should only have two sub-levels. There was an opinion that framework-making and determination of target are the purposes of activity at the *corporate level*. Several German respondents insisted that change of rule is the main activity of innovation management because all of the company activities are performed according to specified rules, but this opinion is a little different from our standpoint.

(6)   Two persons suggested that the *activity level* should be categorized into three sub-levels such as

(a) product R&D, manufacturing, sales & distribution

(b) market segments, product & service, market introduction problem.

The above opinions were included in our proposed table.

(7)   Almost all answered that activity at the *corporate level* included activity to introduce new technology and seek new business opportunities and also someone insisted that construction of an innovation system is the main outcome of the activity at the *corporate level*.

(8)   There was not much difference of opinion on the function of the *business level* because almost all of the innovation activities in so-called "innovation management" are recognized as activities on this level. However, many businessmen listed actual and common activity processes as purposes of this level.

(9)   On the functions of the *activity level*, there were two different opinions as follows:

(a) All activity is performed under the condition that object market and technology are specified by the upper level.

(b) Determination of strategy on the market, technology and production is an activity for this management level.

(10)   There is a suggestion that the managerial problem in a joint venture company is a particular style of management. This suggestion will be taken up in a future study when we examine the variation of basic functions differing depending on the style of company.

(11)   A few were of the opinion that only activities such as R&D, new product development, new technology assessment and project management constitute innovation management. We reached a consensus that every managerial act included production innovation; and that innovation management should be recognized as a whole activity including innovation and processes of idea generation.

5.2   Discussion on innovation process by presentation and discussion at the Working Conference

(1)   Definiton of innovation

There are various opinions on the purpose of making innovations such as to maintain competitive advantage, to obtain an economic merit or to contribute to the society and help to solve ecological problems.

Several participants from Germany disclosed an opinion that innovation is a process that changes the rules.

As a result of discussion on the definition of innovation, the Working Group arrived at the following consensus:

"Innovation is the process of achieving an improvement by means of something new that was unknown or unfamiliar, as a concept, till then".

(2)   Innovation system

1) The importance of a systematic approach to innovation management is emphasized by many participants, especially there was general agreement that „in competition on innovation the company needs an innovation system".

2) Main opinions on the relationship between national level and company level are:

(a)   The national R&D policy supports the key technologies and innovation activities in companies to secure key markets and to create new jobs.

(b)   The company must be a component of the innovation system in a national economy, and the company as a component of the national innovation system has to be considered by designing the international innovation system.

(3)   Innovation process

Against our opinion that the product development process starts from a grasp of user's needs, another opinion which put weight on the management-oriented concept was disclosed, stating that competition is a trigger for promoting the process, too; then the customer care process becomes more and more important for the future organization of management.

(4)   Analysis of innovation process

On the possibility of analyzing innovation process, the following different opinions are disclosed:

1) Innovation cannot be ordered by management. The innovation process is an irrational proceeding. It is not possible to innovate or to invent only by logical thinking.

2) Innovation can be planned. Innovation can be planned more easily and the innovation process becomes more logical.

3) We have to distinguish, in respect of the possibility of planning innovation, between the innovation system and innovation management. In my opinion, the innovation system tends to be a predominantly illogical thing and innovation management a predominantly logical one. So management has to take care of the innovation process by building up an innovation system as a framework which supports an atmosphere of innovation in the company in the first step and the generation of innovation in the second step.

6. Conclusions and future problems

This study revealed the following results on the elements and process of the innovation management system from the discussion and comments issued at the Working Conference.

6.1 Elements of innovation management system

The specified elements of the system are summarized in Table 2.

6.2 The purpose of product innovation

Many opinions were disclosed on the possibilty of analyzing the process of innovation management and the applied method, but a general process of innovation management could not be issued. In order to clarify the above problem, we have focused our analysis on the process of product development (new product development and product improvement). The proposed model is illustrated in Figure 1. On the basis of the basic model, the process of product innovation system is illustrated in Figure 2. As a result of this study, the following conclusions and future problems were revealed.

Level	Purpose	Output	Related Activities
Corporate Level	find out more innovative management vision	corporate beliefs and fundamental concept long range strategy	time series of managerial situation, position analysis, scenario writing, cope with international / national trend of economy and value system
	search for creative new technology and capability	selection of advanced technology	technology forecasting analysis of present technology product-technology matrix
	find out an opportunity as new business	research for new business & new product and market	future business needs analysis of competitiveness analysis of capaticity external / internal situation analysis
Business level	get competive advance position	strategic plan for new market and new product	status map of competition technology-market matrix analysis of self managerial potentials and resources
	increase of profit and expand market	new product development	customer's needs assessment analysis of market and competitive situation, basic product evaluation technology assessment
Activity level	sales promotion	product improvement	life cycle time analysis, product portfolio, radar chart saisfaction analysis
	increase market share promote sales amount	develop service system	sales point, PR of product characteristics of product, product-market matrix
	reduce cost and improve quality for longer life cycle of products	manufacturing (process) innovation	quality control process improvement quality deployment

Table 2: The Elements of Innovation Management in the Company

(1)   This study has taken up only main elements of the innovation management system. In order to develop an investigation on the "system", relationship among such elements and their dynamic properties, the process of managerial activity must be analyzed more exactly.

(2)   The interrelationship between innovation management systems at the corporate level and international level should be clarified in the future.

(3)   Systematic analysis of the innovation process on the basis of the proposed basic model should be promoted in the future.

(4)   Analysis of the effect of corporate strategy on product development and innovation process is needed in the future.

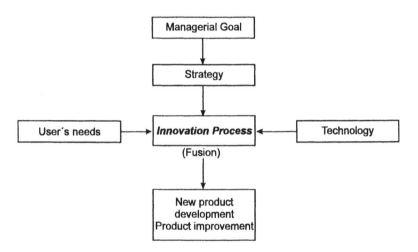

Fig. 1: The Basic Model of Product Innovation Process

116

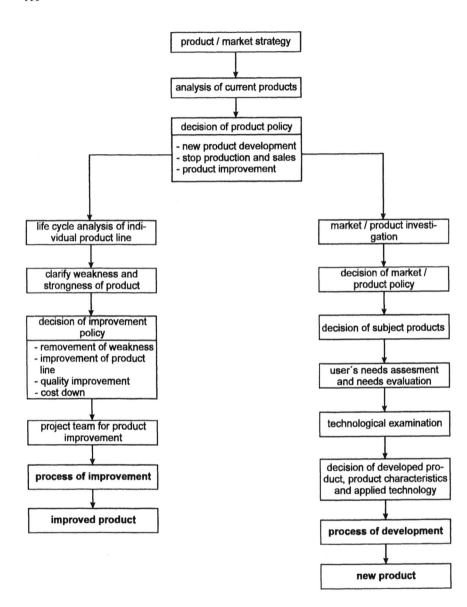

Fig. 2: General Product Innovation Process

References

(1) Peter F. Drucker, "The discipline of Innovation"

(2) Bruce D. Henderson, "The origin of strategy", Harvard Business Review, November-December 1989

(3) Nicolas Danila, "Strategic evaluation and selection of R&D projects", R&D Management, Vol. 19, 1989

(4) Kazuo Sumii, "Innovation management" (in Japanese), Japan Economic Newspaper Press, 1986

(5) Shuji Kondo, "Approach to new product and new business", Japan Management Association, 1989

(6) Knut Holt, "Product innovation management", Butterworths Pub., 1988

(7) U. Koppelmann, "Grundlagen des Produktmarketing zum qualitativen Informationsbedarf von Produktmanagern", Verlag W. Kohlhammer GmbH, 1987 (translated into Japanese in 1984)

(8) Toyohiro Kohno, "Strategy for new product development", Diamond inc., 1987

(9) Heinz Hübner, "How to structure the innovation system", Preprint

Recent Essentials in Innovation Management and Research, edited by H. Hübner / T. Dunkel
Gabler, Wiesbaden/Germany, 1995

Results of Discussion and Fields of Future Research

The Innovation System of the Company as a Frame for the Management of Innovation Projects

Volker Gers, University of Kassel,

Luis Felipe Nascimento, University of Kassel/
University of Rio Grande do Sul, Porto Alegre

Participants:

Moderator: Hans-Dieter Schwabe, Chamber of Industry & Commerce , Kassel (D)

Frank Elsen, Technical University of Darmstadt[*] (D)

Volker Gers, University of Kassel (D)

Heinz Hübner, Conference Chairman, University of Kassel (D)

Takaya Ichimura, Nihon University, Tokyo (JPN)

Markus Krefter, EIDOS Ideenmanagement, Hamburg (D)

Dietrich Legat, Hewlett-Packard, Geneva (CH)

Eckhard Müller, Wintershall AG, Kassel (D)

Luis Felipe Nascimento, University of Kassel and University of Rio Grande do Sul, Porto Alegre (BR)

Matti Otala, Telenorma Bosch Telekom GmbH, Frankfurt/M. (D)

Petteri Piippo, Lappeenranta University of Technology, Finland (SF)

Peter Pinholt, NKT Research Center A/S, Broendby (DK)

Ingo Puhl, Technical University of Darmstadt [*] (D)

Robert Snip, ROSNI Marketing Adviesbureau, Geldrop (NL)

---

[*] only Thursday and Friday

Introduction

The moderator proposed that each participant of the group should present his special interest in this conference. The fields of interest focussed on "implementation of innovation", "concept of innovation", and "basic model of product development".

This discussion contributed to a creative atmosphere in the Working Group. The participants of the Working Group decided to work out a common understanding of innovation at the beginning.

What does innovation mean?

Based on the "working definition" of TWI/University of Kassel (see paper Hübner, Appendix), the participants mentioned the following concepts, which are not only academic but also result from their practical experience in the company:

- Innovation is a process that starts with an idea and ends with a new product or service.
- Innovation is a combination of novelty and improvement to escape competition.
- The goal of innovation is to find the better solution for a problem. Innovation has to fulfill a purpose. It is not necessary to quantify innovation in economic units.
- Innovation is not just for fun. It has not only economic benefits, it is also a contribution to social and ecological issues.
- A process has rules, but the rules can be changed. Innovation is the process that changes the rules, produces new instruments, and creates new paradigms.

There was a consensus on the following definition: "Innovation is a process to accomplish an improvement by means of something new that was unknown or unfamiliar, as a concept, until then".

Discussion after the key note speech of Hübner: "How to Structure the Innovation System of the Company"

The moderator proposed that any questions of the Working Group participants should be asked immediately instead of at the end of the lecture. This procedure proved beneficial to the discussion.

1) What are the problems in carrying out innovative activities in companies?

The Speaker presented practical problems (see paper Hübner) which were discussed, and there was a consensus about his hypothesis.

Speaker (S.): There are difficulties in creating an innovative climate and in establishing innovation projects in companies. The innovation project often depends on chance or power structures: They are delayed and do not succeed because of a lacking systematic application of instruments. The ideas remain hidden due to inadequate organization and innovative climate.

2) What is the National Innovation System?

S.: The national system of innovation is the network of R&D activities in the public and private sectors. The national policy supports the innovative activities of public research organizations and of companies' research departments (see paper Hübner and "Explanation of the Topics").

Participant (P.): The national system is part of the international Innovation System. The innovation process must be efficient in a national as well as in an international perspective.

P.: The national R&D policy supports the key technologies and innovation activities in companies to get key markets and to create new jobs. The Japanese research promotion by MITI of Japan and other institutions, for example, concentrates its support on activities which are orientated on customers' needs.

3) Is there really a competition between nations?

P.: Internationally oriented companies do not understand themselves as part of a country. Competition does not take place among countries but among companies. The viewpoint of these companies differs from the viewpoint of the governmental organizations. Governmental institutions have a vertical point of view. They work out technology policies for their countries. On the other hand, companies have a horizontal viewpoint. They look out for economic possibilities in different countries (see Figure 1).

	Country 1	Country 2	Country 3	Country 4
Company 1	XXXXX		XXXXX	XXXXX
Company 2		XXXXX	XXXXX	XXXXX
Company 3	XXXXX	XXXXX		

Fig. 1: Horizontal/vertical point of view of competition

4) What are the needs for an Innovation System?

Comment (C.): Some axioms and hypotheses about the need for an Innovation System (see paper Hübner) were discussed and the Working Group found consensus:

1) Innovation, especially technical innovation, has an instrumental character to reach economical goals.
2) Thus, scientific and engineering R&D is based exclusively on economic interests.
3) Results of R&D and innovation can be planned.

5) Can innovation be planned?

P.: Yes, look at the "Delphi-Study" worked out for the German Ministry of Research (BMFT, 1993, quoted in paper Hübner). It is a frame for the research goals of a national Innovation System.

S.: If we know the customers' needs, we can use R&D to achieve an innovation. In other words, we have here the discussion: "demand pull" versus "technology push".

The hypotheses are: Concentration on single research projects is not sufficient. To be competitive in innovation, the company needs an Innovation System. The single company has to rely increasingly on co-operation with other institutions. Therefore, a new understanding of the company as a component of the Innovation System of a national economy is necessary. The company as part of the national Innovation System has to be related to the design of the internal Innovation System (see paper Hübner).

P.: For example, companies in Japan operate under tough competition. The majority are competition-drivers and have reduced their innovation costs. They show the way for the other companies which have to adopt this experience.

6) What are the main functions of the company's Innovation System?

S.: We may say: Providing a frame for specific innovations processes; absorption of ideas; integration, based on common need for innovation; collecting ideas for possible use in future; internal co-ordination of projects to prevent delays; (strategic) networking within the (Inter-) National Innovation System, etc. (see paper Hübner).

C.: There was consensus about the main functions of an Innovation System. This is a point of "Fields of future research"

7) What are the borders of a company's Innovation System?

P.: The limits of Innovation Systems depend on each company. In my company, for example, the border of the Innovation System is the border of the company.

P.: How do you deal with external knowledge?

P.: The Innovation System of the company needs to look out for other experiences. The company is not a closed system. It is a part of the national and international Innovation System.

8) How can an Innovation System be designed?

S.: We can use the Aspect System Approach (ASA) that is based on systems theory. Each system can be defined as a set of components which have logical relations with one another. In designing production management systems, one has to observe the aspect system of "functions/methods" (planning of flow-rates, harmonizing flow-rates, scheduling of orders); "responsibilities" (areas of responsibility, responsible departments/persons); "information equipment" (hardware, databases, system/user software) as a means for attainment of the production management goals fixed in the aspect system of "goals" (lead times, service level, inventory; costs). The design based on ASA has been discussed in greater detail in the paper by Hübner.

9) What is the difference between "innovation" and "invention"? (Phases of technological ontogenesis)

S.: There are four phases in technological ontogenesis (see paper Hübner). While discovery is the result of basic research (natural science), invention is the result of applied research. The results are new in an objective sense. As against this, innovation is based on the concept of subjective newness (new from the viewpoint of the company). Innovation is related to technical execution and sale. The last step is diffusion. This step consists in the phase of distribution and marketing.

10) Where do the first phases of technological ontogenesis take place?

C.: On company level, there are different possible beginnings. The company usually starts in the innovation phase, but it may need results of the first two phases. The R&D public policy also supports organizations that are occupied with basic research and applied research. In these organizations, the phases of discovery and invention take place, which sometimes are not profitable within a period, but they are attractive to innovation activities in the companies. The company must identify its "strong point". In which sector is the company competitive?

124

The following model was discussed from several points of view. There was a consensus in the Working Group that this model can be used in several sectors and not only in the technical sector. Invention, for example, is also necessary for the marketing department too (see Figure 2).

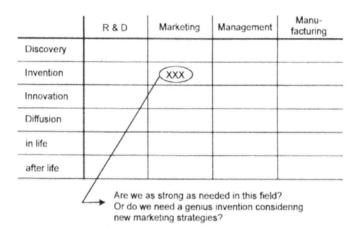

	R & D	Marketing	Management	Manu-facturing
Discovery				
Invention		XXX		
Innovation				
Diffusion				
in life				
after life				

Are we as strong as needed in this field?
Or do we need a genius invention considering new marketing strategies?

Fig.2: Phases of technological ontogenesis to be applied in functions beyond natural / engineering science, too

11) Who is responsible for the Innovation System?

P.: The responsibility is a decisive point (see paper Hübner). The new ideas must go directly to management. For example, people who work with technology look for new ideas and sell these ideas to their companies.

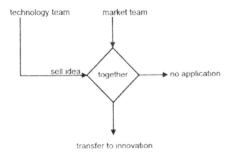

Fig. 3: Possible way of an idea

Therefore, innovation must win in two battlefields: Marketing and technology department (see Figure 3). Somebody who has a new idea must present it immediately to management and discuss it with R&D and marketing departments. As fast as possible, management will have to decide what to do with this idea. On the one hand, the structure must be able to support the innovation process, while on the other hand, it has to be flexible.

Sometimes management does not approve of an idea, but still the people go ahead. An example is the project of a laser printer which was not approved by management. The persistence of some people made this project a market success.

P.: It is necessary to build an "informal" or "oppositional" Innovation System in companies.

P.: The structure supports the innovation process but it cannot produce innovations on its own.

S.: An unpublished study of the situation of an important German group shows that only 15 to 20% of employees of the company are occupied with innovation. The motivation process (see lecture by Otala, pages 100 & seq.) must be part of the innovation structure. We need creative people. There will be an increasing demand for such people in future.

Discussion after the key note speech of Dietrich Legat: "Economic Crisis - Innovation Crisis - Management Crisis?"

The Speaker elaborated that the reduction of cycle times is an irreversible process. The consequences of "superfast processes" are unforeseeable not only for companies but also for society. Of course, this situation caused a lot of questions which were discussed in the following way:

1) What are further reasons in addition to those mentioned by the Speaker for the existence of "superfast processes"?

P.: The reduction of cycle times with respect to business and economy is founded in different tendencies. Of course, **competition** is the most important factor influencing the dynamic of innovation. But on the other hand there are influences caused by the customers: We may call them **"customers' needs"**, **"customers' wants"**, and **pleasure**.

The process of cycle time reduction is also pushed by the fast change of "customers' needs" and "customers' wants". Of course it is evident that only in a very few cases these "customers' needs" are identical with the wants of the customers. To show the difference between "customers' needs" and so-called "customers' wants", let us look at an example: There is no need for a human being to eat caviar or to drink coffee. On the contrary, the consumption of coffee is injurious to health. But we have to respect the preferences of customers like pleasure, fun, and enjoyment.

Besides, we have to take into consideration that **change per se gives pleasure**. It is not necessary to get an improvement as a trigger for change. Change itself provides pleasure, even without improvement. This pleasure in change per se is used predominantly by companies of the consumer industry. Benetton, for example, seems to be a company where "novelty" is considered as more important than "quality" of product.

Furthermore, change is needed to give satisfaction to employees and to the whole company. In this way, change is a potential factor for achieving economic success.

S.: No important invention or development in history has been caused by "customers' needs" or "customers' wants". The exploration of electricity, for instance, was motivated by the thirst for knowledge of some scientists.

However, for a successful survival in the market, the management of a company has to consider the change of customers' needs and wants. So the **"customer care process"** becomes more and more important for the future organization of management.

P.: Even if engineers are convinced of the wrongness of customers' wishes, they have to submit to the "customer care process".

P.: But this acceleration of process caused by "customers' wants", "customers' needs", and "pleasure" is just one explanation for the existence of "superfast processes".

So we have to concentrate on the fact that **competition** is the **most important trigger** for pushing the process. The reasons for this competition-driven acceleration of change are multifarious. For example, overcapacity could be a compulsion to look out for new products and to think about other activities.

S.: Furthermore, the acceleration of processes is based on the aim of a company to attack and to conquer a new market. Or it could be founded on the persuasion of possessing the better solution than the competitor.

2) What are the consequences of the arrival of "superfast processes" for business and economy?

S.: As one consequence, we have to innovate the management process. The cycle times of all economic processes are accelerated and the leaders of companies have to follow this development. This effort becomes more and more impracticable because of the backwardness of traditional management processes.

So the use of the computer supports the acceleration of processes, but the computer cannot help to innovate the management process itself.

P.: Another consequence of "superfast processes" for the company is to **work faster**. Mainly from the point of view of the market introduction of a new product, it becomes necessary to get competitive advantages. If the company is able to develop a product faster than others, it will be possible to start later. So the management may adjust its product innovation to "customers' needs" and "customers' wants" more precisely than the competitors and it will reduce the risk of making wrong decisions.

S.: This development includes an acceleration of the "customer care process", and it is based upon a **quicker feedback** to the market.

P.: Present attempts to handle "superfast processes" are short-lived: Frequently the leaders of companies try to regulate the contents of work. The second step of this strategy is the rationalization of work with the consequences of unemployment and sometimes overcapacity.

Obviously management often brakes the change of economy because it is not interested in change. Management ignores the necessity to adapt the company to "superfast processes".

P.: We have to pay attention to the **ecological impacts** of this development, too. The desire of customers to get the new products will increase if cycle times of products become shorter. The company has to solve this dilemma between pollution of the environment by artificially obsoleted products and the necessity of pushing the innovation process with the aim to create new products which will induce customers to consumption.

3) What would society look like if all "useless" work (or loss of time) had been eliminated?

S.: The pressure for higher efficiency leads to the elimination of rework and all kinds of "useless work". As a consequence, process times will decrease more and more. In this way, whole sectors of the economy will become superfluous. If we introduce teleshopping, shop buildings will become useless. The system of price fixing will become a system of supply and demand like a stock exchange.

P.: It is a **philosophical** discussion **how time should be used.** If people stand in queue their time is wasted only in the economic sense. But there are social components like smalltalk and making acquaintances which cannot be evaluated in terms of efficiency.

The success of the computer in office and household humanizes work and saves time. On the other hand, for example, people may spend this saved time (perhaps!) without sense, playing computer games by themselves or consuming needless things.

S.: In respect of the qualification and training of employees, there are some consequences, too: Useless work has to disappear. The **responsibility** of each employee will grow and **work** will be performed at a higher level of requirement.

But the main problem is ignorance of the responsible politicians and managers who do not realize that this development is no utopia and can only be modified by political changes.

4) What are the limits of the "superfast processes"?

S.: I expect that physical stops will follow and will brake this development. Increasing costs, for instance, could be a hindrance to accelerating a process more and more. For example, the high costs of a new game for Christmas is a counter-argument, or even a physical stop, against quicker development of better games.

But we have to take into consideration the different importance of "superfast processes" for each branch of industry. I suppose the speed of change in the branch of consumer goods is higher than in other branches.

5) Is the development concerning the acceleration of cycle times irreversible?

C.: This question could not be answered by the Working Group. It will be a field of future research.

Discussion after the key note speech of Matti Otala: "Trends in cooperation between industry, R&D centres, and universities"

Introduction

S.: In future, we will probably have a lot of technology changes and faster processes than nowadays. In my opinion, compared to the nineteenth century, we have few technology inventions. Railway, electricity, light bulb, telephone, radio, applications of radioactivity, automobile, aeroplane, etc. were invented within a period of 40 years (1860-1900) . In our century, after 1945, the missile, the transistor, and the computer are major inventions.

1) What are new sources of motivation?

S:: In the eighties, the discussion was about concepts like TQM (Total Quality Management), Just-in-time, TQC (Total Quality Control), etc. The companies used working teams to obtain competition. In the nineties, the discussion is about "how to recycle people?" (how to change their qualifications), i.e. how to push people or how to motivate people? Companies need creative employees to get continuous improvement.

P:: Motivation is a consequence of TQM (Total Quality Management) and team-work.

S:: It is the base for improvement. When teamwork is achieved, the next step is the "open-book management" in which all employees know their tasks.

2) What are the future trends?

S.: There are a lot of trends and changes. Technology and intellectual property are becoming strategic resources to be acquired, shared, and traded. The trend in industry is to concentrate on Cores, Glocal structures, and to built new co-operation schemes and new organizational paradigms (see paper Otala, pages 100 & seq.).

Concentration on "Core Competences"

S.: In the new world scenery, the company is being restructured. Cultural homogeneity and regional factors are very important. They will be concentrated to "cores" (business, markets, customers, products, technologies, and competence). What is outside of cores will be eliminated. Large corporations will be restructured into more manageable units.

C.: The markets will be divided and the companies will look for a new market niche.

S.: The products will be standardized and extremely flexible, technology cycles will be shortening, etc.

GLOCAL *Structures*

S.: Another trend is building of GLOCAL structures. GLOCAL (**GLO**bally lo**CAL**) structure is the definition of an industry trend towards reliance on self-sufficient, semi-autonomous operations located in the area of a homogeneous customer group.

S.: The GLOCAL system permits a reduction of international transport, i.e. industry makes products in the region where they will be sold. The borders of regional systems will be identified by culture. GLOCAL structures in Europe comprise areas like the Scandinavian, Romanic, German-speaking, Anglo-Saxon, and Slavic regions.

New co-operation schemes

S.: The deficit of public budgets will limit the growth of public R&D spending. As a consequence, the public research organizations will be obliged to obtain more funding from industry.

The trend is that research organizations will sharpen the focus of their products and ideas to needs of the companies. Their research will be measured as a business by criteria like productivity and quality. A research organization being awarded with many "Nobel Prizes", but whose research result is not transferred to innovation and to products, will have difficulties to get financing. On the other hand, new co-operation schemes will be built to balance the strong competition. In the GLOCAL system, alliances and joint ventures will grow between and within public (university research group, research institutes, etc.) and private organizations (industrial research laboratories).

New organizational paradigms
S.: The new organizational paradigms will have strategic business units, hierarchically flattened structures, less centralism, and authority will be delegated.

Discussion after the key note speech given by Ichimura and Piippo: "Innovation Management System at Company Level"

During their lecture, Prof. Ichimura and Mr. Piippo introduced a proposal for the **function of Innovation Management** and a proposal for the **process of product development** (see paper Ichimura/Tuominen/Piippo, page 117). The general validity of these proposals was discussed by two questions:

1) What are the functions of Innovation Management in a company?
P.: The distribution of tasks relative to Innovation Management **cannot** be divided clearly between the corporate level, the business unit level, and the product and market level. The decision on management vision, for instance, can be made on corporate level as well as business unit level. Perhaps the corporate level has lost visions, but the business unit level may produce visions because of its greater proximity to the market and to customers.
S.: The problem of describing an Innovation System and its function in a company is based on the multifarious types of companies. Mainly the branch, the size, and the type of strategy of a company are factors that produce these difficulties. The location of a company and the different attributes of each country enlarge this unsolved problem. I believe we need a **"contextual approach"** to find out a satisfying solution and to distinguish more precisely. But the focal point of discussion now is how to find the basic functions and activities concerning Innovation Management in a company.

C.: Concerning a more specific discussion of the functions of the Innovation System of the company, we have to refer the reader to the full paper by Hübner.

2) What about the general validity of the basic model of Product Innovation Management (PIM)?

P.: The model of product Innovation Management cannot be considered as generally accepted! The fixed linkages between the elements of the model are not conclusive. There are other connections between the elements of the basic model of product Innovation Management. Instead of product development, I see **corporate strategy** as the **central element** of the model. Under this aspect, innovation of new products or improved products and consideration of the market trend becomes a part of the corporate strategy.

If we look at the reasons for this linkage, we have to remember the discussion following the lecture held by Mr. Legat (see this documentation, page 126 & seq.). "customers' needs", and especially competition, are the main influencing factors which accelerate processes in a company. Therefore, both factors will partly determine corporate strategy, even if full recording of "users' needs" is impossible.

3) Where do R&D activities take place?

P.: There are three different **areas of R&D activities**. It is possible to distinguish between **external** R&D, **corporate** R&D, and R&D done by **divisions**. Each of these areas differs from the others by its special focal points. I think this may be clarified by showing the example of a German company:

The R&D activities of divisions concentrate predominantly on product development and client adaptation. Divisions do not take into consideration basic research and applied research.

Focal points of the corporate R&D activities are mainly applied research, technical development, and production technology. The importance of basic research and applied research in a company is not so big as in the area of external R&D. The R&D activities of this area concentrate on both fields as well as on production technology (see Figure 4).

	External	Corporate	Division
Basic research			
Applied research			
Technical development			
Product development			
Production technology			
Client adaption			
After sales			

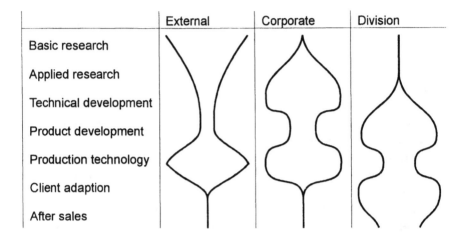

Fig. 4: Example of R&D activities: The breadth of the shapes shows the relative volume of actors in R&D and innovation.

4) How to find future fields for R&D and especially for innovation

P.: There is a great disbelief in marketing. On the one hand, because customers do not know their needs exactly. So marketing **cannot** find out customers' needs. On the other hand, successful companies have to find out customers' needs some years before customers ask for a change because the development of a solution requires a certain amount of time.

P.: Maybe this fundamental problem of marketing can be solved by the following proposal:

We have to distinguish between the basic needs of customers, which are not changing in time, the quality the customer gets, and the customer's expectations. Only quality and expectations are changing in time.

I would like to show you a figure (see Figure 5):

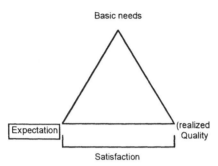

Fig. 5: Aim of innovation: Closing the gap between customer´s expectation and the quality
he gets

Perhaps this figure becomes clear by a fictitious example: A basic need of carriers is the ability
to reach a target point immediately. This aim is not realistic nowadays. But the customer ex-
pects the development of a truck which is able to reach a speed of ninety kilometres per hour.
Today he only gets trucks that drive eighty kilometres per hour.
It is the task of the company to close the gap between expectation and realized quality. If this
intention succeeds perfectly or partly, the satisfaction of the customer will increase. Accordingly, the marketing department has to find out **future expectations of customers**. Maybe this
approach could be a solution for marketing problems in respect of innovation.

5) Can innovation be planned, yes or no?
P.: No, innovation **cannot** be ordered by management. The innovation process is an irrational
proceeding. It is not possible to innovate or to invent only by logical thinking. "Getting the
idea" is the problem, which cannot be planned. In this respect management has to throw the
switches to a positive atmosphere for innovation in the company.
P.: In my opinion, innovation **can** be planned. You have to consider the possibility of an innovation growing slowly. One thousand small break-throughs, for example, are able to build up
one big break-through. The advantages of this system of innovation by small steps are evident:
There is only low risk in practice. Innovation can be planned more easily and the innovation
process becomes more logical.
P.: But on the other hand, great break-throughs caused by this way of Innovation Management
are rare in the recent past.

P.: In this context, the question becomes important how to define a break-through innovation in contrast to an ordinary innovation. The problem cannot be solved unequivocally because of different perspectives of the observers. For instance, the improvement of process engineering could be a break-through innovation for the company. But from the point of view of society or ecology, it could be only a small innovation or it may be considered as a step backwards. So the discussion about the importance of an innovation has to be held under a holistic point of view.

P.: I think with respect to the possibility of planning innovation, we have to distinguish between Innovation System and Innovation Management. In my opinion, the Innovation System in general is a predominantly illogical thing, whereas Innovation Management is a predominantly logical thing. So it is easier to plan the Innovation Management than the Innovation System.

C.: A **consensus** in the discussion about the question whether innovation can be planned or not was found by the Working Group in some points:

The process of innovation is a creative process. It is not possible to plan the innovation itself. But of course the **environment of the innovation process can be planned** by management. So management has to take care of the innovation process by building up an Innovation System as a framework which supports an atmosphere for innovation in the company as a first step and the generation of innovations as a second step.

The question whether Innovation System or Innovation Management is more logical than the other could not be finally answered by the Working Group.

Furthermore, we have to mention that the question whether results of R&D and innovation can be planned was already discussed under another viewpoint related to the key note speech of Hübner; see this documentation, page 122.

6) What is the structure of an innovation process?

C: The Speakers showed their basic model of an innovation process as an example of product development and gave an impulse to the following discussion:

P.: You cannot illuminate a chaotic process.

P.: Maybe it can be done in analogy to the structure of an ordinary management process. In this case, it is possible to distinguish, among other things, between a sequential process which works step by step, a phase process which contains several sequential processes, or a chaotic process which shows no obvious order. But the proof concerning the existence of one of these structures in the innovation process has to be done by future research.

S.: I would like to consider the process more concretely than abstractly. Another possibility to explore the innovation process and the Innovation Management could be the examination of

Innovation Systems, innovation processes, and management methods which were ineffective in the past in respect of the generation of a successful innovation. If it is not practicable to find out the circumstances which promote an innovation, we have to search for reasons of failure.

P.: But this method of examination will be difficult. It is possible to describe the trouble by one sentence: "Mistakes do not have fathers"!

P.: In my opinion, it is impossible to create a model of innovation process which takes into consideration the multifarious attributes of reality. Besides, we hardly know anything about this process. Therefore, it becomes very difficult to develop a model. But on the other hand, the **value of models is high** even if they **are not of general validity,** because they will stimulate and structure discussion.

C.: The question whether we design an Innovation System or an Innovation Management System could not be solved by discussion.

Furthermore, we have to refer to the paper of Prof. Hübner again concerning the tasks of Innovation Management.

7) How to improve the innovation process

C.: Closing the discussion, Mr. Snip presented his current research domain to answer this question. It is called **"meta-innovation"**, meaning the process that improves innovation processes. In this respect, his research domain is a good proposal as one way of thinking in order to discuss the structure of innovation process and Innovation Management.

Mr. Snip regards the whole innovation process from the fuzzy front end which, in the course of time, becomes more and more concrete in an innovation route, to the end of process which includes innovation results. He is interested mainly in the situational influences, for instance sociological or economic factors, which are important with respect to the innovation process (see Figure 6).

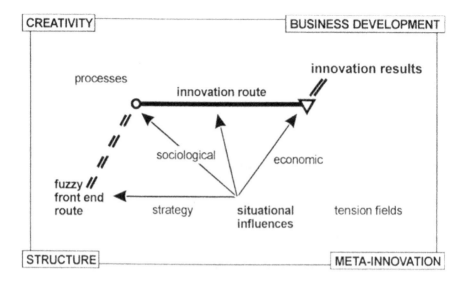

Fig. 6: Research domain of meta-innovation (Rosni Marketing Adviesbureau)

The investigation route of his research has to be characterized as very pragmatic and as practice-oriented. Accordingly, his catalogue of guiding questions refers to fields of unsolved problems of companies concerning innovation.

The examination of the research domain is based on two research methods: On the one hand, literature study is used. On the other hand, Mr. Snip collected case studies of thirty innovation routes with personal involvement during the time between 1968 and 1994.

Maybe this empirical approach will lead to an idea what innovation process and Innovation Management look like.

Finally, we would like to list some **literature** which was mentioned by participants of the Working Group coming **not only** from universities. The books deal with the question of the logic of systems:

Popper, Karl R.: The Logic of Scientific Discovery, 5th ed., London, 1968.
Dörner, Dietrich: Die Logik des Mißlingens. Strategisches Denken in komplexen Situationen, Hamburg, 1993.

Fields of future research

During the discussion, a number of questions could not be answered. These unsolved problems are possibly the trigger for future innovation research. Maybe until the next ISPIM Conferences some of these questions will be enlightened, or they will be a topic in another Working Group. From our point of view, the following questions have to be mentioned as fields of future research :

1. Definition of terms:
We have verified that some concepts have different interpretations. It is necessary to harmonize the language. The goal of this field of research is the construction of a house of definitions.

2. Differences between customers' needs and customers' wants:
There are many kinds of differences in the individual decisions of customers about what they desire and what is best for them. Only in a very few cases, the choice of the customer is identical with the optimal decision, which means low impacts in respect of health, ecology, economy, and so on. Accordingly, science has to seek a solution for handling these bi-partite necessities of the customer.

3. Who defines customers' needs?
What authority is entitled to decide about the measure of the value system of society?. Furthermore, we have to think about criteria of valuation, for example religious, ethical, economic, and ecological criteria. To reduce this problem, future tasks of research would be, among other things, the development of adequate rating models.

4. Development of non-economic criteria for the evaluation of innovation

It is necessary to obtain other criteria for the evaluation of an innovation in addition to economic criteria. We have to discuss concepts for including other influence factors to judge an innovation, for example the social benefit of a (technical) improvement.

5. The Innovation System of a company

a) How to design and implement an Innovation System

We need experience for the implementation of an Innovation System using the Aspect System Approach (ASA) as discussed, which are useful in practice on the one hand and which give us an image of how to realize Innovation Systems on the other hand.

Independently of individual solutions, research has to consider the fact that no general solution exists.

b) What is the structure of an Innovation System?

As a field of future research on the structure of an Innovation System, we may mention the tasks of corporate, business, product and market levels concerning the function of Innovation Management in a company. Influences of the structure on the success of innovation have to be explored.

6. Informal or counteractive Innovation Systems

It is necessary to explore the existence of informal or counteractive Innovation Systems because a lot of successful innovations are initiated by persons who do not belong to the Innovation System or who even work against the established Innovation System. This phenomenon has to be analysed with the aim to find out possibilities of promotion of persons within the informal system. A description of the characteristics of members of the informal Innovation System, like spontaneity and autonomy, is also important.

7. Development of models of Product Innovation Management (PIM) which take into account contextual factors

Because of the difficulties of developing a general model of product Innovation Management, it becomes necessary to develop specific models. They have to take into consideration different situative influences as far as possible. These situative influences change, for example, in respect of the branch of industry or the location of a company.

8. How to manage "superfast processes"?

There are a lot of unsolved questions in respect of "superfast processes": For example, the discussion about consequences of the arrival of "superfast processes" for economy, ecology, and society becomes important concerning the problem how to manage "superfast processes" responsibly.

We have to answer the questions whether the acceleration of processes is irreversible or not and whether any stops to this development exist.

9. How to qualify (empower) people?

The pressure of competition requires companies to think about the promotion process for selecting and pushing innovative people. Qualification of employees has to be "recycled" by life-time learning. Management must play a new role. We have to examine the tasks of management concerning the creation of an atmosphere of innovation. For example, motivation of people becomes more important than control.

10. How to improve the innovation process by "meta-innovation"?

This field of research has to regard the innovation routes as a whole. Research can be done, for example, by exploring the interrelated subjects of the innovation process or by analysing of situative determinants which influence the process.

Instruments as Management Technology[*]

---

[*] For better understanding, it is recommended to read first the particulars on the Topic, given
under Explanation of the Topics (pages 1-6)

Recent Essentials in Innovation Management and Research, edited by H. Hübner / T. Dunkel
Gabler, Wiesbaden/Germany, 1995

From Low-Tech to High-Tech

Product Development Strategies for Finding New Markets and Technologies

Harry Nyström,

Sten Liljedahl

Institute of Economics
University of Uppsala, Sweden

Abstract:
In the context of a strategic model for product and company development a distinction is made between more open and more closed technological and marketing strategies. This framework is then used to discuss how companies may go from more low-tech to more hi-tech development, by technological and marketing upgrading of new products. The empirical analysis is based on interview data from 13 Swedish biotechnical and foodprocessing companies.

1. Introduction

In the product development literature (Urban et al, 1980, Wind, 1982, Crawford, 1991, Kuczmarski, 1992) most models are mainly concerned with the technological and market upgrading of existing products. Such a competitive option focuses on the marginal technical adjustment and selective marketing of established products, without considering the need to develop radically new technologies and markets. This type of low-tech product development is therefore mainly concerned with how to compete with established products and technologies. Focusing on existing market opportunities then becomes more important than developing new knowledge directed towards new customer needs.

In recent years increasing attention is given in the literature to more high-tech product development situations (Gupca et al, 1985, Green, 1991, Ng et al, 1992) based on managing and exploiting technological and market change, rather than on consolidating and defending existing conditions.

The dynamics of going from low-tech to high-tech product development has not been dealt with, however, to any large extent, despite the fact that this is the most pressing strategic issue for many companies, faced with radical environmental change. Particularly in the case of commodity based companies, for instance basic chemical companies and agroindustry firms, we find many examples of companies faced with this need, due to overproduction and stagnation in demand for traditional products.

In the following we will discuss, in the context of an empirical study of 13 Swedish biotechnical and food processing firms (Nyström et al, 1992), how companies may achieve this type of strategic transformation from low- to high-tech, that is from lower to higher levels of technological and market innovation in their new products.

For this purpose we will utilize a strategic development model, based on research carried out since 1975 in a wide range of industries and technology areas in Sweden (Nyström, 1979, 1990). The results of these studies indicate that more open strategies - emphasizing organizational flexibility, external research and marketing co-operation and synergistic technology use (new technological combinations) - are necessary to achieve higher levels of technological and market innovation in developing and marketing new products.

2.   Theoretical framework

Our model for product development is based on two main outcome dimensions (Figure 1), the level of technological innovation and the level of market innovation for new products and related services. In both instances these measures are derived from interviews with company representatives, who have been directly involved in their development.

The level of technological innovation - our measure of technological success - is defined as the degree of creativity companies have had to employ to solve the critical technical problems when developing new products or processes.
The underlying assumption is that achieving a relatively high level of technological innovation is usually a necessary, but not a sufficient condition for achieving a high level of market innovation - that is highly unique and competitive new products - particularly in research and technology intensive industries. The more radical the need for creative thinking and the more successful a company has been in solving the critical problems in a specific development project, the higher the level of technological innovation is.

We have chosen the level of technological innovation as our main indicator of technological success, since it is a more direct and encompassing measure, than other more operational measures often used in the literature, such as patents (Brockhoff). Patent protection is an imperfect indicator of the level of technological success, since for competitive reasons companies often do not apply for patents and therefore should not be used as a single indicator. Development time is also an imperfect indicator, since it reflects effort applied, rather than success achieved.

The relatively high correlation in our data of these more indirect measures with our more valid, but less operational measure, based on the direct questioning of company researchers, give us greater confidence, however, in our direct main measure of technological success.

The level of market innovation - our measure of market success- is defined as the degree of market uniqueness for new products. The less interchangeable a product is perceived to be by buyers when it is introduced on the market, the higher the degree of market uniqueness. The assumption is that the more unique it is - the more that buyers see it as different in features and performance from competing products - the greater the market potential.

An implicit assumption, which finds support in our research, is that companies do not usually introduce highly unique new products, if they have not by pre-testing or market research convinced themselves that customers value the ways in which a new product differs from existing ones.

Examples of products with a low level of both technological and market innovation, as we have defined these terms, are for instance standardized raw materials, such as sugar and grain. With regard to this type of product, efficient production and distribution is the main concern of management. Prices tend to be highly competitive and overproduction often leads to surpluses, as we see in the agricultural area today. Supply and demand situations on the open market are usually erratic to predict. This often leads to efforts by companies to control sales, for instance by using defensive strategies to tie existing customers more closely to their products.

To obtain greater sales and profits, market and technological upgrading of products is usually viewed as desirable by low-tech companies, dependant on products with low degrees of technological and market innovation. To achieve this objective and become more innovative such companies need, however, to open up their marketing, technological and organizational strategies. This, then, also requires that they increase their innovative potential by designing and implementing a more creative culture and climate and more flexible forms of production and distribution. This presents formidable obstacles to change for most low-tech companies.

One way for these companies to achieve a competitive advantage - which is shown in Figure 1 by Product Development Strategy A - is to try to increase the level of market innovation, without having to significantly increase the level of technological innovation. Essentially this type of low-tech marketing strategy requires companies to become more market oriented, by differentiating and positioning their products to achieve competitive advantage (Porter, 1985). Thereby companies, if successful in their efforts, may increase their degree of market innovation by finding market niches, where their products are viewed as superior to competing ones.

Research intensity is in general very low in this type of company and mainly limited to perfecting existing technologies, rather than developing new ones. Technological strategies are usually very closed and mainly based on in-house development and refining established knowledge, which in our framework is called internal orientation and isolated technology use. Marketing strategies are also relatively closed and directed towards existing customers and modifications of existing products. This type of relatively closed development strategy is for instance almost the only strategy used by Swedish food processing companies (Nyström and Edwardsson, 1982) and the main development strategy for companies in the Swedish forest industry (Nyström , 1985).

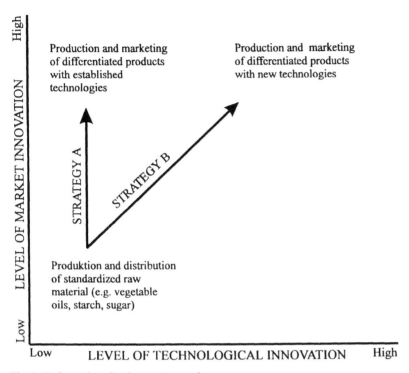

Fig. 1. Basic product development strategies

A more radical and innovative development strategy, shown in Figure 1 as Product Development Strategy B, is necessary in our framework, if companies are to achieve a high level of both technological and market innovation for new products. This strategy involves both high risk and high possibilities for growth and profits.

As our earlier research shows (Nyström, 1979, 1990), this usually requires that companies have relatively open and flexible technological and marketing strategies and high research intensity to generate new knowledge.

More open technological strategies (Figure 2) are characterized by a greater degree of external orientation (that is more research co-operation) and more synergistic technology use (that is more combining and recombining of existing knowledge).

148

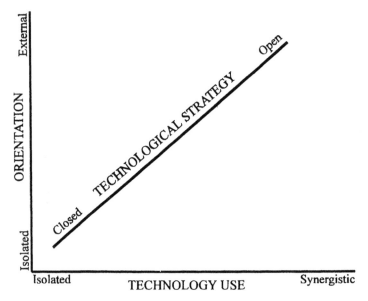

Fig. 2. Main dimensions of more closed and more open technological strategies

Strategic ventures with buyers, universities, other firms or inventors are often used to achieve synergistic technology use and external orientation in development activities. Some companies in this high-tech category, for instance pharmaceutical and eletronic companies, devote upwards of 20 % of sales to R&D, while some low-tech companies, for instance food- and woodprocessing companies, often spend less than 1%.

More open marketing strategies (Figure 3) are strategies which are directed towards new product uses and/or new customer groups. The most open strategies are those which fulfil both these criteria to a large extent.

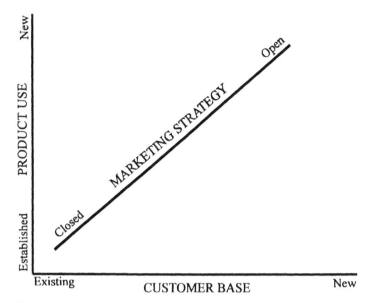

Fig. 3. Main dimensions of more closed and more open marketing strategies

By using more open technological and marketing strategies several companies included in our earlier studies, such as Pharmacia and Perstorp, have historically been able to change their product mix to include many more products with a high level of technological and market innovation. Essentially this has meant going from a more low-tech to a more high-tech development situation, for instance from basic chemicals for established uses to fine chemicals and chemical diagnosis in new applications. Similarly, many low-tech companies with problems today should be able to achieve successful innovative growth by employing more open development strategies.

Agroindustrial companies could, for instance, change in the direction of pharmaceutical companies, either by developing functional foods, that is food products with medical value (Nyström and Mark-Herbert, 1993) or by utilizing their processes and raw materials for developing substances also for medical use (Mark and Wahlgren, 1990, Nyström et al, 1992). As an example Pharmacia finds the basic source for its world unique eye operation substance, Healon, in rooster combs. This is supplied by a farmer / entrepreneur who has helped to breed a suitable stock of roosters with giant combs. This entrepreneur also used eggs to produce antibodies for medical use and has been actively involved in research to develop this technology in a venture company.

A basic assumption in our framework is that it is necessary to consider both the company and product level - and the interaction between the two - if we are to understand how companies may develop radically new products. Open technological and marketing strategies are more concerned with the overall ability of companies to develop and market new products, than with the specific products that may result. At the same time the existing product mix is the baseline companies use to develop their overall competence (Prahalad and Hamel, 1990) and technological potential for finding new products and markets. In the following discussion we therefore will be concerned both with the company level and the product level of analysis.

3. Empirical results

The specific study reported on in this paper deals with product development strategies in 13 Swedish biotechnical and food processing companies. The companies are Cerealia, Juvel and Abdon (grain processing), SSA (sugar processing), VL and SL (grain and farm supply), ABP, BioNova and Lipid Teknik (bioengineering companies), Filium and Binol (vegetable oils), SSP (starch processing) and Svalöf (plant breeding).

Based on personal interviews and company data, detailed information was collected in 1990 on the overall product development strategies of these companies and the new products developed and marketed by these companies in recent years. Our empirical data makes it possible for us to divide our 13 companies into our two categories, based on how closely their actual product development strategies correspond to our theoretical classification.

If we begin with our first example of a company pursuing Strategy A, Cerealia, its main development focus is on increasing the cost efficiency in the Swedish Milling and Bakery Industry, using existing technologies. Most of their R&D cooperation is within these industries, but there are a few examples of inter industry cooperation, for instance with Alfa Laval, Svenska Fläkt and SSP. In our terminology this means that they have a very closed technological strategy, based to a large extent on isolated technology use and internal orientation. Their marketing strategy is also highly closed, since almost all their new products are modifications of existing products directed towards established customers.

Juvel's main objective is also to concentrate on improving its basic assortment of milling and bakery products directed to food retailers. Their main technology is processing grain from the grower to the retailer, using established know-how and little outside R&D co-operation. As in the case of Cerealia their technological strategy therefore is very closed and mainly characterized by isolated technology use and internal orientation and their marketing strategy highly closed, emphasizing product modifications and existing customers.

Abdon, our third grain processing company also has a very closed technological strategy, emphasizing internal orientation, isolated technology use. Although their marketing strategy, as in the case of Cerealia and Juvel, is quite closed and mainly focused on product modifications and existing customers, it is based on more international contacts and a wider network.

SSA, the Swedish Sugarprocessing Company, mainly produces sweetening products for consumer and industrial uses. Historically it has had a relatively open and innovative product development strategy, but since the late 1980:s its technological and marketing strategies have radically changed. They have greatly reduced their research intensity, and moved away from basic research in sugar technology, towards more applied research. Their technological strategy is quite internal and isolated and their R&D co-operation is mainly with other companies in the Sugar Industry . At the same time they have significantly increased their marketing efforts for established products. This means that they now have relatively closed technological and marketing strategies.

VL, a regional grain and farm supply company in Western Sweden , focuses on the distribution and processing of grain for animal feed and human consumption. Its technological strategy is relatively closed, based mainly on and internal orientation and isolated technology use, but with some instances of more synergistic use, by combining fat- and fibertechnology. Its ambition is to achieve a more open technological strategy, by increasing its R&D contacts with universities and other companies. Its marketing strategy is also relatively closed - emphasizing existing products and markets - but here again the company wants to achieve a more open marketing strategy to match its technological aspirations.

SL, a regional grain and farm company in Southern Sweden, also has grain products for animal and human consumption as its main businesses. As in the case of VL, it has a relatively closed technological strategy and marketing strategy, but aspires towards more open strategies by stressing co-operation with other companies, new technological combinations, and new markets.

We thus have classified Cerealia, Juvel and Abdon as clear instances of companies using Product Development Strategy A, with SL and VL as more transitory cases, moving in the direction of Product Development Strategy B. We will now turn to the companies whose strategies are classified as examples of Strategy B in our framework.

BioNova is a small bioengineering firm, working mainly in the area of enzymatic processing of grain. Its business idea is to separate grain into various components, fibers, carbohydrates and proteins, and market them for different applications. It has a relatively open technological strategy, based on synergistic technology use and external orientation. R&D co-operation is mainly with universities and companies in food processing and pharmaceuticals. It also has a relatively open marketing strategy, searching for new markets for its products, for instance in bread mixes, vitamins and protein drinks for body building.

ABP is a small venture company, specializing in microbiology and biotechnology. It has a highly open technological strategy, based on external orientation and synergistic technology use. It has intensive R&D co-operation with universities and other companies and research workers coming from different disciplines. It has an open marketing strategy based on selling its ideas to a wide range of companies in different technology areas.

Lipid Teknik is a bioengineering company, producing and marketing special lipids to the pharmaceutical, food processing and cosmetic industry. Its technological strategy is highly open, stressing external orientation (for instance process development together with customers and joint university research) and synergistic technology use (for instance combining lipid technology with medical and food technology). It also has a highly open marketing strategy to find new customers and applications for special lipids.

Filium is also a company in the rape seed oil processing business, specializing in industrial lubricants. Their technological strategy is relatively open, combining biological and medical technologies in synergistic technology use and emphasizing external co-operation with consultants and other companies. Their marketing strategy is relatively open with regard to finding new customers, but less so with regard to developing radically new products .

Binol is a company developing and selling products based on the processing of rape seed oil. It has a relatively open technological strategy, emphasizing synergistic technology use (for instance combining lipid technology with microbiology) and external orientation (for instance customer co-operation). It also has an open marketing strategy, focusing on new products and market segments, such as vegetable based saw chain oil for the forest industry and hydraulic oil for the food processing industry.

SSP is a starch processing company, developing and marketing its products and applications to the paper, food processing and chemical industry. Its technological strategy is relatively open, stressing external R&D orientation by co-operating with customers and universities and synergistic technology use, by combining for instance fiber technology with starch technology. The marketing strategy is highly open, actively searching for new applications and customers in a wide range of industries.

Our final example of a company is Svalöf, a 50 % government owned plant breeding company. Its technological strategy is highly open, emphasizing external orientation by R&D co-operation with industry and universities in Sweden and abroad and to some extent synergistic technology use, by combining plant breeding with industrial process technology , e.g. starch processing. Its marketing strategy is relatively open in the sense that the company has been successful in finding new customers for its technology, for instance SSP, the starch processing company included in our sample.

4. Conclusions

In Figure 4 we have classsified the 13 companies with regard to how closed or open their technological and marketing strategies are, based on our interview data.

We thus see that BioNova, ABP, Lipid Teknik, Filium, Binol and SPP are all relatively clear instances of companies following Strategy B, that is moving from more low-tech to more high-tech product development, by increasing the level of technological and market innovation in their new products.

We see that the companies most closely following strategy A, Cerealia, Juvel, Abdon and SSA, all have very closed technological and marketing strategies, which is what we would expect from our theoretical framework and previous studies, if they are to be successful in pursuing this strategy. If, however, they want to move in the direction of Strategy B, our research indicates that they need to open up their technological and marketing strategies, to increase their technological and market potential beyond that which is possible with their more defensive Strategy A. VL and SL are evidently working in this direction, but it is still an open question if they will succeed in their ambitions.

154

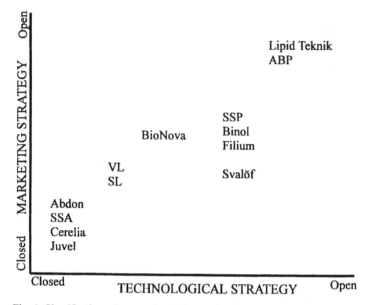

Fig. 4. Classification of companies with regard to how open or closed their
technological and marketing strategies are

The companies classified as being quiet successful in implementing strategy B - which means
that they have already developed and marketed new products with a high level of technological
and marketing innovation - all have relatively open technological and marketing strategies. This
is particularly the case with regard to the most pronounced venture companies, Lipid Teknik
and ABP, but also the other companies in this group have relatively open strategies.

The main conclusion, therefore, which is in line with our earlier studies, is that if companies
want to achieve a more high-tech development strategy, by technological and market upgrading of new products, they need to change towards more open technological and marketing
strategies. This in conjunction with other efforts, such as achieving a more flexible and chal-
lenging organization, to open up their and increase their technological and market potential.

Agroindustry - and other biologically based businesses - seem to have a high potential in this
respect, as is shown in emerging areas of technology, such as bioengineering, and new markets, for instance biologically based medical and environmental products. Our interviews indicate that a number of Swedish companies are well positioned to benefit from these possibili-

ties, and to do this they need to use open strategies to find new markets and technological opportunities.

References

Basberg, B.L., Patents and the Measurement of Technological Change: A Survey of the Literature, Research Policy, pp 131-141, 1987.

Crawford, C.M., 1991, New Product Management, Homewood, Irwin.

Green, K., Shaping Technologies and Shaping Markets: Creating Demand for Biotechnology, Technology Analysts & Strategic Management, pp. 57-76, No.1, 1991.

Gupca, A.K., Ray, S.P. & Wilemon, D.L., R&D and Marketing Dialogue in High -tech Firms, Industrial Marketing Management, pp. 289-300, 1985.

Kuczmanski, T.D., 1992, Managing New Products - The Power of Innovation, Englewood Cliffs, Prentice Hall.

Mark, C. & Wahlgren, K., 1990, Teknologiska strategi - en studie med exempel fran mejeriindustri, Report 32, Department of Economics and Management, Swedish University of Agricultural Sciences, Uppsala.

Ng, S.C.S., Pearson, A.W. & Ball, D.F., Stategies of Biotechnology Companies, Technology Analysts & Strategic Management, pp. 351-361, No.4, 1992.

Nyström, H. & Evardsson, B., Product Innovation in Food Processing - A Swedish Survey, R&D Management, pp. 67-72, 1982.

Nyström, H. & Mark-Herbert, C., 1993, Functional food i Sverige - svensk livsmedelsföretags syn pa produktutveckling och marknadsföring, Report 61, Department of Economics and Management, Swedish University of Agricultural Sciences, Uppsala.

Nyström, H., 1985, Product Development Strategies in Swedish Paper Companies, Report 246, Department of Economics and Management, Swedish University of Agricultural Sciences, Uppsala.

Nyström, H., Liljedahl, S., Mark-Herbert, C. & Wahlgren, K., 1992, Teknologiutveckling i 14 svenska bioteknik - och livsmedelsföretag - strategisk beskrivning och teoretisk modell, Report 51, Department of Economics and Management, Swedish University of Agricultural Sciences, Uppsala.

Nyström, H.,1979, Creativity and Innovation, Chichester, John Wiley & Sons.

Nyström, H.,1990, Technological and Market Innovation, Chichester, John Wiley & Sons

Porter, M.E., Competitive Advantage, London, Free Press.

Prahalad, C.K. & Hamel, G., The Core Competence of the Corporation, Harvard Business Review, pp. 79-91, May-June, 1990.

Urban, G.L. & Hauser, J.R., 1980, Design and Marketing of New Products, Englewood Cliffs, Prentice Hall.

Wind, Y.J., 1982, Product Policy, Reading, Addison-Wesley.

Recent Essentials in Innovation Management and Research, edited by H. Hübner / T. Dunkel
Gabler, Wiesbaden/Germany, 1995

Corporate Strategic Planning

Wolfgang Czerny

Austrian Research Centre Seibersdorf

Abstract:
Corporate strategic planning may serve enterprises as an answer to the challenge made by an increasingly complex business environment. The general aspects of strategy development, such as strategic competence and strategic orientation, are the prerequisites for a strategic approach. Strategy is based on individual viewpoints that are closely connected to the acting/leading person. The main phases of creation and restriction that dominate the process of strategy-development and -specification have to be considered. The inclusion of holistic aspects risis the question of the relevant strategic space that has to be scanned. Under a comprehensive survey aspects of social and ecological compatibility become more pronounced vis-à-vis the otherwise dominating economic and technological approaches.

1. Strategic planning - development and general view

An enterprise and its environment are a system of continuously growing complexity. Enterprises, as well as organizations, groups and individual persons must prove their viability against this background of highly intricate, interlinking patterns in the global network. This complicated networks and interactions call for a holistic approach to strategic planning. A systems-oriented view has become an important task, not only for corporate management, but also on a higher plane, concerning man and society. Human beings as well as enterprises have to face constant changes in their environment. They are increasingly confronted with the variegated structures of a many-faceted, multi-cultural world. On one hand this entails a loss in orientation and dissolution of overall goals on the other hand it increases in the opportunities for a more liberal and creative way of living, working and realizing personal ambitions.

Enterprises have to find adequate answers to the questions arising from the change in economic policies, the internationalization of markets, harder competition, technological challenges, the necessity of innovations, etc., and they have to do this quickly.

158

The call for strategic considerations, forming the basis for decisions and measures of management and control, became loud in the 1960s when it became obvious that planning methods, especially in the operative/quantitative field, can no longer cope with the radical changes transforming technology and market. The concept of strategic planning became influential in devising and implementing strategies that would enhance the competitiveness of each business unit. Since then much effort was put into further development of methods of strategic planning in order to cover the different needs of a company in its complex environment.

If we look at the development of management systems (Figure 1) we can see the request towards new methods and tools in order to handle the rising dynamics and complexity of the systems involved.

future events	1900 1930 1950 1970 1990		
	known - extrapolated events known - new discontinuities		
periodic events	• manual systems and techniques *Management by control*		
	• financial control		
foreseeable by extrapolation	• production budgeting		
	• financial budgeting *Management by*		
	• management by objectives *extrapolation*		
	• long range planning		
foreseeable risks and chances	*Management by anticipation of change* • periodic strategic planning		
	• strategic orientation of the management		
partly unpredictable "weak signals " unpredictable	*Management by flexible / quick reactions* • management of strategic influence		
	• management based on weak signals		
	• management by strategic surprise		
system dynamics	constant linear periodic chaotic		
dynamics of reaction	reactive anticipatory exploratory creative		

Fig. 1: Development of management systems (adapted from Hammer 86)

The question arises:

Is strategic management able to meet the challenge of integration in a system of constantly rising complexity?

In a recently published article "The Fall and Rise of Strategic Planning" Mintzberg points out the limits strategic planning is facing.
Strategic planning has been quite successful and is still a mayor instrument in management and consultancy. Nevertheless managers themselves increasingly opposed against the overall use of strategic planning since "strategic planning is predominantly strategic programming".

Mintzberg: "The main difficulty turns out to be - strategic planning isn't strategic thinking. One is analysis and the other is synthesis".

In using strategic planning managers give up their very essential competence namely synthesis in favour of the analytical aspect. For an effective management, based on and structured by a detailed analytical approach, integration becomes the big challenge.

2. Characterizing the strategic approach

What are the different aspects in strategic management that have to be looked at from a holistic point of view?

First we have to ask: What is a strategy all about? Following v. Moltke[1], strategy is to be characterized as "the art of acting under the pressure of most difficult conditions", as well as "the continuation of the original, leading idea according to the changing circumstances".

The company / the management has to make decisions concerning its future business activities though often little relevant information is accessible.

The **strategic challenge** is to be successful by means of a sequence of decisions and actions. This orientation towards success, which on a very basic level means fighting on order to survive, makes it necessary to define goals. Being successful has to be acknowledged by rewards the measure for the gained success. Since strategies are developed by people, the success of a company closely relates to the success of the acting person, e.g. the manager. Dedication and conviction as well as adequate rewards are necessary in order to match the persons and companies interests.

Strategy may be seen as an instrument, a method, that helps to overcome uncertainty (in acting) through reduction of vagueness by means of calculated risk (this definition stresses the analytical aspect). Developing strategies needs constant learning in order to adapt to changing circumstances, to adopt new methods and to develop new tools.

Considering the various aspects, **strategic competence** (see Figure 2) is characterized by strategic functions concerning the four domains:

strategic thinking, - planning, - learning and - acting.

---

[1] Strategy is "die Fortbildung des ursprünglichen, leitenden Gedankens entsprechend den sich stets ändernden Verhältnissen", as well as "die Kunst des Handelns unter dem Druck der schwierigsten Bedingungen". (Moltke)

160

- The central issue in <u>strategic thinking</u> is to develop a strategy against the background of a vision, of a "leitmotif". Therefore goals have to be defined and criteria for success have to be fixed.

- <u>Strategic planning</u> follows a systematic way in order to achieve success. Emphasis is put on the analysis of external conditions and influences and on internal resources to fix the individual position out of which the problem situation and relevant potentials can be defined.

- The concern of <u>strategic learning</u> is to adapt the basic strategic idea to the rapidly changing conditions and relations by means of scenarios and experiments.

- <u>Action plans</u> as well as suitable measures have to be evaluated on basis of experience and accumulated knowledge.

Identification and commitment are the limitation factors of strategic competence as a whole and of each single strategic function.

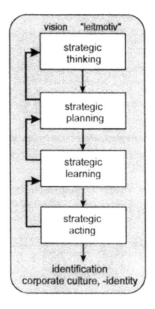

Fig. 2: Strategic competence

The following table (Figure 3) characterizes the strategic versus a non strategic approach.

strategic functions	issues	non-strategic	strategic
- thinking	motives. commitment	passive oriented - responding external and internal needs	active oriented - visions are the basis for fixing goals
- planning	time-frame. information	short range - goals are extrapolated sequentially	long range - goals based on comprehensive analysis
- learning	development	external influence on development is dominant	development is strongly influenced by internal factors
- acting	competition. measures	negative - competition endangers the own position	positive - competition gives a chance to be better

Figure 3: Strategic versus non-strategic approach (adapted from Harasser)

The **strategic approach**, based on the four strategic functions, consists of a creative phase to open up the strategic space through the possible dimensions of activity, as well as a restrictive phase to define the relevant strategic field of action by means of stressing the individual viewpoints (Figure 4).

The creative phase starts with an idea, a vision, expressing the basic goals and success criteria (e.g. the business idea). This idea has to be looked at from various strategic aspects in order to point out possible ways of realization. The aspects correspond to the dimensions that open up the relevant strategic space. In the restriction phase the different aspects are integrated and stressed according to individual- respectively corporate issues in order to achieve synthesis.

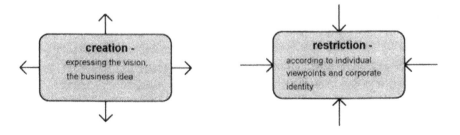

Figure 4: The phases of creation and restriction in strategic approach

162

The phases of creation and restriction express the dynamics in each of the strategic functions and are the basis for the continuous process of strategic orientation.

Strategic orientation connects closely the strategic functions in a continuous process. This may be expressed by means of a control mechanism which is hierarchical organized and inter-linked (Figure 5).

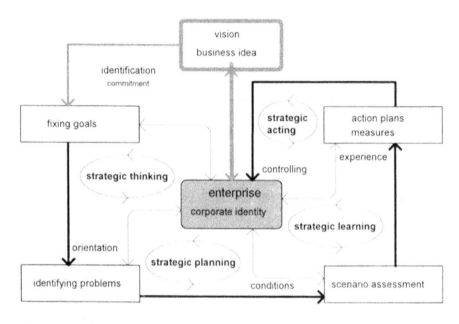

Fig. 5: Strategic orientation

The control mechanism consists of at least four feedback loops to cover:
- thinking - fixing goals on basis of identification (e.g. business idea),
- planning - identifying problems under given orientation,
- learning - evaluating possible scenarios to adept to changing circumstances,
- acting - relying on experience in order to make action plans.

Developing strategies is not an unequivocal process. The procedure of finding the proper strategy, apart from internal and external fringe conditions, will influence the result. There are always chances and risks which - as essential elements of a strategy - open up diverse ways to obtain the desired goals.

3. Corporate planning model

The corporate planning model for strategic management (developed by Czerny[2]) emphasizes a broader understanding in companies decision making. It is based on a holistic approach and addresses the central issues, the main features of strategy and strategic approach. The model is to be used as a framework pointing out the multidimensional strategic space, thus enabling an integrative viewpoint and establishing links towards broadly used methods in strategic planning. It takes into account different aspects as guidelines in decision making and connects the four domains of strategic competence.

The model comprises five central sections/stages (see Figure 6) which respond to the different objectives of strategic management such as strategy finding, strategic planning, experimenting, guiding ...

* Strategic system determination - defining strategic units for the enterprise.
  Strategic planning is based on the strategic units such as strategic business units. The holistic approach distinguishes four strategic dimensions (economy/technology/environment/society) when determining strategically relevant units for the enterprise. The selection of relevant units is closely connected to the selction of a strategy.

* Strategic systems analysis - definition of strategic potentials in view of fringe conditions.
  The strategic units are described by a profile of strengths/weaknesses. The profile is based on the characteristics of the enterprise and its environment (e.g. type of production or organization, equipment, logistics, qualification, structures of supply, market structures, competitors, etc.). Further, relevant potentials are determined and the strategic units are positioned in a portfolio-matrix.

* Strategic systems modeling - setting up experiments and scenarios in the light of relevant trends.
  Trends and developments have to be evaluated for an integrative systems description. This may take place, for example, in monitoring the strategically relevant environment. In addition, effects must be assessed concerning the involvement in / the interrelations of the total system. Finally, forecasts have to be made on the basis of scenarios.

---

[2] Czerny W. Ein integratives Modell zur strategischen Unternehmensplanung. 1994

* Strategic guiding - definition of strategic activities on the basis of goals and problems. Strategic management is primarily concerned with formulating strategic corporate policies. A concept must be developed, establishing priorities and plans of action, considering actors and the relevant units. A hierarchy of problems and goals must be defined, for decision-making, scenarios must be evaluated, strategy paths must be described and the necessary resources must be assessed (mobilized) before measures can be taken.

* Strategic systems integration - selection of fields to be included in the relevant context. This final stage transgresses the individual horizon of a given situation in strategic planning. It involves areas in which individuals or enterprises take part without having possibilities of direct access or control.

In order to serve as a management instrument, the corporate strategic planning model must be established as an in-house system based on the principles and methods of strategic competence.

4. Strategic system determination

In order to develop a strategy, strategic units have to be defined. A strategic unit is a competence domain by which the enterprise successfully acts in the market opposing its competitors. Strategic units are the planning units (e.g. strategic business units) on which the company builds competitive advantage.

In order to fix relevant strategic units the focus has to be put on the individual competencies of the company as well as on the individual strategic viewpoint / orientation.
- Which are the competence domains of the company?
- Which aspects are emphasized in strategic orientation?
Products[3] and corresponding activities determine the specific competencies which have been accumulated in the company.

---

[3] Products are manifestations of the companies business idea, they concern manifacturing goods, services, information, knowledge, etc.

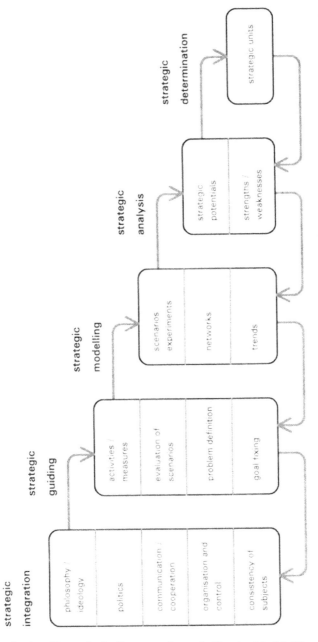

Figure 6: Sections/Stages in the Corporate Strategic Planning Model (Czerny 94)

166

The major activities in a company concern (Figure 7):

    procurement - production - development - sales, marketing

(From a systems point of view these are: input; transformation; maintenance, development; output.)

If an enterprise is analyzed comprehensively, aspects of social and ecological compatibility will become more pronounced vis-à-vis the otherwise dominating economic and technological aspects. Managers developing a strategy have to take these different aspects into account, they serve as guidelines for orientation. A strategy integrates all four aspects, but, out of the companies individual viewpoints and decisions, they will differ in intensity and sequence and thus lead to different strategies.

The individual strategic orientation of a company is formed by selectively putting emphasis on different strategic aspects. The strategic orientation of the company influences the development of competence domains.

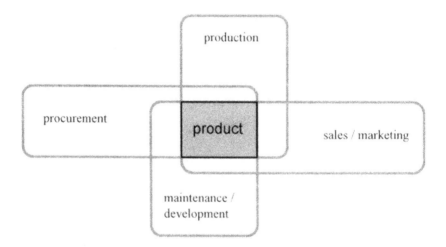

Fig. 7: Strategic space - the four dimensions concerning the major activities in the company

The general aspects for strategic orientation (the following table -Figure 8- gives an overview) can not be distinguished clearly, they supplement each other.

economic aspect	technological aspect
business oriented - sales, turnover, profits *competitive products*	oriented towards product(ion) development, technical solutions *high-tech products*
socio-cultural aspect	**ecological aspect**
oriented towards organization, networks, communication systems *availability of products*	quality oriented benefit for system / customers *individual adapted products*

Figure 8: Strategic aspects

Strategic units are characterized according to the different strategic aspects (Figure 9).

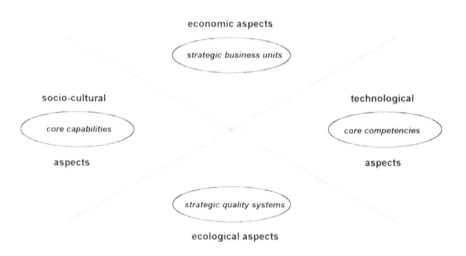

Figure 9: Strategic aspects and corresponding strategic units

economic aspects   - *strategic business units*
technological aspects - *core competencies*
ecological aspects   - *strategic quality systems*
socio-cultural aspects - *core capabilities*

Strategic concepts based on different strategic units have been developed to explain the success of companies (the concept of core competencies[4], competing on capabilities[5], TQM ...).

Strategic business units / product-market combinations

Emphasizing the economic aspect strategic business units are the relevant objects in strategic management. Strategic business units can be described by product-market combinations (differing through products and markets). They correspond to the selling activities of the company, concerning services, products, trade, financing.

Strategic business units are often organized as profit centres (they are success oriented).

Core Competencies

The technological aspect in strategic orientation emphasizes core competencies as strategic units. Core competencies concern the knowledge base of the company, - "streams of knowledge on which to build competitive advantage"[6]. The major points of interest concern the technology incorporated in the product and the production process, R&D and technical logistics and - organization (construction). In order to build core competencies, the technical competencies present in the company have to be concentrated, amplified and stressed. The question to be put is:

Which competencies are the basis for (past, future) success?

Starting from core competencies, core products are developed. They are the basis for the business (business units) with a wide spectrum of emerging products.

Strategic Quality Systems

An ecological point of view puts system compatibility into focus[7]. The systems concerned are hierarchical organized[8]. For the company the relevant systems outside are predominantly customers, next to them their environment has to be taken into consideration, concerning

---

[4] Prahalad C. K., Hamel G. The Core Competence and the Corporation 1990
[5] Stalk G., P. Evans, L.E. Shulman Competing on Capabilities 1992
[6] N. Checker (CHEM Systems, London) Seminar: Einheit in der Vielheit - Das Konzept der Kernkompetenzen Wien, Mai 1992
[7] Czerny W. Qualität - ein Schwerpunkt im Rahmen einer integrativen strategischen Planung 1994
[8] Seghezzi H.D. Europe as Part of the Triad 1993

individual-, group-, local-, regional-, and global aspects. The corresponding systems inside the company are the relevant strategic units. (this are the employees / the customers inside the company as well as functionally organized working groups, but also production units have to be seen as a system). The main areas concerned by strategic quality systems are

- quality in production
- quality in service
- quality in design
- quality assurance.

The main aim in using strategic quality systems as a basis for strategic orientation is to optimize towards internal and external compatibility.

Core Capabilities

The socio-cultural aspect emphasizes the capabilities of a company concerning organization and communication. Political aspects become important. Politics on a global / national level sets the relevant frame for the company, politics inside the company fix competencies, influence communication and corporation as well as corporate culture. Competing on capabilities puts emphasis on

- business processes
- business politics
- business contacts
- networks and marketing.

Strategies are directed towards improvement of organization and communication structures in order to serve the customers.

From the holistic point of view the different aspects in strategic orientation which stress different success factors leading to different corresponding strategic units have to be explored in order to develop strategies.

References

Czerny W.: Ein integratives Modell zur strategischen Unternehmensplanung, ÖFZS-A-2834 1994

Czerny W.: Qualität - ein Schwerpunkt im Rahmen einer integrativen strategischen Planung, ÖFZS-A-2916 1994

Hammer R.: Strategische Planung und Frühaufklärung, Habil. Innsbruck 1986

Harasser C., O. Thuile: Was ist Strategie, Moderne Methoden der Unternehmensführung, Bd. 1, Südtiroler Sparkasse, o.J.

Mintzberg H.: The Fall and Rise of Strategic Planning in: Harvard Business Review 1 / 1994

v. Moltke H.: Ausgewählte Werke Hrsg. F. v. Schmerfeld. Berlin 1925

Prahalad C. K., Hamel G.: The Core Competence and the Corporation, in Harvard Business Review 3 / 1990

Stalk G., P. Evans, L.E. Shulman: Competing on Capabilities, in Harvard Business Review 2 / 1992

Seghezzi H.D.: Europe as Part of the Triad, in EOQ `93 World Quality Congress Proceedings Vol. 1 Helsinki 1993

Recent Essentials in Innovation Management and Research, edited by H. Hübner / T. Dunkel
Gabler, Wiesbaden/Germany, 1995

Future R&D Management: Challenges, their Impacts and Selected Tools

Dorothea von Wichert-Nick

Fraunhofer-Institute for Systems and Innovation Research (ISI)

Karlsruhe, Germany

Abstract:

The examination of future challenges that arise from the areas of economic changes, technological trends, internationalisation, the growing importance of human resources and the need for environmental protection as well as sustainable development prepares the ground for new approaches towards the management of R&D within companies. A generalized model of R&D management in the past and in the future gives rough guidelines for the design of new and advanced management techniques. As an example technological forecasting is discussed as a management technique that is growing in importance. Traditionally, forecasting was used only as a means to collect information. By taking the need for organisational learning into account, finally a new forecasting paradigm is developed.

During the last years R&D management has turned out to be crucial for the competitive position both of single companies as well as for whole countries. New concepts for an advanced R&D management are needed in order to meet future challenges. As everybody knows, there will be no simple solution for all cases, but a variety of tools that have to be chosen according to the specific, situational needs.

This contribution is based upon a recent conceptual study of "Best Management Practices and Tools for R&D Activities" that was carried out for the Commission of the European Union, DG XIII by Guido Reger, Kerstin Cuhls and Dorothea von Wichert-Nick (1994). The aim of this study was to identify different types of R&D management as well as tools that are used by firms to support acquisition of scientific and technical knowledge. The linkages between future challenges and management practices were also to be investigated.

1. Future Challenges and their Impacts

The complexity of recent trends and their future developments makes it impossible to identify and explain the whole range of challenges R&D management has to face. Only a few tendencies which will definitely have a major impact on R&D management now and in the future are described briefly. These challenges can - pessimistically - be seen as problems which have to be solved, but also as a positive chance to find new ways and create new management tools to cope with a changing environment through research and development (cf. Reger/Cuhls/von Wichert-Nick 1994). The main challenges and their impacts can be summed up in five groups:

1.1 **Economic challenges:** global markets are dominated by demand rather than by supply. **Changes in consumer demands,** high quality standards and the growing competition on the international markets force companies to provide a broadened range of products (diversification) or one product in a larger variety. Therefore, **flexible specialisation,** fast reactions to consumer demands and rapid changes in the production and assembly facilities as well as in R&D are necessary, whereas the **life cycles** of products and whole industries are increasingly shortening (cf. for instance OECD 1991; Bullinger 1992; Ernste/Meier 1992). These economic trends lead to a growing importance of **time** as a factor in R&D management, to higher R&D expenditures and the need for efficient and effective R&D activities.

1.2 **Technological challenges:** a growing **complexity** of technologies in products is the consequence of changes in consumer demands and taste. The development of technology no longer corresponds to traditional classification schemes isolating one single technology, but in the context of an early and intensive networking bet-ween different areas of science and disciplines (cf. Grupp 1993; BMFT 1993). This **overlapping of technologies** is a challenge that has to be faced by **inter- and/or multidisciplinary approaches** of R&D activities combining the knowledge of different scientific and technical disciplines. Since some technologies are more science-based than others, there is a shift to more **science-based technologies**. Therefore, more research in pure science inside the companies or external knowledge from the scientific community is necessary.

1.3 **Internationalisation:** trade frictions are one of the limiting factors in the **global trade** of goods and force companies to decentralise their production and marketing and to invest abroad. The increasing convergence of consumer tastes not influenced by culture, the capability to provide goods in larger varieties, as well as new transportation and communication possibilities, has made the exploration of international markets possible. This leads to a

growing competition of internationally operating companies. **Global sourcing** (cf. Soete 1993), that means, combining production factors from all over the world, is a crucial driving force in the internationalisation of production and R&D. The internationalisation of **science and technology** leads to investments in decentralized R&D facilities abroad (techno-globalism) to make full use of the best available knowledge in specific technological fields, but evokes concern about free access to scientific institutions and the know-how about certain product components which are dependent on specialist knowledge.

1.4 **Human Resources: a higher threshold of competence** is required in general to create new technology. **Higher qualification and new skills** are necessary which are not only based on the specialized technical knowledge provided by the natural sciences, but also on social abilities, skills to communicate across functions and disciplines, problem-solving orientation and the ability to adapt to teamwork (cf. OECD 1991). As the amount and quality of information and knowledge increases rapidly, **continuous learning** and **re-training** of skills are necessary. As a result of a **change in the social values** of societies, new methods are needed to **motivate** personnel and improve **creativity**, innovation and its application in products.

1.5 **Environmental protection and sustainable development:** both goals are one of the major tasks of the future (cf. Brundland Report 1987; Meadows et al. 1992). Enterprises will have to orientate their R&D, their products and production processes towards economic as well as ecological needs. In order to fulfil these requirements R&D management needs a multidisciplinary and systemic view, has to link environmental goals with R&D aims and strategy. All in all, a post-modern organisation has to be created.

2. Generalized Model of R&D Management

Before considering special tools, the question can be posed if there is a "best practice" or ideal model for R&D management. Such a model will not have to fit all enterprises, as their situations are rather diverse, but it can serve as a rough guideline. Several of these models have been developed, e.g. the "Third Generation R&D", the "Three Paradigms Scenario" and finally, the "Fifth Generation Innovation Process". All of them not only describe general trends of management practices for the future, but also take the past into account by formulating preceding stages of R&D management.

The **Fifth Generation Innovation Process** was presented by Rothwell (1991, 1993). He describes five generations of perceptions of the innovation process which were derived by the evaluation of empirical studies and theoretical literature. These generations recapitulate the development R&D management has taken from the 1950s until today (see Figure 1).

The **first generation** was characterized by simple linear sequential technology-push assumptions. It was followed by the need-pull dominated **(second) generation**. Coupling of these two basic paradigms has taken place in the **third generation**, in which the thoughts are focused on the interaction between marketing and R&D. The **fourth generation** began in the mid 1980s and can be marked as "integrated model". In this stage, which is still dominant today, sequential-process- was replaced by parallel-process thinking. The emphasis of R&D management was placed on working simultaneously across business functions and on integrating the R&D/manufacturing interface technologically by CAD/CAM and organisationally by integrated development teams (so-called "rugby teams"). The "integrated model" cannot only be characterized by interfunctional integration within the enterprise, but also by growing integration with other companies.

The **"systems integration and networking model"** (**"fifth generation"**) is regarded by Rothwell as a somewhat idealized development from the fourth generation model that is going to match the upcoming challenges. For most companies this model is still in its evolutionary phase and describes the (near) future of the management of innovation and R&D. In this model, innovation is seen as a multi-institutional networking process. It encompasses strong linkages with leading edge customers, strategic integration of primary suppliers, and strong horizontal linkages. The most significant feature of this model is the electronification of innovation. R&D management will mainly aim at higher flexibility and increases in the development speed. Another focus will be on quality and other non-price factors, such as environmental sustainability. Besides that, there are further challenges for R&D management: since the complexity of the innovation process and the number of actors are increasing, the ability for cooperating and networking is of growing significance for managing R&D. This also includes "... the requirement for innovation/technology strategy to be at the leading edge of corporate strategy is greater than ever before" (cf. Rothwell 1991, 22). Not included in this model, but nonetheless of growing importance, is the company's ability to develop own long-term visions instead of following existing technological or economic trends.

Figure 1 The Fifth Generation Innovation Process

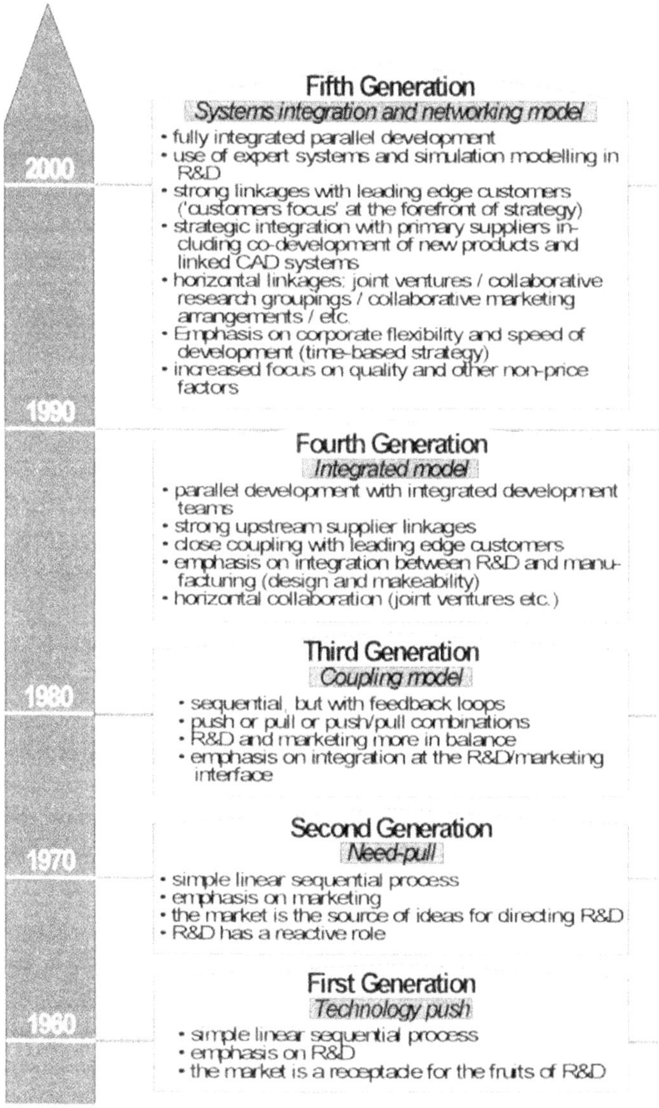

Fifth Generation
Systems integration and networking model
- fully integrated parallel development
- use of expert systems and simulation modelling in R&D
- strong linkages with leading edge customers ('customers focus' at the forefront of strategy)
- strategic integration with primary suppliers including co-development of new products and linked CAD systems
- horizontal linkages: joint ventures / collaborative research groupings / collaborative marketing arrangements / etc.
- Emphasis on corporate flexibility and speed of development (time-based strategy)
- increased focus on quality and other non-price factors

Fourth Generation
Integrated model
- parallel development with integrated development teams
- strong upstream supplier linkages
- close coupling with leading edge customers
- emphasis on integration between R&D and manufacturing (design and makeability)
- horizontal collaboration (joint ventures etc.)

Third Generation
Coupling model
- sequential, but with feedback loops
- push or pull or push/pull combinations
- R&D and marketing more in balance
- emphasis on integration at the R&D/marketing interface

Second Generation
Need-pull
- simple linear sequential process
- emphasis on marketing
- the market is the source of ideas for directing R&D
- R&D has a reactive role

First Generation
Technology push
- simple linear sequential process
- emphasis on R&D
- the market is a receptacle for the fruits of R&D

2000 · 1990 · 1980 · 1970 · 1960

Source: Rothwell 1993, 39; Reger, Cuhls, von Wichert-Nick 1994, 12.

3.   Selected Tools for R&D Management

In the study on which this contribution is based six groups of tools were discussed (cf. Reger/Cuhls/von Wichert-Nick 1994). Corporate culture and its significance for R&D, the structure of the organisation, the development, leveraging and renewal of core competencies, as well as instruments for technological forecasting were introduced as modes for managing internal R&D activities. The acquisition of external scientific and technical know-how was described by means of cooperation, e.g. co-development, strategic alliances, and networking. The management of scientific, technical and functional interfaces within companies and between them was the last topic of concern. In the following only technological forecasting shall be examined more closely.

4.   Technological Forecasting in the Enterprise

Today the techniques of technology forecasting are focused on the task of improving the company's information base. They encompass exploration and prognosis methods that can be used in the analyses of parameters affecting the development of specific technologies. These parameters can be derived out of technical, economic, and social contexts (Gerybadze 1991).

In the past years the **interest in forecasting techniques has been steadily rising**. Four possible reasons can be named for this tendency (cf. Murdick/Georgoff 1993, pp. 2):

- New conceptual advances in areas such as economics, theoretical and applied statistics.
- New capabilities in data accumulation, access, and processing.
- The attempt to get a better understanding of the underlying structures of events or states.
- Emerging problems such as accelerated environmental dynamics and the growing importance of extended planning horizons.

As technology strategies gain in importance for the companies' well-being, economic and technical issues get more intertwined. A company using adequate forecasting techniques is able to discover new technology at an early stage of the life cycle. Information on upcoming technologies enables the company both to **gain time for the development of new strategies** as well as **provide a timely start into the development of this technology.**

If used alone, forecasting techniques only deliver informational raw material. The forecast and its results only will have an impact if embedded in analysis, interpretation, communication and resulting actions (see Figure 2).

Figure 2. Process of Forecasting in the Enterprise

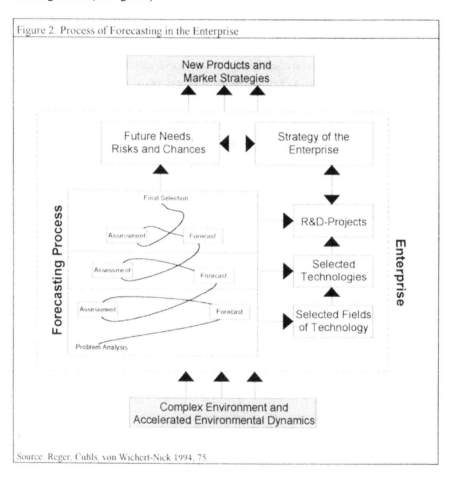

Source: Reger, Cuhls, von Wichert-Nick 1994, 75

Meanwhile, although analysis and interpretation usually are achieved rather effortlessly, communication of the results is a sore point in many companies (cf. Gerybadze 1991). **Organisational integration of forecasting** in the R&D activities of the enterprise starts with the right monitoring system. Every member within a company should monitor his environment with respect to discontinuities or changing trends. Quality circles and service members can be "tools" in the collection of data. Interpretation of outcomes should be done by those levels of the company that need the results most, otherwise the results often will not reach their user. A bottom-up process could be initiated that integrates the forecasts from all different levels of the company. Furthermore it has to be ensured that outcomes result in action as indicated by the forecast.

Another topic of importance is the **integration of technology forecasting and technology assessment**. Over the last decades society's sensitivity concerning the impact of technology has increased greatly. Technology can have an impact on a broad variety of areas: social life, ecological and environmental impacts are just the most obvious (cf. Porter et al. 1991). In order to take responsibility for the impact of new technologies in an early stage of their development as well as following upcoming regulations, new models of forecasting cycles have to be developed which iterate both forecasting and technology assessment.

5.   Development of a New Forecasting Paradigm

The use of technological forecasting techniques as described up to this point follows the traditional result-focused paradigm: forecasts are seen as tools that uncover latent knowledge and transform it to explicit information which will be used in decision-making. A **new paradigm** can be developed if **organisational learning, its improvement and support** are regarded (for the learning organizsation see: Garvin 1993, Levitt/March 1988). From this position the process of forecasting can be utilized in order to diffuse the latent knowledge of a few experts which is extracted by the classical use of forecasting methods to a broader public, a process in which the total organisational knowledge is enlarged (see Figure 3).

With this conception the mere information and result orientation of forecasting techniques is enlarged by its **use as communication or learning device**. Following this new paradigm, the process of forecasting should be performed within interdisciplinary teams that do not only consist of specialists for the the subject of interest, but also of people who are experts for other technological fields or even for other disciplines, as for example social sciences. By means of group interaction the participants will indirectly "teach" each other. If general understanding differs within the group, **creative recombinations of existing, latent knowledge and new, explicit information** develop which enhance the individual creativity and inno vativeness (cf. Kogout/Zander 1992). As organisational learning needs a high degree of freedom the only general guidelines for the process should be company visions and lead capabilities.

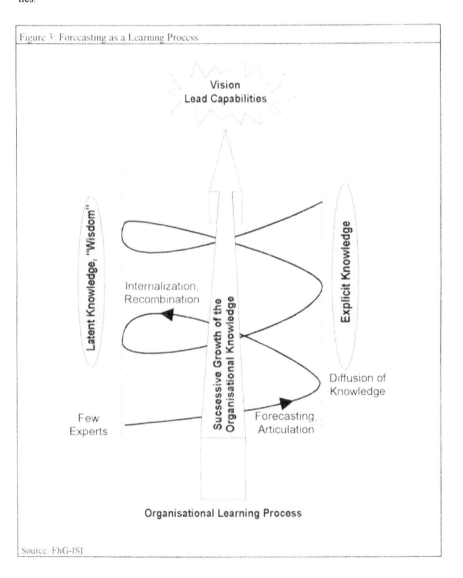

Figure 3: Forecasting as a Learning Process

Source: FhG-ISI

If the process of forecasting is changed as described the **process of assessment has to be changed accordingly.** The integration of organisational members from different disciplines will enlarge the variety of criteria that are used for the choice. Especially the integration of social and environmental aspects can be obtained by this approach.

With its ability to support organisational learning, the possibility to integrate various stakeholders as well as alternative issues (e.g. environmental and social), and its foundation on company visions, this new forecasting paradigm will be a helpful tool in order to meet the future challenges. It also fits well into the "systems integration and networking model" as described by the Fifth Generation Innovation Process.

References

BMFT - Bundesministerium für Forschung und Technologie (Ed.) (1993):
  Deutscher Delphi-Bericht zur Entwicklung von Wissenschaft und Technik, Bonn.
Brundland Report (1987):
  Weltkommission für Umwelt und Entwicklung: Unsere gemeinsame Zukunft. German Edition by Hauff, V. (Ed.), Greven.
Bullinger, H.-J. (1992):
  Neue Produktionsparadigmen als betriebliche Herausforderung. In: IAO-Forum, Bullinger, H.-J. (Ed.): Innovative Unternehmensstrukturen, Berlin, Heidelberg.
Ernste, M./Meier, V. (Eds.) (1992):
  Regional Development and Contemporary Industrial Response, London, New York.
Garvin, D.A. (1993):
  Building a Learning Organization. In: Harvard Business Review, July-August 1993, pp. 78-91.
Gerybadze, A. (1991):
  Technological Forecasting. In: Technologie-Management: Ein Erfolgsfaktor von zunehmender Bedeutung, Zürich, pp. 71-100.
Grupp, H. (Ed.) (1993):
  Technologie am Beginn des 21. Jahrhunderts, Schriftenreihe des Fraunhofer-Instituts für Systemtechnik und Innovationsforschung, Vol. 3, 1993.
Kogout, B./Zander, U. (1992):
  Knowledge of the Firm, Combinative Capabilities, and the Replication of Technology. In: Organizational Science, Vol. 3 (1992) 8, pp. 383-397.
Levitt, B./March, J.G. (1988):
  Organizational Learning. In: Annual Review of Sociology, Vol. 14, 1988, pp. 319-340-
Meadows, D.H./ Meadows, D.L./Randers, J. (1992):
  Beyond the Limits of Growth, London.

Murdick, R.G./Georgoff, D.M. (1993):
Forecasting: A Systems Approach. In: Technological Forecasting and Social Change, Vol. 44, pp. 1-16.

OECD (Ed.) (1991):
Technology in a Changing World, Paris.

Porter, A.L./Roper, A.T./Mason, T.W./Rossini, F.A./Banks, J. (1991):
Forecasting and Management of Technology, New York.

Reger, G./Cuhls, K./von Wichert-Nick, D. (1994):
Best Management Practices and Tools for R&D Activities. Study on behalf of the Commission of the European Union. Brussels/Luxembourg/Karlsruhe.

Rothwell, R. (1991):
Successful Industrial Innovation: Critical Factors for the 1990s. Extended version of a paper presented to the Science Policy Research Unit's 25th Anniversary Conference, Brighton, University of Sussex, 3-4 July 1991-

Rothwell, R. (1993):
The Fifth Generation Innovation Process. In. Oppenländer, K.-H./Popp, W. (Eds.) (1993): Privates und staatliches Innovationsmanagment, München.

Soete, L. (1993):
Die Herausforderung des "Techno-Globalismus": Auf dem Weg zu neuen Spielregeln. in: Meyer-Krahmer, F. (Ed.): Innovationsökonomie und Technologiepolitik, Forschungs- ansätze und politische Konsequenzen, Heidelberg.

Recent Essentials in Innovation Management and Research, edited by H. Hübner / T. Dunkel
Gabler, Wiesbaden /Germany, 1995

An Expert System for Strategic Technology Management

Brigitte Reminger

Siemens AG, Munich

Abstract:

Selecting the most promising technologies or research projects is an important step in innovation management. Portfolio technique is a mean to select the right projects. A critical issue in applying the portfolio technique is defining the appropriate criteria for the portfolio axis named potential and position compared to the competitor. These criteria have to be appropriate to e.g. the structures of the branche or the strategy of the company. It is very useful to show the weakness and strengh of the projects to be selected in a profile. To be able to draw an objective profile the projects have to be analyzed very thoroughly. The expert system supports this analysis and takes the certainty of the results into account. There are advantages in using the system, e.g. objectivity of the results, shortening the time of analysis or the flexibility of data update. But the use of a computer-based system also causes some problems.

1. Technology Management as Part of Innovation Management

A considerable share of innovations is based on the results of the research and development process, as Figure 1 shows. The selection of the most promising technologies and projects for scientific research has a significant influence on the creation of inventions. Technology evaluation is a precondition to select the right projects. It is also an instrument of innovation management if it takes the possibilities of technological and economical realization and diffusion of the inovation into account.

2. Different Approaches to Technology Evaluation

In general there are three ways to do technology evaluation.

2.1. The Fully Centralized Approach

This procedure provides for a team consisting of five to fifteen experts conversant with the technologies used in the company. The team evaluates the technologies and does strategy formulation. Each member has an own view of the problem and its interpretation. This raises the problem that task distribution can cause different evaluation criteria to be used.

The results will most probably not be accepted by the researchers and developers. While affected by the decision, they have no influence in finding the results. Moreover there has to be additional well-trained staff in the planning department.

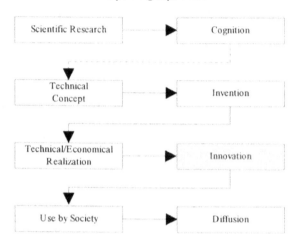

Fig. 1. Stages of technological Innovations[1]

2.2. The Fully Decentralized Approach

Another way is that every researcher is responsible for the strategic planning of his particular technology. The most important advantage of this method is the very high technological competence of the researchers who do the evaluation and planning. But there is no coordination with the strategic planning on a corporate level[2]. This evaluation is not objective.

2.3. The Combined Approach

A very practical approach is to do technology evaluation centrally coordinated by only a few employees. They collect basic information concerning the technologies in very well-structured interviews with the researchers who gain their knowledge by doing research and interacting

1 s. Ropohl, G.: Eine Systemtheorie der Technik. Zur Grundlegung der allgemeinen Technologie, München .etc. 1979, p. 273

2 [2]Brockhoff, K.: Schnittstellenmanagement: Abstimmungsprobleme zwischen Marketing und Forschung und Entwicklung, Stuttgart 1989.

with the scientific community. This knowledge can be combined with external information such as patents or publications.

3.   Using an Expert System

The combined approach however requires the collection, analysis and interpretation of a plenty of information. The use of data processing is obvious. The type of information used in technology evaluation however can only be processed with a new kind of software: expert systems.

3.1.   What is an Expert?

An expert is able to accomplish something because of training and experience that the rest us is not able to. He has got a large amount of domain-specific knowledge. A real expert does not only produce good solutions but often finds them qicker. The expert uses tricks and caveats to solve problems. He is not only proficient, but also smooth and efficient in his actions and he is able to explain his lines of reasoning. He is good at plowing through irrelevant information to get to basic issues and can recognize problems as instances of types with which he is familar.

3.2.   What is an Expert System?

Knowledge-based or expert systems employ the above described knowledge to solve problems similar to the way that human experts would. In the late 1970s scientists realized that the problem-solving power of a computer program is mostly based on the knowledge which is embedded in it, not just its formalisms and inference schemes. The intelligence of a program is determined by the quality of the specific knowledge about a problem area. The most important characteristic of an expert system is that this knowledge is explicit and accessible because it is separated from the control mechanisms about the knowledge. This separation is a main characteristic of this new kind of software.

3.3.   Comparison of Data Processing and Expert Systems

Although conventional computer programs support decision making, they are not comparable with expert systems. Programs consist of algorithms and data. Algorithms determine how to manipulate the data, and data characterize parameters in the particular problem at hand. Expert systems manipulate knowledge, not by using algorithms, but by the use of heuristics and inferential processes. Furthermore they differ in their architecture from conventional programs as shown below.

Data Processing	Expert Systems
Representation and use of data	Representation and use of knowledge
Algorithmic	Heuristic
Repetetive process	Inferential process
Effective manipulation of large data bases	Effective manipulation of large knowledge bases
Input has to be complete	Input can be incomplete

Fig. 2. Comparison of Data Processing and Expert Systems

3.4. The Kind of Information needed to do Technology Evaluation

Technolgy evaluation requires a special type of information[3]:

- information is often not complete

- information is fuzzy, not sure

- mostly qualitative information

- not well-structured information

As outlined above this is the kind of information processing expert systems are made for.

---

[3]   Kirsch, W.: Einführung in die Theorie der Entscheidungsprozesse, Wiesbaden 1977; Zangemeister, C.: Werturteil und formalisierte Planungsprozesse - Zur Notwendigkeit und praktischen Möglichkeit einer systematischen Integration menschlicher Urteilskraft und Erfahrung in modell- und computergestützte Planungssysteme, pp. 107. In: Grochla, E., Szyperski, N.: Modell- und computergestützte Unternehmensplanung, Wiesbaden 1973 pp. 97-123

4. Advantages using the Expert System

The expert system provides the following specific features and advantages:

4.1. Consensus Management

First of all, the expert system supports the evaluation by the R&D experts. Methods for technology evaluation can be developed together with the researchers and implemented in the system. This makes sure that every user runs the process in the same way.

4.2. Considering Certainty of Evaluation

The certainty of evaluation is taken into account in two different ways. On the one hand, after answering a question, the system asks the user to estimate the certainty of his answer (s. Figure 4). On the other hand, the user has the opportunity not to answer a number of questions, if he does not want or is not able to do. The certainty of the evaluation increases with the amount of information given (s. Figure 3).

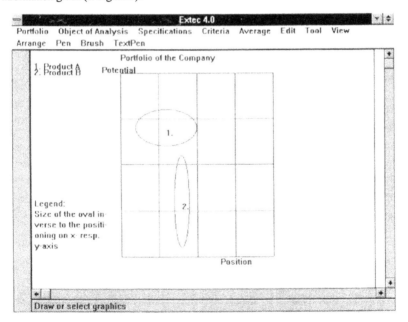

Fig. 3. Portfolio Concept

4.3. Objectivity of the Results

Objectivity is guaranteed by a deeply structured analysis procedure. Patents, publications, R&D funding and some well-known methods of technology management such as the S-Curve or technology life cycle concept are used.

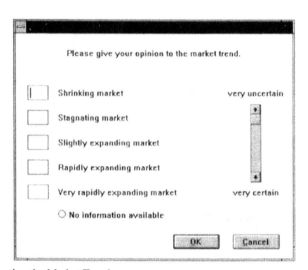

Fig. 4. Estimating the Market Trend

4.4. Taking the different Significance of the Evaluation Aspects into Account

Some criteria like the volume or the attractiveness of the market are relevant for nearly every project in R&D or innovation. The potential for further technological development however is only of importance for a company which follows the strategy of a technological leader. The criteria also differ in their importance which is reflected by their weight.

4.5. Reducing the Time for Evaluation

Using an expert system diminishes the time technology planning and evaluation takes. This is a real strategic advantage. The expert system reduces the time for example for the evaluation of 22 technologies from one year to three weeks (s. Figure 5).

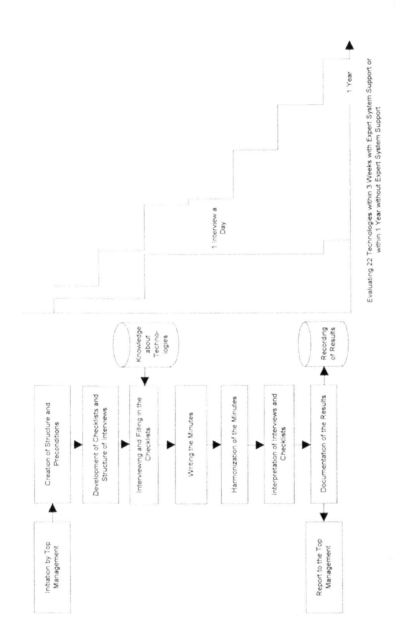

Fig. 5. Process Steps of Technology Evaluation with/without the Expert System

4.6. Explanation and Reproduction of Results

The results of the evaluation can be declared and reproduced. The system provides help texts for the user. Every question of the system and every answer of the user is recorded. After each session all the data are stored and can be used for the next session.

4.7. Flexible Data Update

The users of the system are top level managers. The interviews must take as little time as possible and the structure of the interview has to provide as much flexibility as possible. In same cases it is not neccessary to update all the data. The system has to provide this by giving the opportunity only to update the information the user wants to.

5. Conclusion

The main advantage is that strategic discussions within the management are put on an argumentative level. They are no longer characterized by eloquence and political power. In this respect the expert system does not replace entrepreneurial decisions but diminishes the risk of dissipation of resources.

Instruments can be used as political instruments. But instruments are also a mean to reduce the complexity of the innovation process. One of the most important conclusions of the discussion was that we need instruments and we should develop them. Developing and using instruments however needs a clearly understanding of the possibilities and limits of the instruments.

References

Ropohl, G.: Eine Systemtheorie der Technik. Zur Grundlegung der allgemeinen Technologie München u.a. 1979.

Brockhoff, K.: Schnittstellenmanagement: Abstimmungsprobleme zwischen Marketing und Forschung und Entwicklung, Stuttgart 1989.

Kirsch, W.: Einführung in die Theorie der Entscheidungsprozesse, Wiesbaden 1977

Zangemeister, C.: Werturteil und formalisierte Planungsprozesse - Zur Notwendigkeit und praktischen Möglichkeit einer systematischen Integration menschlicher Urteilskraft und Erfahrung in modell- und computergestützte Planungssysteme, in: Grochla, E., Szyperski, N.: Modell- und computergestützte Unternehmensplanung, Wiesbaden 1973, pp. 97-123

Recent Essentials in Innovation Management and Research, edited by H. Hübner / T. Dunkel
Gabler, Wiesbaden/Germany, 1995

INNOVA

An Instrument for Strategic Innovation Analysis

Heinz Hübner

Torsten Dunkel

Management Science - Technology Impact & Innovation Research
University of Kassel

Abstract:
INNOVA, a software programme for strategic planning, enables the user to assess the need for and the urgency of innovative measures in the company. Urgency codes, priority lists, innovation profiles as basis for innovation balances are provided for prospective actions to be taken in the areas of product innovation, innovation in the production system, organizational innovation and other measures.

1. Introduction

An increasing pressure for innovation, the necessity of permanent cost reductions and corporate restructuring expressed in concepts like Lean Management and Business Re-Engineering, as well as the consideration of ecological aspects, are forcing companies to exploit all possibilities of operational innovation to the best possible extent. The most critical issue facing companies today is how to manage in an increasingly complex and unpredictable environment. The more uncertain und instable the world becomes, the more companies must rely on the management of innovation to create their desired future.

Although the importance of innovation is generally known, many companies have difficulties in identifying the need for innovation and planning adequate innovation strategies related to several possible fields of innovation.

2. Description of INNOVA

INNOVA, a comprehensive software for personal computers, has been developed for computer-aided planning. The software consists of a total of 10 main criteria such as "users' needs" and "competitive position of the product" (see Figure 1). The application of INNOVA enables the user to determine the need for and the urgency of innovation from the company's viewpoint regarding the product, the division, or the strategic business unit (SBU).

(1) Customers'/Users' needs

(2) Competitive position of the product/product group

(3) Economic position of the product/product group

(4) Ecological Quality of the product/product group

(5) Management

(6) Technical development

(7) Production system

(8) Cases of warranty/complaints

(9) Availability and supply reliability of resources for
   the own production (diminuation of dependencies!)

(10) Legislation

Fig. 1: Main criteria of innovation analysis

Overall four possible fields of innovation will be considered as shown in Figure 2:

⇒ PRODUCT INNOVATION:	new and/or improved problem solutions in the form of products and/or services
⇒ INNOVATION IN THE PRODUCTION SYSTEM:	new and/or improved production systems in a broader sense, i.e. also physical and non-physical innovation as part of the planning and management (manufacturing innovation)
⇒ ORGANIZATIONAL INNOVATION:	new and/or improved adjustments concerning the company's structural organization and the organization in charge of operational procedures (i.e. organization/ administrative procedures)
⇒ OTHER MEASURES:	to eliminate weaknesses concerning concepts and systems (i.e. management, marketing, etc.)

Fig. 2: Possible fields of innovation

In the course of quantifying the urgency for measures of innovation, two kinds of urgencies will be distinguished as shown in Figure 3 (cf. Hübner/Hübner, 1991).

EXISTENTIAL URGENCY	EXPANSION OF THE COMPETITIVE POSITION
The need for innovation to guarantee the continuance of the company as stabilization.	Active use of innovation to gain competitive advantages combined with the expansion of the market position as well as its turnover and ROI.

Fig. 3: The two kinds of urgencies

Each main criterion will be explicated in detailed sub-criteria.

194

Using the example of the main criterion "Competitive position of the product", Figure 4 shows the breakdown of a main criterion into sub-criteria.

1.1 Do the products presently offered on the market by different companies meet the user's needs?

1.2 Does our product meet the user's needs?

1.3 To which extent do we know the user's needs?

1.4 How are the chances to open up new markets for our present product?

1.5 How are the chances to open up new user problem definitions for our technological know-how (solution finding knowledge)?

1.6 Do the product-related supplementary services currently offered by different companies (i.e. terms of delivery, services, etc.) meet the user's needs?

1.7 Do our additional services meet the actual problem definitions and requirements of our customers?

1.8.1 Do additional requirements, wishes of our (potential) user's exist in relation to APPLICATION FUNCTIONS?

1.8.2. Do additional requirements, wishes of our (potential) user's exist in relation to PRESTIGE FUNCTIONS?

1.8.3 Do additional requirements, wishes of our (potential) user's exist in relation to ADDITIONAL SERVICES?

1.9.1 Degree of satisfaction in relation to quality of APPLICATION FUNCTIONS of our product?

1.9.2 Degree of satisfaction in relation to quality of PRESTIGE FUNCTIONS of our product?

1.9.3 Degree of satisfaction in relation to quality of ADDITIONAL SERVICES of our product?

1.10 How significant is the danger of a change of our user to other competitors (loyalty, commitment, dependence of customers)?

Fig. 4: Sub-criteria for the module "competitive position of the product"

3. Procedure of applying INNOVA

An interdisciplinary team is formed for the purpose of discussing and recording the specific company data; this team is headed and directed by a staff member of the company or an external consultant. The sequence of processing the individual main criteria according to Figure 1 is to be determined by the team; they can also be used as modules.

The input of specific company and product information is effected by referring to several sub-criteria per module. The assessment per sub-criterion as well as the evaluation will be performed, just as the judgment on consequences, by the team made up of competent representatives at least from the Product Development, R&D, Materials Purchase/Production, Marketing/Sales, and Controlling departments.

Figure 5 shows the input mask of INNOVA for one sub-criterion. The elaboration of each sub-criterion will be carried out in 5 steps as indicated:

Explanation of Figure 5:

Step 1: Assessment of the specific situation of the product (selection of the impact per sub-criterion).

Step 2 and 2.1: Derivation of the consequences concerning

- the kind of urgency
- the fields of innovation measures.

Step 3: Input of the rate of urgency from 0 = without any influence to 5 = very high urgency for the measures of innovation.

Step 4: Input of evaluation (weighting) from 0 = this sub-criterion is not important to 10 = very important

Step 5: Collection of remarks concerning data collection or first ideas that could be considered as a possible solution to the problem.

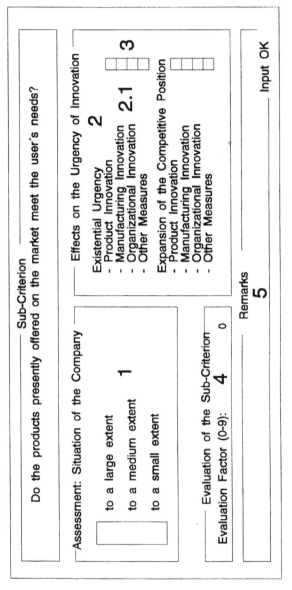

Fig. 5: Input mask of INNOVA for the sub-criterion "Do the products presently offered on the market by different companies meet the user's needs?"

The interdisciplinary analysis team will discuss and elaborate these sub-criteria for all relevant modules within a data collection phase in the firm. This data collection is the first of a **total of 3 subsequent phases**:

(1) Data collection by an innovation analysis team in the firm.

(2) Data processing and analysis/print-out of the results. Interpretation and derivation of measures.

(3) Presentation and discussion of the results, common development of measures in concrete innovation projects.

It is recommended to have the first use supported by an INNOVA expert from university or a consultant.

The qualified consulting on INNOVA (phases 1 and 3) will be organised within the firm. Phase 2 takes place outside the company. It is possible to set up an "application know how" within the firm, so as to carry on analyses independently , for this purpose, the TWI offers a short-time training. In case of periodical application of INNOVA and the presentation of innovation balances for a progressive optimization of the corporate innovation process, the TWI offers qualified assistance as accompanying and post-application research .

4. Results

INNOVA provides a complete documentation of the compiled data. The analysis of these data will be achieved by calculating urgency codes for both kinds of urgencies, presenting priority lists as well as graphical visualizations in the form of innovation profiles as displayed in Figure 6 .

As a result of the strategic innovation analysis, the company will be provided with "Innovation Profiles", i.e.

- the combination of innovation profiles of each examined product/examined product group per business period,

198

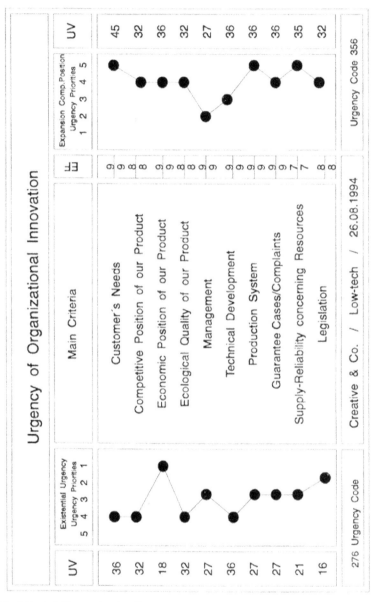

Fig.6 Typical "Innovation Profile"

Legend: EF = Evaluation Factor
UV = Urgency Value

- the calculated urgency-values and
- the urgency-codes,

which are the basis for the elaboration or derivation of innovation strategies and recommendations for future business policy.

The innovation analysis constitutes an important basis for **strategic planning**, distinguishing between "existential urgency" and "expansion of competitive position". If applied repeatedly, the software provides for stepwise creation of so-called "Innovation Balance Sheets", allowing to control the success of actions taken and, as a result, **optimizing the innovation behaviour** of companies. Thus, the application of the software achieves additional integrative effects for the company as displayed in Figure 7.

Horizontal integration among the different departments of the company will be achieved by the interdisciplinary innovation analysis team. Vertical integration into the strategy will be performed by the concept of INNOVA itself. Thereby, the software takes into account Innovation Management as corporate cross-sectional function with crucial strategic importance within the company.

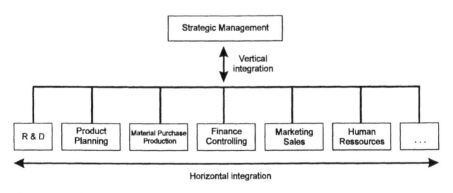

Fig. 7: Integrative Effects of INNOVA

200

References:

Hübner, Heinz/Hübner, Heimo: The Determination of the Need for and the Urgency of Innovation from Company's View, in: Allesch, J. (Ed.): Consulting in Innovation, Amsterdam 1991, pp. 25-30.

Hübner, Heinz/Hübner, Heimo: INNOVA. A User Programme for Innovation Planning, Kassel 1992. (Handbook of the Software available with Demo Disk at: TechnikWirkungs- und Innovationsforschung, FB Wirtschaftswissenschaften, University of Kassel, D-34109 Kassel)

Recent Essentials in Innovation Management and Research, edited by H. Hübner / T. Dunkel
Gabler, Wiesbaden/Germany, 1995

Results of Discussion and Fields of Future Research

Instruments as Management Technology

Andreas Eichler, University of Kassel
Brigitte Reminger, Siemens AG, Munich

Participants:

Moderator: Dale Littler, University of Manchester (GB)
Wolfgang Czerny, Austrian Research Center Seibersdorf (A)
Torsten Dunkel, University of Kassel (D)
Andreas Eichler, University of Kassel (D)
Harry Nyström, Institute of Economics, University of Uppsala (S)
Brigitte Reminger, Siemens AG, Munich (D)
Dorothea von Wichert-Nick,
  Fraunhofer Institute for Systems and Innovation Research, Karlsruhe (D)

The group work was structured in the following way: After one lecture, the Group asked the Speaker (S.) about unclarified points. Then there was a discussion about several points mentioned in the lecture. Before listening to the next lecture, the most interesting points were summarized.

Discussion after the key note speech given by Nyström "From Low-Tech to High-Tech: Product Development Strategies for Finding New Markets and Technologies"

Mr. Nyström gave a report on how to change a company from producing and marketing "low-tech" goods to "high-tech" goods.

After Prof. Nyström´s lecture, several questions arose:

1) Is there a possibility or a necessity for companies to develop from "low-tech" to "high-tech" companies?

S.: There is a possibility, not a necessity.

2) How is a "low-tech" and a "high-tech" level to be defined?

S.: For defining a "low-" and a "high-" tech level, it is necessary to compare the company (or the product or the marketing etc.) level to the level of other companies (or products, etc.). Thus, "low-tech" and "high-tech" are used in a relative sense.

3) What are the sources of the study?

S.: The study is based on personal interviews with 13 Swedish biotechnical and food processing companies.

4) Is it an "ex-post" or an "ex-ante" analysis?

S.: Case studies - on which this analysis is based - looked at the past, but out of these, strategies for the future have been derived.

5) Had the strategies of the companies analysed in the case studies been planned, or had they been developed without planning?

S.: Strategies had been developed "organically", that means without planning.

Participant (P.): Could enterprises be more successful with such an "organic" strategy than others with a formulated, clear strategy?

P.: Yes, I think so. Look at systems which have been created by natural evolution and compare them with man-made systems, e.g. artifical intelligence with the human brain. It seems to me that such systems have not been planned. Nevertheless, they are quite perfect, I think.

P.: I am not sure if it is useful to compare the way of creating natural systems with man-made systems like enterprises. In my opinion, there are two reasons contradicting this comparison: Firstly, the forming of systems by natural evolution takes a long time, e.g. billions of years - enterprises do not have so much time. Secondly, no enterprise will survive with such a high rate of unsuccessful attempts as natural evolution made before building the "perfect" systems that exist today.

P.: There might be a risk in substituting "planned" systems for "organic" systems because you often do not know much about the efficiency of the organic system, its elements and the interactions between these elements. So you risk destroying an efficent system or a system with a lot of elements that you might need for your planned system.

P.: In my opinion, the main problem is not the problem of destroying an efficient system. If the organic system were efficient, I am sure you would not destroy it. The problem I see is that you often do not know which system - organic or planned - is more efficient. A second point is that it is not easy to substitute a system that people do not know for a system they know. I think it is possible that a system known by people for a long time - planned or organic - is often more efficient. So you have to take the time and expense for adapting your new strategy to your calculation.

P.: We talk as if a "planned" strategy would be more successful than an "organic" strategy. But: Where are the important differences between a realized "planned" and a realized "organic" strategy? I think that this question is not useless because the realization also of a "planned" strategy is influenced by so many factors that - in my opinion - the result of a realized "planned" and a realized "organic" strategy is the same in a lot of cases.

6) **Is there - apart from strategies A and B - a strategy C, in which the level of technological innovation becomes higher without a higher level of market innovation? One example for such a strategy C could be present strategies of Japanese camera manufacturers.**

S.: Such a strategy C might be possible, but is not analysed in Prof. Nyström´s investigations.

As a result of the discussion, questions were formulated by the Working Group as fields of future research:

1. Does the climate and culture of a company support or hamper the change from a "closed" to an "open" (see paper Nyström) strategy?

2. How is creativity - as a requirement of the "open" strategy - to be integrated in a company?

3. Are companies more successful with a formulated, clear strategy than others without it?

Discussion after the key note speech of Czerny "Corporate Strategic Planning"

After Dr. Czerny´s lecture, there were a few questions from participants of the Working Group:

1) How is creativity to be integrated in that analytical model?

S.: The creative part of the described model is the aspect. The ordinary point of view is asking what could be improved in the strategic business units. In contrast to the ordinary point of view, the new point of view is asking for the existence of core competences which could be developed.

2) What are the differences between the old model (strengths and weaknesses) and the model of core competences?

S.: The difference between the two models is that the holistic model integrates the four dimensions of strategic thinking, namely:

- economy
- technology
- environment
- society.

P.: I think there is one problem you have in the new "holistic" model as well as in the old model: The problem how managers could find the core competences or the strengths and weaknesses, if they only see what they want to see. And that is a problem not only for managers.

P.: So you need an additional instrument to find the real core competences or the real strengths and weaknesses. Expert systems might be such an instrument. Such an expert system will be presented later by Mrs. Reminger, so the discussion about that point might be ended here.

P.: There is another point I would like to mention: In so many theoretical models - not only in Mr. Czerny´s - merely reality is described. People have acted in such a way as the models advised them for a long time. So there is nothing new in this model for them. Thus, even if nobody has described this aspect of reality before you, everybody is acting as if they knew the model.

In the following discussion, a few (unsolved) problems were mentioned:

1. The holistic model says nothing about the question how to develop the core competences. So there might be the risk that applying this model will support a "closed" strategy.

2. How can one plan against surprises in that model?

3. People only see what they want to see. So how could managers find the real core competences, if they only see what they would like to see?

Discussion after the key note speech of von Wichert-Nick "Future R&D Management: Challenges, their Impacts and Selected Tools"

In the following discussion, a few points were mentioned:

1) What is the main issue?

S.: The major issue is that the forecasting model is a formalized model for handling the change.

2) Is there a necessity of consensus in that model?

P.: The model forces a consensus.

P.: Consensus between experts would be desirable.

P.: Experts might have different aims, especially if they come from different departments within the company. So it might be quite difficult to get a consensus about forecasting between different experts.

P.: Not consensus, but contradiction is a necessity for the learning of organizations and for finding realistic forecasts.

3) How can you find experts if you do not know the technology and the area, e.g. emerging technologies?

S.: You cannot find experts from fields which are not known to you. In such situations, it would be useful to ask experts from many fields.

P.: You will not find any new expert by that method. Only established experts can be found by it.

P.: It is said that you will have to engage experts from many fields if you do not know the fields you are looking for. My question is, how to find the "many fields" in which there might be the experts you would like to ask?

4) How is that method of strategic planning to be organized?

S.: By forming teams.

Discussion after the key note speech given by Dunkel "INNOVA - An Instrument for Strategic Innovation Analysis"

After Mr. Dunkel's lecture, a few questions of understanding were asked by the Working Group:

1) What are the advantages of "INNOVA"?

S.: The first advantage of "INNOVA" is that it allows to identify urgencies for innovations in several fields of innovation without focussing only on product innovation, but related to strategy. A second advantage is that it supports the integration between different departments of the company.

2) What is the reason for using numbers instead of words like "large", "small", etc?

S.: Numbers as part of a qualitative scale are a requirement for the calculation of urgency codes.

3) What is the empirical outcome of the project?

S.: "INNOVA" has been developed together with, and used within, some companies. We are planning to apply it in some companies in a periodically repeated way to optimize the innovative behaviour of the firms, using Innovation balances.

Apart from these questions, the problem was mentioned how to proceed from analysing problems to implementing the results in practice.

Discussion after the key note speech of Reminger "An Expert System for Strategic Technology Management"

In the following discussion, a few points were mentioned:

P.: When discussing Mr. Czerny's lecture, we talked about the problem how managers could find facts and/or problems if they only see what they want to see. In my opinion, using an expert system presents the same problem: The results of the expert systems cannot be better than the data which is entered into the system.

P.: I agree with you. But I would like to ask you, where could be the reasons for a manager to put in the wrong data into the system?

P.: There are a lot of reasons why managers might put the wrong data into an expert system. The first reason - but in my opinion not the most important one - is that they do not know the correct data. Another - which is most important, I think - is that they are **afraid of the consequences** which **analysing the right data** by the system might have. A third reason might be that they are afraid that using an expert system might restrict their creativity.

P.: Another problem I see is: Who decides which data is important? Is it the computer that decides, or the managers who put the data into the expert system, or the managing director?

As a result of discussion in the Working Group, some problems were identified to be discussed in the plenary session:

1. The input into such an expert system by users in the company influences the results of using the expert system.
2. The kind of input in the expert system (by users) depends on the consequences which the users expect from entering the information into this system.

3. People in the company might be afraid that using such an expert system might restrict their creativity.

In the plenary discussion on Friday afternoon, Prof. Dale Littler gave an overview over the lectures and the discussion within the Working Group. In addition to the aspects discussed in the Working Group, the problem arose that instruments can be used as political instruments, too. But instruments are also a means to reduce the complexity of the innovation process. One of the most **important conclusions** of the discussion was that we **need instruments** and we should develop them. Developing and using instruments, however, requires a clear understanding of the possibilities and limits of the instruments.

Fields of future research

1. Are companies with a formulated and clear strategy more successful than others without it?

2. To what extent does the structure and culture of a company influence the possibilities of using external resources and know-how, e.g. cooperation in R&D?

3. If so, how can creativity be integrated in the company?

4. What could be an appropriate mixture and interchange between the analytical and the creative approach of management?

5. It would be interesting to see if there is an influence of the companies'culture on this mixture!

6. People - and therefore also managers - see what they want to see!
   How do the internal structure and the goals of a person influence the way of looking at things and the selection of instruments?

7. How can one plan against surprises?

8. Forecasting methods tend to produce consensus!
   But contradiction might be very helpful for finding new or different ways!
   A problem of future research could be how to deal with contradiction.

9. Another success factor for applying forecasting methods is the identification of (new) experts for emerging technologies.

10. First of all, it is important to differentiate between the process of innovation and the instruments.
    On the one hand, it is important to know the possibilities and the limits of the instruments.
    On the other hand, the characteristics and the structure of the process should be known.
    Integration of the instruments is an important point.

In the concluding session, the following comments on fields of future research mentioned above were given:

Referring to

Item 2. A problem for the managers of medium-sized companies, who often are the proprietors: How to deal with the large volume of information, which implies unwanted disclosure of information?

Item 7. What is a "surprise"?

Ecological Problems

as a Trigger for Innovation[*]

Recent Essentials in Innovation Management and Research,edited by H. Hübner / T. Dunkel
Gabler, Wiesbaden/Germany, 1995

Qualitative Evaluation of the Environmental Effects of Companies' Strategies

Harald Hiessl

Uwe Kuntze

Michael Schön

Fraunhofer-Institute

for Systems and Innovation Research (ISI)

Karlsruhe

Abstract:

In order to reduce environmental burdens, enterprises will be increasingly forced to change the use and lifespan of their products. Different strategies can be distinguished: Production of more durable goods, extension of the effective life or serviceable life of products and product components by reusing, repairing, re-manufacturing, etc., production of multifunctional goods, recycling of materials, and different commercial strategies for avoiding waste, e.g. selling the use instead of the product or shared use etc.. These strategies are distinguished according to their environmental effects in the different phases of the product life cycle. First subjective estimations of these effects are discussed and critical strategies with a potential increase of negative environmental effect are identified.

1 Strategies for structuring the use and lifespan of products

Enterprises in Germany and other industrial nations will be increasingly forced to take on not only the hitherto external costs of production, but also the external costs of their products. In particular, due to the emerging obligation to accept the return of their products after use, they will be increasingly confronted with the issue of optimizating the use and lifespan of these products.

In line with Stahel (1991), the following strategies for structuring the use and lifespan of products can be distinguished:

Strategy A: Production of more durable goods

Strategy B: Extension of the effective life/serviceable life/ of products by

     B1   reusing
     B2   repairing
     B3   re-manufacturing, general overhaul, product recycling
     B4   technical upgrading

Strategy C: Prolongation of the lifespan of product components by
     C1-C4   analogous to B1 - B4

Strategy M: Production and use of more multifunctional goods

Strategy R: Recycling the materials

     R1   direct recycling of manufacturing waste
     R2   graded recycling of material ("end of pipe")
     R3   recycling of materials from mixed waste

Strategy V: Commercial strategies for avoiding waste

     V1   selling the use instead of the product
     V2   shared, combined or repeated use
     V3   selling the service "quality control" instead of selling product replacements

2   Environmental effects in the phases of the product life cycle

These strategies are distinguished according to their environmental effects. Environmental effects arise primarily in the areas of

- Material consumption (consumption of raw materials, non-renewable resources)
- Land consumption in terms of actual area used
- Change in monetary and nonmonetary value of surrounding land
- Energy consumption
- Waste

- Water resources
- Sewage
- Air pollution
- Climate changes.

In principle, not only effects which relieve the stress on the environment (alleviating effects), but also additional burdens are conceivable in these areas, if one considers that the type as well as the strength of these environmental effects can differ extensively in the different phases of the product life cycle. For example, the following differentiation of product life cycle is used here:

1. Raw material production (resource recovery and material generation)
2. Production and fabrication
3. Use
4. Decomposition (dismantling, separation of materials)
5. Disposal (e.g. thermal, material recycling, landfills)

A further distinction has to be made between specific and absolute effects. Specific effects are related to the individual product, absolute effects arise from the multiplication of the specific effect by the number of units present in the product life cycle at any one time. Absolute alleviation can, for example, arise from increased efforts in production processes in spite of the specific additional burdens occurring at the level of individual products due to the reduction in production numbers.

The possible specific and absolute effects of the different strategies in the various stages of a product's life-cycle are represented qualitatively in the Table 1, which summarizes our subjective estimations as a hypothesis for discussion. Here, to start with, only first estimates of the "environmental effects" are regarded which represent a subjectively weighted aggregation of the above mentioned environmental effects in the individual areas. To this extent, the evaluations of the strategies derived from this representation are subjective, too. In the course of a planned research project we are aiming to collect objectivizing information and develop quantifying and evaluating procedures based partly on models.

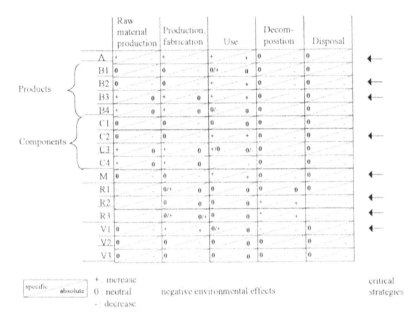

	Raw material production	Production, fabrication	Use	Decomposition	Disposal
A	+	+	+	+ 0	0
B1	0	0	0/+	0 0	0
B2	0	0	+	+ 0	0
B3	+ 0	+ 0	+	+ 0	0
B4	+ 0	+ 0	0/-	0 0	0
C1	0	0	0	0 0	0
C2	0	0	+	+ 0	0
C3	+ 0	+ 0	+/0	0/- 0	0
C4	+ 0	+ 0	-	0	0
M	0	0	+	+ 0	0
R1	0/+ 0	0	0	0 0 0	0
R2	0	0	0	0 +	+
R3	0/+	0/+ 0	0	-	+
V1	0	+	+	0/+ 0	0
V2	0	0	0	0 0	0
V3	0	0	0	0 0	0

specific — absolute

+ : increase
0 : neutral
- : decrease

negative environmental effects

critical strategies

Tab. 1: Qualitative estimation of negative environmental effects during the phases of the product lifecycle and their dependence from different strategies available to reduce material flow rates through an economy.

Different combinations of the specific and absolute effects can be observed: specific alleviation, invariance and additional burdens combined with absolute alleviation, invariance or additional burdens. In our preliminary judgement, *absolute additional burdens* do not occur at any stage in the life-cycle *with specific alleviation or invariance*. This would be the case if alleviating or invariant measures at the individual product level were overcompensated by a large increase in the number of units. This should - when regarding the entire life cycle of the product - be excluded as a strategy a priori, but does not even occur in individual life cycle stages. The same is true for the combination of *specific alleviation/absolute invariance* with which no improvement could be expected from an environmental viewpoint. Only the combination *specific additional burden/absolute additional burden*, which is possible in certain life cycle stages, occurs in individual cases with which, in an integral approach, it is hoped to procure alleviation throughout the entire life cycle of the product.

Many strategies lead to an absolute additional burden during the operational life of the product, or, at the most, have a neutral effect. Only variant C4 (prolonging the effetive life of components by technical upgrading) makes a continuous technical adaptation possible and thus opens up the prospect of reducing the environmental load when the product is used (*specific and absolute alleviation*).

However, *alleviating effects and/or cases of invariance* dominate in the pre and post-use stages of the product's life cycle wherein a certain symmetry can be observed. Frequently, the effects from resource recovery and material generation on the one hand, and those of disposal on the other are equally weighted. The same is true for production and fabrication, as well as the decomposition processes which work in a reverse direction (e.g. strategies B1, B2, C1, C2, M, V2, V3). However, greater efforts are also frequently found on the material side and in production and fabrication which do not necessarily lead to additional efforts in decomposition and disposal (e.g. strategies A, B3, B4, C3, C4).

The recycling strategies R1-R3 are given the status of special cases as they obviously result in alleviation on the raw material and material sides. In production and fabrication, as well as use, no environmental effects are expected, merely in the area of decomposition is an additional effort and thus an additional burden conceivable (strategies R2 and R3). The remaining specific and absolute effects are always constant here, as there is no alteration in the effective life or no intensification of use and, therefore, no influence on the number of units.

In Table 1 socalled "critical strategies" are identified. These strategies are defined to be those with a potential increase of negative environmental effects (both specific and absolute) in at least one phase of their respective life cycle. Critical strategies are strategies A, B2, B3, C2, M, R2, R3, and V1.

According to this first qualitative evaluation strategies B1, C1, R1, V2, and V3 are the only strategies that do not seem to produce any negative absolute effects throughout the overall lifecycle. Of those only R1 is widely applied on an industrial scale. The reuse-strategies (B1 and C1), the strategies of a more "intelligent" use of products (V2), their professional maintenance and "quality control" (V3) are only of marginal importance today. These strategies have a potential for environmental relief. Their implementation seems to be worth to be intensified on a wider scale.

Literature

Stahel, W. R.: Langlebigkeit und Materialrecycling - Strategien zur Vermeidung von Abfällen im Bereich der Produkte. Vulkan Verlag, Essen 1991

Recent Essentials in Innovation Management and Research, edited by H. Hübner / T. Dunkel
Gabler, Wiesbaden/Germany, 1995

Increasing the Duration of Product Utilization as a Strategy to Meet Ecological Needs

- Some Results of an Ongoing Project [*] -

Volker Sporr
Christoph Witzenhausen

Management Science - Technology Impact & Innovation Research
University of Kassel

Abstract:
The current environmental situation requires a more efficient utilization of existing resources which could be solved by a sustained product utilization. It should be the aim to oppose those factors that limit the product utilization and which are initiated by producers and consumers. Therefore, firms are responsible for using their capital and human resources as efficiently as possible. Simultaneously, the strategy of extending the phase of product utilization can offer an enormous innovative potential for securing the existence of enterprises in the long term. The following results are based on two case studies.

1. Initial Situation

Increasing ecological problems are putting pressure on science and industry to look for concepts which will enable an economy in the sense of sustainable development. The current measures applied by enterprises are mostly preventory. They concentrate on reducing emissions of harmful chemicals and pollutants, and they try to improve the recyclability of products as well as their packagings.

---

[*] "Possibilities of extending the period of product utilization, considering economic implications as well as the ongoing technical development". Development of theoretical models together with concrete analysing of products with a view to (technical) adaptation and upgrading is effected in a special product workshop run by the TWI.

Up to now, the phase of product utilization has not been taken into consideration sufficiently. As a product generally incorporates material and energy, high potentials for saving material and energy could be achieved by extending the phase of product utilization; this requires to introduce a reconditioning loop as shown in Figure 1.

To allow a more efficient utilization of resources (material, energy), it is necessary to extend the phase of utilization of products prior to recycling.

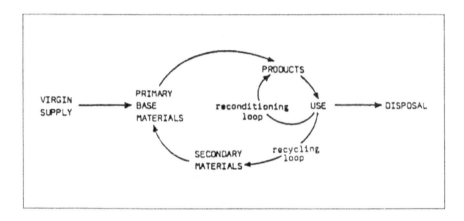

Fig. 1.: Reconditioning Loops versus Recycling Loop
    comp. Stahel, 1991., p.

The object of the investigation are technical consumer durable utility goods with a decreasing efficiency*) .

In consideration of the utilization phase (UP), the following questions arise:
• **What has to be understood by UP?**
• **Which factors influence the UP?**
• **What possible solution can be derived from this for the enterprise?**

---

*)   Products with decreasing efficiency are characterized by the fact that every failure of the system is
      linked with alternatives, which are either reconditioning or exchange of subsystems, or replacement
      purchase of the entire technical system. In contrast to that, products with a constant efficiency do not
      offer any alternative of replacement purchase after failure.

2. What is the utilization phase?

In general, the UP of a product can be understood as the space of time that lies between its first use by its owner and its final decommissioning[*]. In literature, a distinction is often made between an economic and a technical service phase of products. The technical UP is related to products that cannot be reconditioned (e.g., bulbs, electronic units), which means that a minimum of reliability is taken as a basis (is assumed). A case of damage occurs when the minimum reliability no longer exists and therefore the product will have to be replaced.

Products with decreasing efficiency that can be reconditioned are characterized by the economic UP. Economic UP marks the space of time in which the consumer believes this product to be the best alternative for the achievement of an aim he pursues. This implies an economic weighting between the alternatives of reconditioning[**] and replacement purchase that can be represented in terms of a graph of reliabiltiy.

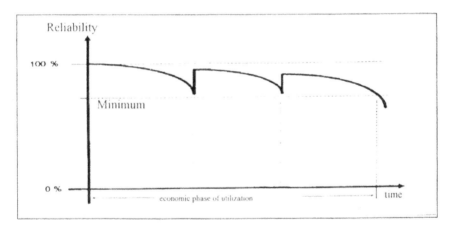

Fig. 2: Course of the economic UP (utility phase) of a product with decreasing efficiency comp. Bellmann, 1990, p. 18

As it is evident from Figure 2, it is possible to reach a theoretically unlimited UP by repeated measures of reconditioning. In consideration of products that can be reconditioned, it is not

---

[*]   K. Bellmann, Langlebige Gebrauchsgüter, Wiesbaden 1990, p.2
[**]   The task of reconditioning is restoration of the target state and functioning order after break-down of t he product.

possible to determine a technical UP through early repair or renewal. Therefore, only an economic UP will make sense for those products.

3. Which factors influence the utilization phase?

The UP of products is influenced by a great variety of factors, which can be divided into three categories. These categories are:

- **S - social factors,**
- **T - technical factors,**
- **E - economic factors.**

A significant social phenomenon that leads to shortening of the phase of product utilization of many products is often designated by the term "physical obsolescence"[*]. Therefore, a fashion-oriented measure that is supported by enterprises leads to stimulation of customers and ends up in the premature substitution of products, e.g., in the automobile industry, a steady change of secondary features like shape and equipment of car types causes a stronger demand for new cars.

The technical factors of influence can roughly be divided into two spheres, namely further technical development and physical ageing processes.

The technical process in the sense of qualitative improvement leads to a functional devaluation of already existing products. This devaluation causes a substitution of a product that could still be used and is also designated, in literature, by the term "functional obsolescence"[**]. Physical ageing processes result from the scientifically/technically limited phase of product utility of the materials that were used, e.g., the phase of service is limited by corrosion and wear and tear.

The substantial economic factors of influence incorporate the weighting between costs of reconditioning and costs of replacement purchases in case of damage that will become necessary in case of failure (breakdown) of the product. In general, aspects of costs and utility are the basis for the decision of the user.

---

[*]   By physical obsolescence we understand that manufacturers plan to let their products pass out of date in consideration of the function of value. An example that is often stated is the fashion branch which intention ally causes a devaluation of old collections through permanent change of design.

[**]   Functional obsolescence is a goal-directed process. It means that an existing product becomes old-fashioned because a new product with an improved ability to fulfill the functions of the existing product is introduced to the market, and/or because product innovation satisfies additional needs of customers.

In conclusion, one can say that some of the influential factors could be described as a system of operations. On the one hand, an interdependence between the elements of the system of operation exists, on the other hand, consumers as well as enterprises are taking the initiative.

4. What possible solution can be derived from this for enterprises?

The factors mentioned above contribute more or less intensively to a devaluation of already existing products which is dependent on their kind in comparison to current alternatives. This could be counteracted by an enterpreneurial strategy of long UP. The task of this concept is to prevent a premature devaluation through suitable means.

Therefore, it is not only necessary to aim at the maintenance of the original efficiency of the products, but far beyond that, to provide possibilities for measures of adaptation to current product demands. According to the philosophy that not every new need will absolutely require a new product, this means that an extension of product utility is based on a product that already exists and can be reached through measures of functional upgrading or additional equipment (comp. Figure 3). The demands mentioned above can only be fulfilled if enterprises meet certain preconditions. These could be divided into the following areas:

- **Technical requirements**
- **Demanded-object-oriented services (*in German: Nachfragerobjektbezogene Dienstleistung*)**
- **Innovative management of information.**

4.1. Technical demands

The technical demands are determined in such a way that the future development of products is characterized by a "preventive development", which means that the evolutionary development, which is technically foreseeable to a certain degree, may be absorbed by a variable product structure**) .

---

*)   *Nachfragerobjektbezogene Dienstleistung* are services that are oriented towards consumer demands on objects they have bought and which need future care by the firm, e.g. measures of overhaul, upgrading etc.

**)   In this context, Ropohl uses the term of 'dynamic conception' which means a repertoire of formation elements that can result from a different kind of product structures. G. Ropohl, Flexible Fertigungssyteme, Mainz 1971, p.252.

222

A variable product structure contains the option to correspond to increasing requirements of customers without binding it up to the purchase of a totally new product. Hereby, all measures of adaptation are described that reflect the dynamics of development and can be divided into four areas (comp. Figure 3).

function technology	existing function	new function
existing technology	additional equipment	additional functional equipment
new technology	technical upgrading	upgrading

Fig. 3: Possible forms of measures of adaptation
comp. Hübner/Witzenhausen/Sporr, internal Working Paper, TWI, Kassel 1994

- 'Additional equipment' includes measures of adjustment that are obtained under consideration of techniques and functions that already exist, e.g., a PC's RAM which is provided with additional capacity.
- 'Additional functional equipment' includes measures of adjustment by which a new product function is made available through already existing techniques, for instance, the installation of catalytic converters in cars.
- 'Technical upgrading' will introduce new techniques that will execute already existing functions, e.g., the installation of electric instead of manual window operation in a car.
- 'Upgrading' is related to measures of adjustment that will equip the product with a new function with the help of a new technique, e.g., the installation of fax modems into PCs which neither had the appropriate technique nor the function.

With these measures of adjustment, enterprises have instruments at their disposal

- to integrate new demands of customers into existing products;
- to take existing products into consideration despite technical progress and to guarantee that those older product types are compatible with their successor models;
- to minimize costs of maintenance;
- to make sure that the product has a pleasing design (e.g., timeless design) or that design changes can easily be made.

The measures of adjustment imply that product innovations have to be made according to a certain aim and have to correspond to an extended use for clients.

4.2. Demanded-object-oriented services

Providing measures of adjustment has to be understood as being a service granted by a company, rendered to the object by order of its user. These are demanded-object-oriented services[*], which are used for the process of transformation from the current phase of utilization into a sustained phase of product utilization.

Because of structural changes in the field of industry and handicrafts[**], it is necessary to newly define the term 'service' for producing enterprises, because the old definition is no longer sufficient.

Berekoven has developed a new typology of firms that offer services, which demonstrate that a strict separation between service and production cannot be maintained any longer, because future services will have to be increasingly taken into account during the development of products (comp. Figure 4).

Every offer of a firm includes a service, which is always a certain part of the firm's entire range of products offered. On the basis of this total offer of material and immaterial services, Berekoven has specified the phase of services anew. The meaning of services has been extended by the relationship between supplier and customer[***].

The nature of demanded-object-oriented services lies in the coupling of material and immaterial services, which is expressed in the accentuation of the relationship between supplier and customer.

---

[*]   L. Berekoven, Der Dienstleistungsmarkt in der Bundesrepublik Deutschland, Göttingen 1983, p.44
[**]   ibid, p.276
[***]   According to Berekoven services are processes in the broadest sense. They are used to cover the requirements of third persons with material and/or immaterial results whose performance and utilization requires a synchronous contact between the supplier of a service and the customer of a service respectively whose objects require the coverage of requirements.cf. L. Berekoven, Der Dienstleistungsmarkt in der Bundesrepublik Deutschland, Göttingen 1983, p.23

4.3. Innovative management of information

The strategy of extending the phase of product utilization requires special skills from firms according to decisions concerning its product policy. In so far, innovations are the result of collecting information, which means that the forecasts assumed must comprehend the current and future relevant demands of clients and to direct entrepreneurial activities accordingly. Therefore, a qualified way of collecting information is needed, which embraces the inside view (the firm) as well as the outside view (market, society) and will lead to an innovative management of information.

The innovative management of information is an essential part of a market-oriented entrepreneurial management. On the one hand, the tasks of these instruments are to transform immaterial collecting of information into material output (cf. Figure 5) and, on the other hand, to analyse foreseeable developments as early as possible in order to exclude asymmetrical developments*) .

reciprocally oriented toward persons (person : person)	demanded object-oriented services (person : object)

health care
body care
education
supervision
entertainment
prostitution
consultation
	object: - completion
	      - installation
	      - fitting
	      - servicing

supply-oriented object (object : object)	reciprocally oriented toward objects (object : object)
travel conveyance of passengers lodging and catering	delivery of goods textile care land and forest services data-processing motor-vehicle cleaning
education and entertainment performances fairs and exhibitions medical bath institutions	motor-vehicle recovery motor-vehicle tuning deep-freeze storage undertaking
short-term (object) letting short-term (personnel) letting	

Fig. 4: Typology of business, comp. Berekoven, 1983, p. 45

---

*)   By 'avoidance of asymmetrical development' it has to be understood, that inside a firm individual depart ments like organisation, technique, staff, planing and supervision have to be coordinated in order to work efficiently.

5. Some approaches for solutions

The result of every new unit of commodity production and its consumption forcibly leads to a deterioration of environmental qualities as well as a deterioration of the life-quality of society. The strategy of extending the phase of product utilization would oppose this dangerous development because it would improve the efficiency with regard to the consumption of resources and would force society to paradigmatically change its outlook on life.

The implementation of the strategy of a sustained product utilization set high demands on enterprises. So, the realization of

- **M - measures of adjustment,**
- **D - demanded-object-oriented services,**
- **I - innovative management of information**

requires a radical change in the structure of firms. Because every single department in the enterprise is concerned, a philosophy of management as a kind of superstructure could be useful. This is, at last, led by the idea that not every new need can be satisfied by a new product only . This special result shows that the direction of the entrepreneurial aim lies only in the sale of utility instead of selling physical products, e.g., the cascade principle includes the idea of a sustained product utilization for consumers, while product utility is maintained or improved by appropriate means (upgrading, additional equipment).

Moreover, it has to be said that the present relationship between firms and consumers is not sufficient and that an extended definition of the term 'service' is needed. Demanded-object-oriented services are urgently needed and should lead to better relations between supplier, consumer and product.

Furthermore, external and internal collecting of information will become more and more important, since they will guarantee the transformation from information into goal-directed innovation.

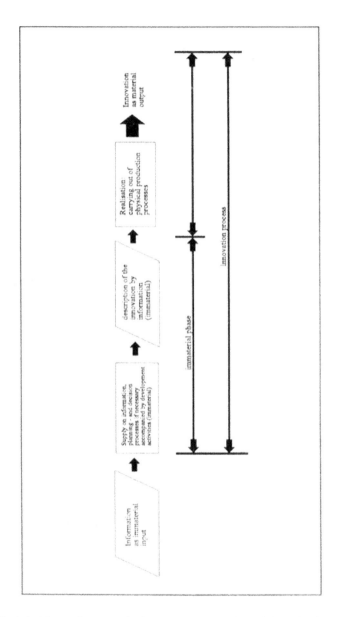

Fig. 5: Technical innovation as result of a process that transforms information into material innovation, comp. Hübner, 1990, p.33

From the strategy of extending the phase of product utilization that is described above, the following advantages can be extracted:

- To realize the measures of adjustment the return of products could be planned by the firm and should not be dependent on consumer decisions.

- The moment of overhaul work and measures of adjustments could be adapted to the firm's cycles of innovation. As a result, the expenses of work and costs could be calculated, too.

- The production plants themselves can also be used for a long period of time provided that measures of adaptation can be applied. Thus, the period of amortization can eventually be sustained.

- The general return includes an optimization of measures of adjustment and will result in the firm's specialization in this area.

- Furthermore, a close contact to customers will exist, enabling the firm to find out the real use clients have of its products and services and to align future innovation to it.

6. Case study on diesel-driven railcars

A case study was made to complement the theoretical treatment of the topic. The subject of the study were diesel-driven railcars that are used by the Deutsche Bahn AG (types VT 624/634 and VM 924/934), and which could easily be seen as fine examples of how the strategy of extended product utilization is realized.

The "works" division of the Deutsche Bahn AG has carried out measures of adjustment and maintenance on the vehicles throughout their service lifetime, so that an extremely long phase of utilization of 20 up to 30 years has been reached. It was the aim of the study to demonstrate how these measures have been realized over decades, and what problems arise in connection with those measures.

The works division of the Deutsche Bahn AG is not the producer of the vehicles. Its production is organized according to the job-shop principle to cope with the tasks mentioned above, with measures of adustment being made by a special kind of flowing production that is called "flow-cycle production" (German: Fließtaktproduktion). Flow-shop operation is impossible, because too few units are produced, and in spite of various studies in wear-and-tear and fixed intervals of maintenance, items of work will occur that cannot be planned in advance. Therefore, a very flexible structure of production is needed which is able to carry out the various kinds of work occurring (e.g., damages caused by accidents, prototypes etc)

The study has shown that a strategy of extending product utilization is economical, too. The current measures of adjustment cause about fifty per cent of the prime costs of a new vehicle. It must also be emphasized that great quantities of energy and raw materials can be saved. Even if the measures of adustment are extensive, at least seventy percent of the old substance can be kept.

The following points have been proved as contraproductive according to the concept of extending the phase of product utilization:

• Technical progress

• Very few units of production (about 1000 vehicles)

• A wide variety of different types

• Obtaining of spare parts (in most cases spare parts are only delivered up to ten years)

The works division of the Deutsche Bahn AG considers the following aspects as preconditionial for a realization of the strategy of extending the phase of product utilization that is as efficient as possible:

1. The demands of maintenance and reconditioning should already be taken into consideration when the product is being developed (e.g., easy dismantling, high quality materials etc).

2. The production of too many types and incompatible product groups should be avoided. This would facilitate carrying out measures of adjustment at favourable costs (modular design).

3. High units of production and a high value of the basis substance would offer good conditions for a long phase of utilization.

A positive company result in the long term will be granted if the requirement of the works division of Deutsche Bahn AG for an intensive cooperation with the vehicle producers is assured and supported by them.

7. Case study on heating boilers

The case study was made in an industrial company that is a leading producer in the area of heating technology in Europe. The object of the study was a boiler provided with a newly developed burner that has set new standards in heating technology in respect of ecological criteria (low emission of air pollutants). The company is characterised by quality and long phase of utilization of its products, and it aims at an efficient exploitation of its resources by using high-quality and environment-friendly materials.

The aim of this study was to show possible problem areas that derive from a realization of the strategy of extended product utilization. Two areas in which problems can arise have crystallized:

- **Costs of measures of adjustment,**
- **Technical problems.**

7.1. Costs of measures of adjustment

A boiler is an immobile good and requires extensive fitting work that causes high costs and will be carried out by a craftsman's business instead of by the company itself. Because of high costs of transportation and assembly, it is not adequate to build up a central workshop for carrying out measures of adjustment. The scale of measures of adjustment is limited to such extent that they can performed at the site of the consumer, because decentralized workshops are regarded as economically irrelevant .

Moreover, the company is put under pressure to hold down costs, because the consumer normally does not estimate the value of his economic goods, for example a boiler that is in working condition. Losses of value and efficiency of the equipment are not considered, so that a cost-and-benefit analysis of measures of adjustment is distorted and complicates the price-fixing process of the company.

7.2. Technical problems

Technical product development as well as production are the focal point of the problem. In view of the realization of a longer phase of product utilization, the components of existing products should be considered as a starting point for the production of new products. On the other hand, companies aim at the development of new technologies based upon know-how that concerns the non-physical parts of the products. Therefore, the product is a compromise between profiles of demands and thoughts of profitability which are influenced exogenously as well as endogenously.

Primary influences make up market demands that are transformed into high-quality products. Therefore, it is the intention of the company to develop products according to a distinctively variable product structure. Indeed companies are realising products that are highly modularised constructed, but limitations exist, where individual demands for products impair the compatibility of single components. This is connected with the development of new technologies that often result from legal provisions.

Thoughts of profitability crucially influence the use of new production technologies that are integrated into the products, too. The companies get new product technologies that will change the product structure and impair the compatibility of the physical parts of their products.

The study has shown that it should be in the company's interest to manufacture products on the basis of existing technologies, provided that changing demands for products can also be realized. Currently, the solution of adequate research and development has only a theoretical character for the company. However, these considerations can be seen as a chance for a future profile of companies to meet the growing demands of society for an environment-friendly economic process.

Under the given circumstances, the company does not see an economic alternative that guarantees its aim of a positive company result in the long term. Besides legal provisions, for example the bill named "Kreislaufwirtschafts- und Abfall Gesetz" - KrW/ABG (circulation and waste law), general regulations create the preconditions for social acceptance of extending the phase of product utilization.

References:

Bellmann, Klaus. *Langlebige Gebrauchsgüter: Ökologische Optimierung der Nutzungsdauer.* Wiesbaden: Deutscher Universitäts Verlag, 1990.

Berekoven, Ludwig. *Der Dienstleistungsmarkt in der Bundesrepublik Deutschland.* Band I, Göttingen: Vandenhoeck und Rupprecht, 1983.

Hübner, Heinz. *Technologie- und Innovationsmanagement unter Berücksichtigung der Technikwirkung.* 2., überarbeitete Aufl., Kassel: Universität Gh-Kassel, 1990.

Ropohl, Günter. *Flexible Fertigungssysteme zur Automatisierung der Serienfertigung.* Mainz: Krausskopf - Verlag, 1971.

Stahel, Walter. *Langlebigkeit und Materialrecycling.* Essen: Vulkan-Verlag, 1991.

Recent Essentials in Innovation Management and Research, edited by H. Hübner / T. Dunkel
Gabler, Wiesbaden/Germany, 1995

Problems of Changing from Additive toward Integrated Environmental Protection

Krystof Kurek

Zentrum für integrierten Umweltschutz e.V.
Kassel

Abstract:
The presently often practised environmental protection in companies is normally the additive way, in which the polluters are acting in an after-care way more than in a provisional one. The symptoms of the damages to the environment are most times removed but the causes remain the same, which only means a displacement of the "burden" between two environmental media. The integrated environmental protection follows the principle of provisions. The whole company and its activities are directed to the avoidance or reduction of ecological damages. Social requirements and those referring to competitional strategies, which result from the growing interference with environment, are taken into consideration within this concept. Several problems result from the introduction and implementation of integrated environmental protection in smaller and medium-sized companies. Some of the possible problems are the following: Lack of responsibilities for the interests of environmental protection, insufficient ecological awareness, lack of capacities to work out and to translate integrated solutions, lack of environmental information and management systems, lack of interdisciplinary education of the responsible persons, lack of concluded solutions.

1. Main points of integrated environmental protection

Integrated environmental protection puts its main emphasis on the following points /1/:

- Development and production of ecologically friendly products;
- Use of economically and ecologically sensible rough and raw materials and primary products;
- Production processes with high emission standards;
- Development of concepts for the analysis and judgement of production processes with a view to the environment;
- Optimization and assessment of circulation processes.

The consequent realization of integrated environmental protection within a company means, in this context, that all internal company function areas are orientated to construct in a recyclable way, to produce energy-saving and to optimize the used material referring to its ability to function and to be re-usable /2/.

All these measures guarantee that environmental protection is taken into consideration at all levels of the processes within a company so that the necessity of reprocessing or disposal of a product afterwards is already taken into account in the construction phase.

2. Innovation by investigations in environmental protection

Big sums, which are invested in environmental protection, offer the possibility to develop and use innovative technologies. This has led to considerable results in additive environmental protection in the past.

In 1994 1,7% of the gross national product **(gnp)** have been used for environmental protection. Considering the investigations in former East Germany, Germany would reach the same level of expenses as Denmark. The adopted standards, mainly in the field of prevention of air pollution, have achieved that energy producers, industry and households have constantly reduced their emission of air contaminants such as sulphur dioxide, carbon monoxide and dust. Considerable progress has been made in the field of prevention of water pollution. The optimized industrial sewage treatment and the construction of several biological sewage treatment plants have led to a significant reduction of the pollution of surface waters. Modern technologies of waste disposal and decontamination have made progress with the soil conservation.

Although big success has been made, subsequent costs are estimated at 10% of the gnp /1/.

Figure 1 shows the international investigations in environmental protection referring to gnp.

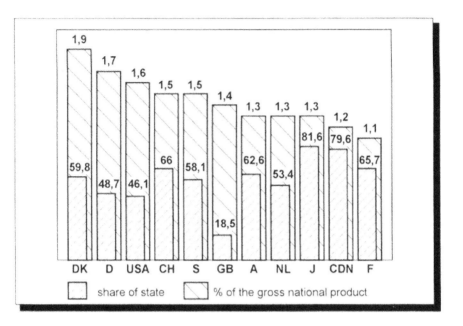

Fig. 1: Expenses for environmental protection and current expenses of the state and private economy in 1994, gnp in prices and rates of exchange of 1985 (D = West Germany) /3/.

3. Necessity of transition

Figure 2 shows the division of the investments in environmental protection in Germany from 1975 to 1988. 75% of the investment volume are secondary and additive measures (end-of-pipe-technologies) while investments integrated in the process and product are mostly insignificant.

Additive technologies of environmental protection show a high efficiency referring to contaminants on the one hand but have still weak points on the other hand:

- Change in emphasis of ecological damages between the media (from air to water into soil, e.g. filter technology);
- Additive technologies of environmental protection being susceptible to interference (the contaminants are first produced and then treated, so they might be released in case of an interference);

- Most times high investment costs and overhead expenses of the site for additive protection of the environment;
- Disproportion between supplementary investments and degrees of purity planned at the existing sites;
- Disregarding of innovation orientation referring to the product.

A further development of additive environmental technologies is in general possible but often uneconomic due to the complexity of problems. Therefore new attempts have to be made to reduce industrial production of pollution. Included in these attempts is the idea of an environmental protection referring to production as well as a product-integrated environmental protection to ensure that the environmental protection is considered in each step of the production process, the extraction of raw material and production, the reprocessing and the waste disposal. The aim is to limit emissions respectively to avoid them.

The consideration in all phases of the production leads from an economically shaped market cycle to an additional ecologically shaped product-life-cycle /5/.

The producer is consequently confronted with an expansion of his responsibility for his product and the changed demands on the development of his products.

The necessity of transition to integrated environmental protection definitely results from a comparison of the additive and integrated conservation technology under different aspects (Table 1).

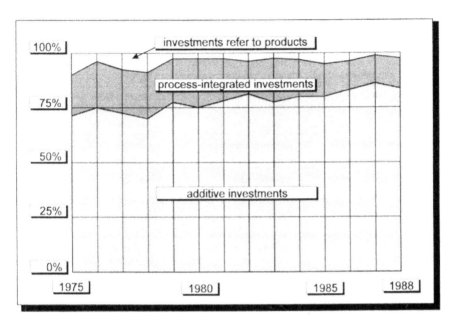

Fig. 2: Division of the industrial investments in environmental protection /4/

It is understood that integrated environmental protection needs a longer perspective with reference to preoccupation as well as an investment instrument. It causes most times higher costs for a short term, but long-term effects are much more favorable compared to additive environmental protection.

238

	additive technology	integrated technology
ecological efficiency	lower	higher
efficiency of resources	lower	higher
aspects of financing and realization	mostly easier	mostly a higher investment volume, more time is needed for adaption
productivity in general	drop in production	potential for higher productivity
effects on preoccupation in short terms	probably higher	probably lower
effects on preoccupation in long terms	lower	higher
international competitiveness	presently very high	potentially high due to the whole industry being effected
present use	definitely bigger	presently only 20% of the investment volume for environmental protection of producing industry
present regulation of environmental protection	favors industrial adaption via additive technology	hinders indus.adaption integrated technology
low possibility to foresee and lack of long-term-planning of env. prot.	favors industrial adaption via additive technology	hinders indus.adaption integrated technology

Table 1: Comparison between additive and integrated conservation technology under different aspects /6/

4.   Process of innovation

The variety of possibilities to implement a process of innovation to reduce the emissions within the production process continuously may be divided in four categories /7/:

-    to operate economically
-    substitution of materials
-    new production procedures
-    recovery of resources

To operate economically has the aim to use machines and production systems in the most efficient way. The according use and regular maintenance of industrial sites can often avoid an unnecessary consumption of material, loss of material or waste of material. EDP offers big advantages in this context for the recovery of saving potentials in environmental protection through an economically operating way. It allows the integration of management systems with environmental data and an effective control of the stocks. The substitution of a material often allows to substitute the emission source completely.

The abandonment by several car producers of solvent-based paint is only one example. The production of solvents can even be reduced by the application of water-soluble paint.

Emissions can be reduced through new production procedures and reduction of the number of production phases. The realization of "industrial eco-systems" is one way for the recovery of resources. The material remains within the production system and is reused in the same or in another process. Environmental protection referring to integrated products offers as well several possibilities to structure the process of innovation for the reduction of emissions /8/:

- to substitute the product or take it off the market;
- to substitute or remove noxious materials;
- to use more ecologically friendly materials or processes;
- to produce a concentrate;
- to produce in big quantities;
- to combine the functions of more than one product;
- to produce only a few models or types;
- to redesign for a more efficient use;
- to increase the life span of a product;
- to reduce unnecessary and expensive packaging;
- to improve the possibilities to repair a product;
- to redesign for reprocessing by the user;
- to reprocess the product.

240

5. Environmental law as an innovation factor

Implementation of environmental protection in the whole industry practice should be made on a wide basis. Therefore the planned inclusion of environmental protection in the Constitution is in this context a sensible federal aim.

Environmental legislation has also to accompany the transitional process to integrated environmental protection. The verdict based on a ban has to be substituted by integral legislative initiatives.

Regulation	Internal company consequences (examples)
Wasserhaushaltsgesetz (water conservation act)	Inspection, renovation of sewage sites under consideration of the state of technology. Inspection of the company with reference to the dealing with materials, dangerous to the water measures to save water
Abwasserabgabengesetz (act on fees for waste water)	measures to reduce the amount of harmful substances
Gefahrstoffverordnung (dangerous substances regulation)	stock-taking of chemical stock (stock list)
Verordnung zur Lagerung wassergefährdender Stoffe (regulation on storage of water polluting substances)	concept for protection against fire detain of water for fire fighting
Bundes-Immissionsschutz-Gesetz (federal immission control act)	inspection if official approval is required for the sites inspection of the state of official approval if changes were made in the sites
TA-Luft (technical guidance air)	renovation of old sites to fulfil the new requirements
TA-Siedlungsabfall (technical guidance settlements´waste)	recyclable materials have to be separated in domestic waste and to be reprocessed

Table 2: Internal company consequences resulting from environmental legislation /9/

Regulation	consequences for companies
Kreislaufwirtschafts- und Abfallgesetz (act of circuit economy and waste)	More responsibility for the entrepreneurs for production and products. Duty to inspect the production processes with emphasis on ecology
EU-Richtlinie über Verpackungsabfälle; (EC guidelines of packaging waste)	Obligation to avoid packaging waste indicating minimal and maximum rates for reprocessing Using ecologically friendly materials
Entwurf einer Elektronikschrott-, Altautoverordnung (Draft of electronic and car scrap regulation)	Obligation to reorganize products and production. Obligation to take back and reprocess materials
52s BImSchG in combination with 5.BImSchV (BImSch-federal immission control act)	Responsible persons have to be named in the management. Obligation to build an environmental management organization
Umweltinformationsrichtlinie der EU, (EC guidelines of environmental information) Entwurf eines Umweltinformationsgesetzes des Bundes (UIG), Hessisches Umweltinformationsgesetz (environmental information law of Hessia)	Pressure through public concerning the obligation of information.
Produkt- Umwelthaftungsgesetz (Product and environmental liability law)	Pressure through liability of the producers. Obligation to introduce an internal company environmental management organization (similar to 52a BImSchG in combination with 5.BImSchV but generally for all products)
EG-Verordnung über die freiwillige Beteiligung gewerblicher Unternehmen an einem Gemeinschaftssystem für das Umweltmanagement und die Umweltbetriebsprüfung vom 29.6.1993 (Eco-Audit)	Pressure to permanently optimize the production process through: public, competition, insurance of being credit-worthy, amount of insurance premiums)

Table 3: Legislation initiatives for strengthening integrated environmental protection.

The numerous legislative measures for protection of the environment are gaining more and more influence on entrepreneurial thinking and acting. Not only short-term decisions are affected by this but also long-term strategic concepts within the companies. In Table 2, some internal company consequences which result from environmental legislation are shown.

Several bills already exist which should support integrated environmental protection. Some of these bills with the resulting internal company consequences are shown in table 3.

Several of the laws or legislation initiatives overlap and complement one another. The decisive factor is that these regulations actually initiate long-term processes of permanent innovation concerning the products and production processes.

6. Innovation strategy of integrated environmental protection

The transition from additive to integrated environmental protection needs a development of strategies to translate this idea into practice. Such strategies have to be formulated globally on the one hand in order to be able to be used in as many fields as possible, but they have to be concrete enough in order to be able to be translated on the other hand.

Strebel /10/ proposed in this context the following:

- Orientation referring to function rather than to the product;
- Reduction of the variety of materials by simplification and standardization;
- Substitution of ecologically harmful product elements;
- Prolongation of the products´ life;
- Construction referring to products and disposal;
- Consideration of the future technical progress through unit construction systems and similar functioning components parts with homogeneous material;
- Consideration of recyclability of materials;
- Use of secondary raw materials;
- Improvement of material exploitation and efficiency of energy;
- Use of regenerating energy sources;

These strategical hints could be the basis for entrepreneurial strategies to be translated into integrated environmental protection.

7. Basic conditions for the realization of integrated internal company concepts of environmental protection

To make progress with the ideas of integrated environmental protection it is necessary to take several steps at the same time, including all social groups in this process.

The basic conditions are determined by public, politicians and market:

Responsibilities for the public:

- Strengthening of ecological awareness;
- Popularization of the idea of integrated environmental protection in public.

Responsibilities for the legislator and politician:

- Preferential treatment of integrated environmental protection in future bills;
- Support (also financial) of the idea of integrated environmental protection;
- Support of interdisciplinary education;
- Support of independent institutions which work out the scientific basis for translation scenarios for integrated environmental protection;
- Better identification of problems, negative tendencies and faster reactions.

Pressure through competition:

- Successful translation of marketing strategies in view of integrated environmental protection;
- Successful translation of internal company motivation concepts in view of integrated environmental protection.

The introduction of integrated environmental protection requires special efforts at an entrepreneurial level. Some of these "immediate measures" are:

- to implement environmental protection in the entrepreneurial strategy;
- to work out environmental management systems;
- to introduce structures for permanent optimization of products and processes in view of ecology;
- interdisciplinary education of employees;

- to work out tools (e.g. on a EDP-basis) which make the communication between the different departments easier;
- to work out tools for a fast and reliable decision-making in view of ecological aspects in all parts of the company.

8. Small and medium sized companies and integrated environmental protection

The idea of integrated environmental protection has first been picked up by bigger companies and groups of companies and partly been translated in view of marketing aspects and TQM (total quality management) /10/.

Several problems result from the introduction and implementation of integrated environmental protection in smaller and medium sized companies. The diversity of problems which are partly confused requires a precise examination. Some of the possible problems are the following:

- Responsibilities are often lacking for the interests of environmental protection; the manager does not have enough time for additional tasks.
- The ecological awareness is insufficiently shaped (in contrary to private life) as turnover and profit are pushed to the fore, therefore only reactions are shown on the difficulties in environmental protection.
- Capacities are lacking to work out and to translate integrated solutions; the necessary outside capacities are often too expensive.
- Environmental information and management systems are lacking.
- Interdisciplinary education of the responsible persons is lacking.
- Concluded solutions for translation are lacking on the market.

This is certainly not a complete list of all problems of the small and medium sized companies with the translation of the idea of integrated environmental protection. Nevertheless, some of the points listed may help to work out a strategy to reduce the problems.

9. Sustainable development as an aim

Sustainable development can be understood as an economic process which can be maintained in the long term without putting too great a strain on the "Eco-System of Earth". To reach such a development, a lot of negative global trends (as population explosion, waste of resources, restriction of eco-systems) have to be avoided.

The producing industry can make its contribution to this development by consequent saving of environmental goods such as air and water, by using energy-saving production processes and by avoiding unnecessary waste.

In order to be able to keep the balance, the complete energy consumption has to be on one level with the solar energy irradiation.

The entropy production has to be minimized in order to reach a result which corresponds to the entropy emittance of the earth.

The reduction of the entropy production requires a "third dimension of market relations". The disposal of by-products of the industry in the form of ecological damages normally assumes new market relations and infrastructures. To establish these is one of the most important responsibilities for management. Furthermore it is necessary to reuse the variety of residues (including the "remaining energy") for the economic process /11/.

Integrated environmental protection may make an important contribution to the global contemplation and optimization of the production processes by an integral way of acting. The demand of the thermodynamical balance of the eco-system of Earth, which is certainly a bit complicated, can also be put in other words /6/:

- The use of raw materials is to be brought back to a level which does not change the influence of raw materials in a negative way.
- The damage to the environment by emissions or residues is to be reduced to a level which does not exceed the processing capacities of the eco-systems for these residues.

This is the only way for us to leave the earth, for future generations, in a condition which is at least comparable to the present one. Therefore a cultural change in values is certainly necessary, which should orientate towards values such as creativity, activity (spiritual and physical) and relationship, trying to reuse the variety of residues (including "remaining energy") for the economic process.

246

Bibliographical reference

1. Kühner, W.; Kurek, K.: Integrierter Umweltschutz and Konsequenzen für die strategische Ausrichtung des ZiU. Internal paper, ZiU Kassel, February 1994
2. Bauer, G.: Umweltgerechte Produktion und Regionalentwicklung. HLT Gesellschaft für Forschung Planung Entwicklung mbH, Wiesbaden 1994
3. N.N.: Umweltschutz-Ausgaben. Westdeutschland auf Platz 2. iwl Umweltbrief, 6 (1994), S. 7, Data from OECD
4. N.N.: Produktionsintegrierter Umweltschutz, Förderkonzept des BMFT, Bonn, January 1994
5. Hübner, H.; Simon-Hübner, D.: Ökologische Qualität von Produkten. Ein Leitfaden für Unternehmen. Hessisches Ministerium für Umwelt, Energie und Bundesangelegenheiten. Wiesbaden, September 1991
6. Coenen, R.; Kopfmüller, J.; Seibt, C.: Die Bedeutung der Umweltschutztechnik für die wirtschaftliche Entwicklung der Bundesrepublik Deutschland. Verstudie erstellt für das Büro für Technikfolgen-Abschätzung beim Deutschen Bundestag von dem Kernforschungszentrum Karlsruhe, Abteilung für Angewandte Systemanalyse, Karlsruhe, February 1994
7. Schmidheiny, S.: Kurswechsel, Artemis & Winkler Verlag, München 1992
8. N.N.: Getting at the Source: Strategies for Reducing Municipal Solid Waste, World Wildlife Fund/Conservation Foundation, Washingtion, D.C., 1991
9. Brinkmann, T.; Ehrenstein, G.W.; Steinhilper, R.: Umwelt- und recyclinggerechte Produktentwicklung, WEKA Fachverlag, Augsburg, 1994
10. Strebel, H.; Integrierter Umweltschutz. Merkmale, Voraussetzungen, Chancen, in: Kreikebaum. H. (Hrsg): Integrierter Umweltschutz. Eine Herausforderung an das Innovationsmanagement. Wiesbaden, 1992.
11. Steger, U.: Umweltmanagement: Erfahrung und Instrumente einer umweltorientierten Unternehmensstrategie. FAZ und Betriebswirtschaftlicher Verlag Dr. Th. Gabler GmbH, Frankfurt, Wiesbaden 1988

Recent Essentials in Innovation Management and Research, edited by H. Hübner / T. Dunkel
Gabler, Wiesbaden/Germany, 1995

Implementing Technology and Product Assessment into the Company

- Outline for a Project -

Heinz Hübner

Stefan Jahnes

Management Science - Technology Impact & Innovation Research
University of Kassel

Abstract:
The nowadays necessary sustainable development of industry involves meeting the needs of the present without compromising the ability of future generations to meet their own needs. To carry through this aim, it is necessary to do assessments concerning the effects of economical acts (production and consumption). The present paper works out the need for this assessment and shows features and concepts for the implementation into companies' acting in the context of a planned research project.

The concept of Technology Assessment (TA) is established in various industrialized countries all over the world, e.g. with the Office of Technology Assessment (OTA), US-Congress, Washington D.C. or with the "Büro für Technikfolgenabschätzung" (TAB), Bundestag (the German Parliament), Bonn. The essential aims of the concept are:

- to research and assess systematically the conditions and potential effects of the introduction and utilization of a technology;
- to identify and analyse social fields of conflict concerning the utilization of a technology; and
- to enlighten and check possibilities to act, improving the examined technology and its utilization[*] (the kinds of effects of technology development and utilization are shown in Figure 1).

---

[*] comp. Paschen/Petermann, 1991, p. 20

TA is positioned on the level of political economy and public welfare with the task of consulting for politicians. The object of research is, of course, technology: physical technologies on the one hand and non-physical technologies, such as social technologies or thought-technologies, on the other hand. So TA has to analyze not only „hardware" like product and production technology, but production-oriented and use-oriented acting, too.

A similar concept regular by law in the states of the European Community is Environmental Impact Assessment (EIA). EIA tries to forecast impacts and effects that specific projects (e.g. a planned long-distance road or a power station) might have on the environment and to find ways to reduce unacceptable effects. It is positioned on the same level as TA.

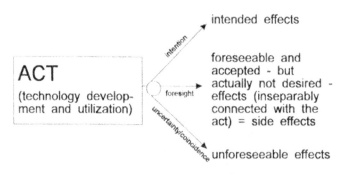

Fig. 1: Connection between act and effect/impact
(comp. Böhret/Franz, 1982, p. 10)

The sequence and tasks of TA and EIA could be the following:
- problem definition
- technology description
- technology forecast
- social description
- social forecast
- impact identification
- impact analysis
- impact evaluation
- policy analysis
- communication of results[*] .

---

[*]   comp. Porter et al., 1980, p. 54 & following

Most of the technological development happens in companies - so it seems only natural to establish TA/EIA in the company's acting in the form of Technology and Product Assessment. In this case, the object to be examined should be the product, because it is the (volume) production and consumption of products as economic acting that causes the basic negative ecological effects :

- increase of consumption of natural ressources including energy and decrease of available resources and
- the increase of harmful materials and waste.

These effects may be caused by the material and immaterial conditions of a product and their moulding in the production process (necessary processing techniques involving environmental damages involved and necessary resources for production and product) and in consumption (necessary energy for operation of the product or waste after its utilization). To prevent these negative effects, products have to become more compatible with environment protection needs. In this connection, results of an impact analysis of information technology should be mentioned which was carried out on the example of the personal computer (PC) (Source: "Environmental Consciousness", a study ordered by the US environment authority EPA in 1994; taken from "Die Presse", Vienna/Austria, 10 Dec., 1994, spectrum, p. XIII). According to this study, the production phase is most problematic under ecological aspects: The manufacture of one (!) PC

- causes the 20-fold of waste, compared with its own weight, during production;
- requires 5335 kWh of energy, which is approximately the 60-fold (private users) or 8-fold (professional users) quantity of mean annual energy consumption during the phase of usage;
- requires a water quantity of 33,000 m³;
- causes emissions amounting to 3 metric tons of CO_2 and pollutes 56 million m³ of air by hydrocarbons, carbon monoxide, NO_x, SO_2, and dust.

Products having a better environmental compatibility are designated - very pragmatically - in a study of OTA (1992), as "Green Products". Essential requirements on so-called „green" products are:

- avoidance of scarce, unrenewable materials;
- recycling of the product;
- energy efficiency of the product;
- avoidance of hazardous substances;
- minimizing the consumption of energy, water, and polluting substances during the production process;
- durability of product;

250

- product and process quality*).

To develop and design products with these features, possible product-specific impacts have to be assessed systematically. Hereby the product should be seen under a holistic approach (product biography, model of a Holistic Product Life Cycle, comp. Figure 2). A holistic approach involves the following environmental issues:

- development and design;
- application of energy, ressources, and materials/components;
- production process;
- product performance during utilization and consumption;
- trigger for (in this case: ecology-oriented) innovation concerning product, production process, and/or organization).

Further reasons beyond the output of „green" products for carrying out ecology-oriented TA/EIA in the company are:

- assurance of adequate procedures for managing environmental risks, and compliance with procedures;
- improved statutory compliance;
- identification of environmental risk/problem areas, early warning and prevention of potential adverse environmental effects (risk identification, assessment, and management);
- improved financial planning by identification of future and potential capital, operating, and maintenance costs, associated with environmental activities;
- improved preparation for emergency and crisis situation management;
- improved corporate image and positive public relations;
- enhancement of environmental awareness and responsibility throughout the corporate hierarchy;
- improved relations with regular authorities or
- facilitating of insurance coverage for environmental impairment liability**) .

To achieve these advantages, a concept of TA/EIA on company level has to be developed on the base of a holistic approach. A concept worked out at the University of Kassel (Department of Management Science: Innovation Research & Impact Analysis) is based on the following guiding ideas:

- model of the Holistic Product Life Cycle;
- holistic inclusion of possible assessment-aspects and

---

*)   comp. North, 1992, p. 52
**)   comp. North, 1992, p. 99

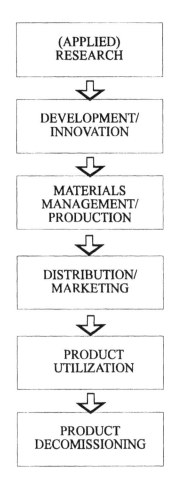

Fig. 2: Model of a Holistic Product Life Cycle
(Source: Hübner, 1990, p. 852)

- consideration of economic and non-economic aspects of assessment[*] - Figure 3 shows an overview concerning this concept.

---

[*]   comp. Hübner/Jahnes, 1992, p. 654

252

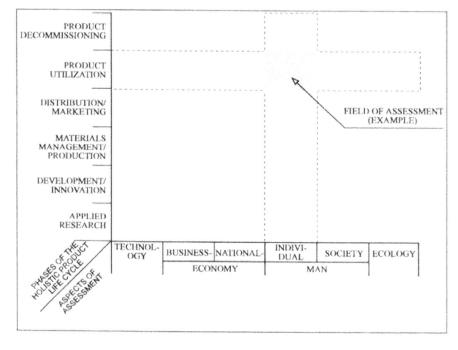

Fig. 3: Overall concept of Technology Impact Analysis
(Source: Hübner/Jahnes, 1992, p. 655)

The use of this concept requires the fulfilment of the following tasks:

- selection of the object of analysis (technology/product);
- laying down the relevant fields of assessment (combination of a phase of the Holistic Product Life Cycle and an aspect of assessment);
- laying down the time and spatial limits of the analysis;
- laying down criteria for assessment per field of assessment and selection of suitable "management technologies" (e.g. risk analysis or value analysis);
- carrying out the analysis by using the assessment-criteria and by usage of suitable "management technologies";
- documentation of results;
- derivation of urgent fields for acting and taking action[*].

---

[*]   comp. Hübner/Jahnes, 1993, p. 23

Though there are a lot of reasons and concepts for carrying out TA/EIA in the company, a practical concept for this level is missing up to now. An **oncoming project** will close this gap by reaching the **following goals**:

- The essential aim should be the development of a practical concept for TA/EIA and product assessment for use in the company (task to be performed, organizational implementation, subdivision of responsibilities, suitable instruments as "management technologies"). The concept should be oriented on the model of TA on the societal and economic level;
- working out economic conditions and limitations for use of the concept in the company (integration in existing controlling systems);
- working out organizational prerequisites, conditions and qualification structures;
- working out chances and risks caused by the existing environmental laws;
- working out technical prerequisites, conditions and limitations for the use of the concept (technical risks, "unknown unknowns");
- working out the conditions, possibilities and limitations of a company's environmental information system (purchase, processing, and evaluation of information).

The information pool at the end of a TA/EIA could be a base for corporate environmental business management: Especially the function fields of R&D, innovation management, production and marketing can use the information for identifying and designing their goals and for further action.

Companies interested in the project are invited/requested to contact the authors at TWI, University of Kassel.

References

Böhret, C./Franz, P.: Technologiefolgenabschätzung, Institutionelle und verfahrensmäßige Lösungsansätze, Frankfurt am Main/New York 1982

Congress of the United States, Office of Technology Assessment: Green Products by Design. Choices for a Cleaner Environment, Washington D.C., 1992, OTA-E-541

"Environmental Consciousness", a study done in 1994 by order of EPA (US), taken from "Die Presse", Wien, 10 Dec. 1994, spectrum, p. XIII

Hübner, H.: Competition in Innovation: Meeting the Challenge of Innovation and Ecology by Use of the Holistic Product Life Cycle, in Khalil, T.M./Bayraktar, B.A. (Ed.): Management of Technology II, Norcross/Georgia 1990, p. 847-857

Hübner, H./Jahnes, S.: Perspektiven und Lösungsansätze für ein Ökologie-orientiertes Wirtschaften (II), in WISU 8/9, Düsseldorf 1992, p. 653-657

Hübner, H./Jahnes, S.: Notwendigkeit und Methodik der Technik- und Produktfolgenabschätzung im Unternehmen, in Management Zeitschrift io Nr. 5, Zürich 1993, S. 21-23

North, K.: Environmental business management - An introduction, Geneva 1992

254

Paschen, H./Petermann, T.: Technikfolgen-Abschätzung: Ein strategisches Rahmenkonzept für die Analyse und Bewertung von Techniken, in Petermann, T. (Hrsg.): Technikfolgen-Abschätzung als Technikforschung und Politikberatung, Frankfurt am Main 1991, p. 19-41

Porter, A.L. et al: A Guidebook for Technology Assessment and Impact Analysis, New York/Oxford 1980

Recent Essentials in Innovation Management and Research, edited by H. Hübner / T. Dunkel
Gabler, Wiesbaden/Germany, 1995

Results of Discussion and Fields of Future Research

Ecological Problems as a Trigger for Innovation

Stefan Jahnes
Christian Kupke
Management Science - Technology Impact & Innovation Research
University of Kassel

Claus Seibt
University of Kassel

Participants:

Moderator: Renate Hübner, Austria Recycling, Vienna (A)

Matthias Diemer, University of Kassel (D)

Helmut Gehrke, Evangelische Akademie Hofgeismar (D)

Stefan Jahnes, TWI/University of Kassel (D)

Bernd Kahmann, Innovation Assistant, Kassel (D)

Christian Kupke, TWI/University of Kassel (D)

Krystof Kurek, Center for Integrated Environmental Protection, Kassel (D)

Claus Seibt, University of Kassel (D)

Michael Schön, Fraunhofer-Institute for Systems and Innovation Research (ISI), Karlsruhe (D)

Christoph Witzenhausen, University of Kassel (D)

The group work was structured as follows: After each key note speech, participants of the group asked the Speaker (S.) about items of special interest or unclarified points. Final conclusions or comments are listed before proceeding to the next lecture.

For organizational reasons, the sequence of lectures had to be changed in this case.

Discussion following the key note speech given by Witzenhausen: "Increasing the Duration of Product Utilization as a Strategy to Meet Ecological Needs"

1) **In your paper, you gave a view on the product development at a company producing heating boilers. But this highly environment-conscious company does not apply the strategy of extending the period of product utilization. Why do they not establish the strategy, for example with their heating boiler equipment?**

S.: The designers defend the opinion that quality standards, product regulations, and security-certification standards for the complete heating boiler unit do impede the re-use of upgraded components. They argue: Because the main product components deteriorate heavily, it is not effective to re-use or upgrade them. You cannot negotiate the different interests related to product use and the advantages or disadvantages concerning product-life extension.

2) **Did another company implement the strategy? Could you explain the pros and cons going along with the implementation?**

S.: Hewlett-Packard, e.g., manufactures copiers in a highly modular design. This design facilitates re-manufacturing and upgrading components of the copiers to extend the utilization phase of the entire unit.

Product life-extension will imply different transformations in product development; first the product use, and not the product itself, has to be considered. If a company's turnover depends on receipts for the product use, the company possibly will be more interested to design and manufacture a product that is durable and easy to repair.

Comments of the group:

In addition to the configurations listed in the paper, we identified the following two topics as further restrictions:

- inflexible quality standards,
- financial interests: e.g. the consumer's higher sensitivity on initial costs of a product rather than its lifetime costs .

3) **When you talk about extension of the product utilization phase, which products do you think are applicable?**

S.: The utilization phase of high-value consumer items may be extended, while mass consumption goods are probably less appropriate for this feature.

4) Re-manufacturing is an option to extend product life. It involves the restoration of old products by refurbishing usable parts and introducing new or upgraded components. What basic differentiations in product disposal do you think are necessary to sustain the re-manufacturing process?

S.: For manufacturers, it is still expensive to get their products back for re-manufacturing. Another distribution concept is to sell the product utilization instead of the product, while the product stays active property of the manufacturer. The related product design is focussed on functional values and supports the new relationship between manufacturers and customers: For instance, fixed periods of re-manufacturing are the base of reliability for customers and calculability for manufacturers. A worse problem going along with this distribution concept is the experience that customers are not as motivated to care as for personally owned products.

5) In your paper, you explained the "cascade-concept" by Walter Stahel as a strategy of product-life extension. Could you give us your estimate about the prospects of realization?

S.: The main feature of the cascade-concept (Stahel, 1991) is an ongoing process, re-using various re-manufactured components and product subsystems as replacement parts or in new equipment. Worn-out components are restored and re-used according to the product-quality standard, otherwise recycled with a high energy efficiency. Further opportunities are upgrading or introducing new product subsystems according to present technology standards.

Hewlett-Packard has implemented the cascade-concept in manufacturing. Some products are designed in such a modular fashion that a lot of standardized components can easily be replaced and re-manufactured as well as re-used in a variety of different H.P. products. The definable functionality of standardized modules opens up the opportunity of replacing subsystems of the product without affecting other components. So a high-quality product performance is maintained over a longer utilization phase.

Comments of the group:

The process-oriented "end-of-pipe" strategies forced by politicians and legislation in the past obviously are not sufficient to solve environmental problems. Product design is being viewed as another important focal point to provide satisfactory and cost-effective environmental protection in the future. Extending the period of product utilization is one possible design strategy for more environment-protective action. It will massively transform the economical, technical, and societal patterns of production as well as consumption and will heavily influence the whole innovation process. Figure 1 points out various problems discussed by the Working Group concerning an extension of the period of product utilization.

258

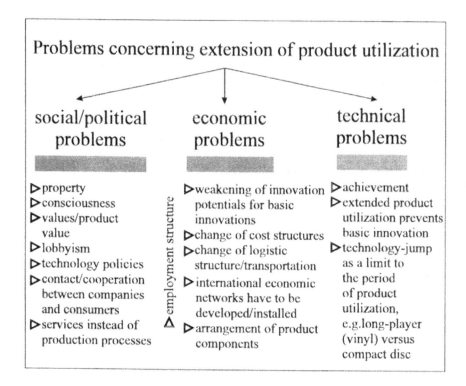

Fig. 1: Problems caused by extension of the period of product utilization

Conclusion:

Nowadays, environmental problems are important triggers of innovation. Environmental concerns are inseparably linked with public, political, economic, and technical aspects. They obviously trigger innovations in products, manufacturing processes, and management organization. In Figure 3 (page 267), the "triggers of innovation" remain in a "Black Box" to point out the importance of further innovation research on the subject.

Discussion following the key note speech of Kurek: "Problems of Changing from Additive toward Integrated Environmental Protection"

1)   **In which case is it unattractive to close material cycles by a recycling process?**

Speaker:

- Transport and material management for recycling operations is ineffectively coordinated.
- The recovered materials do not facilitate their re-use in products with the same product quality standards.
- The disassembled 'stuff' consists of a material mix that can hardly be recycled and recovered.

These topics characterize, for instance, problems concerning the German waste managment system (Duales System Deutschland/"Grüner Punkt").

If the *integrated environmental protection* strategy is solely explained as a principle to close material-cycles by recycling, this will possibly cause more disadvantages than benefits for the environment: e.g. inefficient material transport to 'feed' recycling operations.

2) Integrated environmental protection (IEP) or so-called clean technologies are obviously more effective to provide the protection of environmental quality than additive "end-of-pipe" solutions. Is there a systematic change visible in the formulas of environmental management strategies?

S.: *Additive* "end-of-pipe" strategies are not likely enough to provide satisfactory and cost-saving protection of eco-systems and human health. Strategies addressing environmental problems in a proactive manner are being introduced. Integrating environmental concerns into production and product design may be more effective and cost-saving in the long run than relying solely on remedial or "end-of-pipe" solutions.

3) Does the strategy of extending the period of product utilization make reference to clean technologies?

S.: Product-life extension is a product-design oriented tool within clean technologies. Other opportunities are, for instance:

- Designing products so that they can have a longer utilizaton phase;
- Coordinating design with remanufacturing and recycling options;
- Substituting and reducing toxic constituents in products and waste; making products entirely out of biodegradable materials;
- Increasing energy efficency and using less material to perform the same function.

Comments of the group:

The Working Group points out the following problems of introducing "integrated environmental protection" into practice:

- In many cases, tools are missing to introduce the incentives of the concept into management, production, and product development;
- Differentiated information for specific industrial branches frequently are not available;
- There is still a lack of 'systematic forecasting' examining future tendencies in product development;
- In many countries, reliable environmental policy plans for long-term planning in manufacturing and product development (like the NEPP in the Netherlands) are not available;
- There is a need to develop qualification and motivation strategies for environment-oriented manufacturing;
- Universities are hardly providing interdisciplinary environmental education for future qualification standards.

Discussion following the key note speech given by Schön: "Qualitative Evaluation of Environmental Effects of Companies' Strategies"

1) The environmental impacts of companies' strategies (product design objectives) are extremely diverse at different stages of life-cycle and are difficult to evaluate. Do you think it is possible to compare the aggregated results and define an 'optimum' product design?

S.: To prognosticate the environment-friendliness of a product design, you necessarily have to assess the environmental impacts at every stage of its life-cycle. It is very expensive and time-spending to objectively evaluate product impacts at specific stages of the life-cycle. So we made a subjective attempt to assess the environmental effects and to aggregate the results.

The aim of this research is to accumulate objective information about product impacts and to develop evaluation methods to quantify environmental effects caused by product design. In line with Stahel (1991), we set up different strategies or environment-friendly design objectives, not in order to define an optimum solution, but to give a conceptual overview for further orientation in product development.

Comments of the group:

- The definition of an optimum environment-friendly strategy can cause immobility by generating new design objectives.
- An environmental design may not be applicable during various product generations, but it may be an optimum strategy in further product development.

- Reliable standards for objective and comparable evaluation of environmental effects are hardly existing.

Discussion following the key note speech given by Jahnes "Implementing Technology and Product Assessment in the Company - Outline for a Project"

1) What do you intend by realisation of the project?

S.: By this time, technology assessment (TA) is introduced as a method of policy analysis created to support public-sector decision-making. The concept of TA uses various research instruments and unites different evaluation techniques to analyse present or future environmental, economical, and social effects.

Instruments for analyses designed to assist decision-making in companies are still insufficient: The existing instruments and techniques are either too generalistic or too specific. We intend to design a concept of Technology Assessment (TA) and Environment Impact Assessment (EIA) for assistance of planning and decision-making processes in companies. The project will hopefully start next year with contribution of science and management.

2) Please give a general view on how to manage analyses of private-sector Technology Assessment and on the costs involved

S.: A major volume of a private-sector TA analysis is to scan the actual and to prognosticate the future environmental effects of companies' activities. When doing a TA analysis, you have to consider how production and distribution activities as well as product design affect the natural environment. Supported by a holistic approach, an environment-friendly (re-)designing process of products and production activities will follow. The design process causes hardly 7-8% of a product's initial costs but determines 70% of the later expenses. By giving the designers incentives to consider the economic, environmental, and social impacts of their choices, you will get a high benefit, e.g. by generating less waste and pollution, by reducing production costs and improving product quality.

3) How important are mathematical methods and techniques applied to Technology Assessment?

S.: Mathematical techniques for TA-analyses are mainly applied to singular classes of assessment studies: By way of an example, for Risk Assessment you can realize the Equi-Risk Contour Method or the Probabilistic Event Analysis. An emphasis on mathematical modelling and quantitative measurings precludes an adaequate treatment of a great deal of information central to the TA process. It is probably more effective to use qualitative evaluation instruments like Delphi-techniques and Benefit-Value Analyses.

The application of mathematical techniques to simulate a physical system is a conceptual approach closely related to system analysis and Technology Assessment. More general than simulation is modelling. Especially dynamic modelling is a specific technique which has received a wave of public awareness by the computer-assisted analyses of Meadows et al.: "The limits of growth". But dynamic modelling can only be applied to systems in which a relatively small number of variables can be identified and a few mathematical relationships between components defined. Unforeseeable impacts interacting over time can hardly be identified as variables or defined as mathematical relations. A computer-assisted analysis is not really applicable to be used as a heuristic instrument, e.g. to set up future options and alternative scenarios.

Results of the final group discussion on all papers presented:

As we get more serious about environmental threats, traditional approaches of environmental protection have to be re-assessed. Mankind has to be aware that, whenever touching an ecological system, this causes effects which can only be "forecasted, but not predicted". The pyramid in Figure 2 portrays different levels of environmental protection. The stage at the bottom is mainly characterized by zero environmental protection and the highest consumption rates of natural resources. The stage at the top is ironically characterized as Olympus, the residence of Greek gods and goddesses. Zeus, Hera and their friends feed on heavenly ambrosia: They do not need any natural resources. But when we listen to the tales about the escapades of Chief Zeus on earth, his divine life on Olympus seems to be boring and not really enjoyable.

The strategies we discussed are mainly positioned on the third level. But they set the beginning of a transformation process moving towards the fourth stage with sustainability as a paradigm of further orientation. The fifth level characterized by two question marks is still undefined, but possibly a future strategy following sustainable development. Vertical movements from the pyramid's bottom to the top imply transformations in societal values and human lifestyle. In our opinion, they stand as synonyms for a development of cognition, a paradigm change, and a broad public acceptance of the holistic idea.

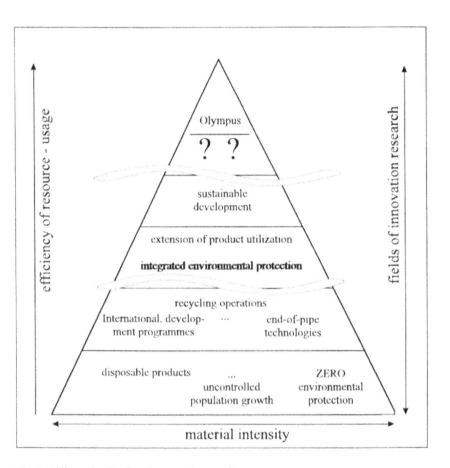

Fig. 2: Different levels of environmental protection

The next illustration (Figure 3) portrays a conclusion of our ideas. It shows again Figure 2 on the right side. This figure portrays environmental concerns as triggers for innovation to product design, manufacturing processes, and management organization. The triggers are still undefined (Black Box) and constitute an important field of further research. Not all demands for environment-oriented innovation give rise to the creation or use of environmental protection strategies. That point/argument is portrayed by a so-called filter on the left side of the Figure 2 pyramid.

264

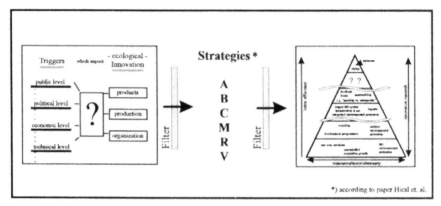

Fig. 3: Triggers, strategies, and environmental protection

The illustration shows, on the right, the pyramid (Figure 2) with the different levels of environmental protection. These levels are designed by the various strategies (e.g. the environmental protection strategies summarized in the paper of Hiessl/Kuntze/Schön); vice versa, the strategies are only designed to meet the needs of environmental protection. The list of possible environmental protection strategies has an open end. The filter in this place symbolizes the fact that not all of the strategies are significant for realization or have a chance of being accepted by the public.

A lot of instruments offering problem solutions are designed at universities. But they are mostly impracticable for companies. This is probably caused by the different reception of problems by academics and managers. A lot of indicators support this point; for instance, communicating at different stages of problem reception will cause a lot of misunderstandings and, in the long run, will stop feedback and information exchange between partners. Missing cooperation causes a lack of powerful interaction not only between "academics" and "managers" but also, for instance, between manufacturers and consumers.

A participant of the **plenary discussion** complained that the public gets more information about negative ecological effects, but hardly any information about the implementation of environmental protection strategies in industrial practice. Another participant commented on the lack of assessment techniques for environment-oriented decision-making in companies.

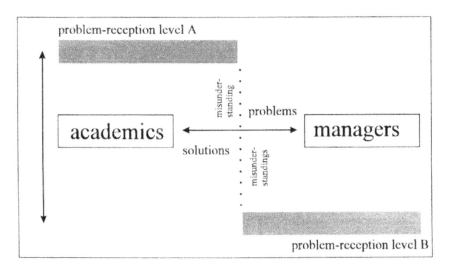

Fig. 4: Communication barrier between "academics" and "managers"

Fields of future research

An important field of further research is designing of acceptable research instruments and evaluation techniques. We propose especially the following items for future innovation research:

1. Strategies to stop rapid product devaluation;
2. Environmental design strategies concentrating on durable and modular design and multi-functional product use;
3. New working and cooperating concepts for a better quality of work;
4. Feedback structures in cooperation;
5. Environmental qualification standard(s);
6. Organization of relationship between manufacturer, distributor, and consumer;
7. Analyses of the specific impacts causing changes in societal and individual values: Research on analytic instruments and evaluation techniques;
8. Policy instruments or so-called "instrument mixes" to internalize external effects on a regional, national, or international level (e.g. laws, taxes, market-based instruments);
9. Reliable policy plans for long-term oriented decision-making in companies;
10. Research on TA and EIA instruments, especially those adaptable for companies.

References

Stahel, W.: Langlebigkeit und Materialrecycling, Strategien zur Vermeidung von Abfällen im Bereich der Produkte, Vulkan Verlag, Essen 1991

Meadows, D./Meadows, Donella,/Randers, J.: Beyond the limits, Chelsea Green Publishing Co., Vermont (USA), 1992

Authors and Participants

Czerny, Dr. Wolfgang
Austrian Research Centre Seibersdorf
Dept. Systems Research
Technology - Economics - Environment
A-2444 Seibersdorf

Diemer, Matthias, Dipl.-Oec.
Graduate Student
University of Kassel

Dunkel, Torsten, Dipl.-Oec.
TechnikWirkungs- und Innovationsforschung (TWI)
University of Kassel
Nora-Platiel-Str. 4
D-34109 Kassel

Eichler, Andreas, Dipl.-Oec.
Graduate Student
University of Kassel, TWI

Elsen, Frank
Doctoral Student
Technical University of Darmstadt/Germany

Garrelfs, Rick
Van der Meer & Van Tilburg
Innovatie Adviesbureau
Postbus 247
NL-7500 AE Enschede

Gehrke, Dr. Helmut
Head of Evangelische Akademie Hofgeismar
Postfach 12 05
D-34362 Hofgeismar

Gers, Volker, Dipl.-Kfm.
Doctoral Student
University of Kassel, TWI

Hiessl, Harald, Dr.-Ing.
Kuntze, Uwe, Economist *(co-author, absent)*
Schön, Michael, Dipl.-Ing. *(co-author)*
ISI ,see Reger, Guido
Breslauer Str. 48
D-76139 Karlsruhe

Hop, Louweris
Post, Dr. Ger *(co-author)*
Senior Lecturer
Eindhoven University of Technology
Graduate School of Industrial Engineering
Postbus 513
NL-5600 Eindhoven

Hübner, Heinz, Dipl.-Ing. Dr. habil., Professor
Head of Department TechnikWirkungs- und
Innovationsforschung (TWI)
University of Kassel
Nora-Platiel-Str. 4
D-34109 Kassel

Hübner, Renate, Mag.
Austria Recycling
Obere Donaustraße 71
A-1020 Wien

Hübner, Richard
Graduate Student
University of Innsbruck/Austria

Ichimura, Takaya, Professor
Nihon University
Department of Management/School of
Business and Commerce
3-1, Kinuta 5-chome Setagaya-ku
JPN-Tokyo 157

Jahnes, Stefan, Dipl.-Oec.
TechnikWirkungs- und Innovationsforschung (TWI)
University of Kassel
Nora-Platiel-Str. 4
D-34109 Kassel

Kahmann, Bernd
Innovation Assistant
Kassel

Krefter, Marcus
EIDOS Ideenmanagement GmbH
Neuer Wall 44
D-20354 Hamburg

Kupke, Christian, Dipl.-Oec.
Project Assistant
TWI, University of Kassel

Kurek, Krystof, Dr. Ing.
Managing Director,
Centre for Integrated Environmental Protection (Ziu)
Landgraf-Karl-Str. 2
D-34131 Kassel

Legat, Dr. Dieter
Planning & Quality Manager Europe
HEWLETT PACKARD S.A.
CSO Quality Dept.
150, Rte du Nant d'Avril
CH-1217 Mayrin/Genève

Le Mouillour, Isabelle
Doctoral Student
University of Kassel

Littler, Dale, Professor
Manchester School of Management
University of Manchester
PO Box 88
GB-Manchester M60 1QD

Maier, Hendrik, Dipl.-Ing.
Chamber of Industry & Commerce
Technology Department
Kurfürstenstr. 9
D-34117 Kassel

Médevielle, Jean-Pierre
Directeur Delégué - INRETS
Case 24
109 avenue S. Allende
F-69675 Bron Cedex

Müller, Dr. Eckhard
Wintershall AG
Head of Department
Executives Planning &Development
Postfach 10 40 20
D-34112 Kassel

Müller, Hartmut
Doctoral Student
University of Kassel

Nagel, Arie, Dr.ir.ing.
Eindhoven University of Technology
Graduate School of Industrial Engineering
and Management Science
P.O. Box 513
NL-5600 MB Eindhoven

Nascimento, Luis Felipe Machado, Dipl.-Ing.
Doctoral Student
University of Kassel
Amelia Telles, 505/203
BR-90.430 - Porto Alegre/RS

Nyström, Harry, Professor
Liljedahl, Sten
(co-author, absent from the Conference)
University of Uppsala, Institute of Economics
Box 7013
S-75007 Uppsala

Otala, Dr. Matti, Professor
Bosch-Telecom
Senior Vice President
P.O.B. 10 60 50
D-70049 Stuttgart

Piippo, Petteri *(co-author)*
Tuominen, Markku, Professor
(co-author, absent from the Conference)
Dept. of Industrial Engineering & Management
Lappeenranta University of Technology
P.O. Box 20
SF-53851 Lappeenranta 85

Pintholt, Peter
NKT Research Center A/S
Bldg. 61 - Sognevej 11
DK-2605 Broendby

Puhl, Ingo
Doctoral Student
Technical University of Darmstadt/Germany

Reger, Guido, Dipl.-Sozialök., Dipl.-Volksw.
Fraunhofer Institute for Systems
& Innovation Research(ISI)
Breslauer Str. 48
D-76139 Karlsruhe

Reminger, Dr. Brigitte, Dipl.-Kfm.
Siemens AG
Operating Revision & Project Control
Otto-Hahn-Ring 6
D-81730 München

Schwabe, Hans-Dieter, Dipl.-Ing.
Chamber of Industry & Commerce
Head of Technology Department
Kurfürstenstraße 9
D-34117 Kassel

Seibt, Claus, Dipl.-Ing.
University of Kassel

Shaw, Dr. Brian
Oxford Brookes University
GB-Wheatley Oxford
OS33 1HX

Snip, Robert
ROSNI marketing adviesbureau
Evene 8
NL-566AL Geldrop

Sporr, Volker, Dipl.-Oec. *(co-author)*
Witzenhausen, Christoph, Dipl.-Oec.
TWI, University of Kassel

von Wichert-Nick, Dorothea
Dipl.-Wirtschafts-Ing., Research Fellow
Fraunhofer Institute for Systems
& Innovation Research (ISI)
Breslauer Straße 48
D-76139 Karlsruhe

GPSR Compliance
The European Union's (EU) General Product Safety Regulation (GPSR) is a set
of rules that requires consumer products to be safe and our obligations to
ensure this.

If you have any concerns about our products, you can contact us on

ProductSafety@springernature.com

In case Publisher is established outside the EU, the EU authorized
representative is:

Springer Nature Customer Service Center GmbH
Europaplatz 3
69115 Heidelberg, Germany